The importance of music both [...] and their [...] into Ame[rica]

Start out with church music

How Shall We Sing in a Foreign Land?

THE IRISH IN AMERICA
Studies sponsored by
the Ancient Order of Hibernians and
the Cushwa Center for the Study of American Catholicism

How Shall We Sing in a Foreign Land?

Music of Irish Catholic Immigrants in
the Antebellum United States

ROBERT R. GRIMES, S.J.

University of Notre Dame Press
Notre Dame and London

Copyright 1996 by
University of Notre Dame Press
Notre Dame, Indiana 46556
All Rights Reserved
Manufactured in the United States of America

Book design by Wendy Torrey and Jeannette Morgenroth
Set in 10.5/13 Granjon by Books International
Printed and bound by McNaughton & Gunn, Inc.

Library of Congress Cataloging-in-Publication Data

Grimes, Robert R.
    How shall we sing in a foreign land? : music of Irish Catholic immigrants in the antebellum United States / by Robert R. Grimes.
       p. cm.
    Includes bibliographical references and index.
    ISBN 0-268-01110-9 (cl. alk. paper)
      1. Irish Americans—Music—History and criticism. 2. Music—United States—19th century—History and criticism. 3. Music—Ireland—19th century—History and criticism. I. Title.
ML3554.G75 1996
780'.89'9162073—dc20   95-18803
                                                                                       CIP
                                                                                        MN

The paper used in this publication meets the minimum requirements of the American National Standard for Information Sciences—Permanence of Paper for Printed Library Materials, ANSI Z39.48-1984

Contents

	Acknowledgments	vii
	Introduction	ix
1	The Irish Immigrant and the Catholic Parish	1
2	Music in the Press	13
3	Change and Adaptation in the 1830s, Boston	29
4	Canonical Music of Ritual: Art Music and the Immigrant	59
5	Popular Music of Ritual: The Tradition of Vernacular Song	96
6	Music of Popular Ritual: Song and Parish Organizations	138
7	"We Hung Our Harps on the Willows"	173
	Appendix	185
	Notes	197
	Bibliography	221
	Index	233
	About the Author	237

Acknowledgments

An individual's work is never the result solely of his own efforts, but benefits from the support, advice, and critique of many others. The present work was originally part of my dissertation written at the University of Pittsburgh under the direction of Professor Deane L. Root, curator of the Stephen Foster Memorial and adjunct associate professor of music. I am indebted to him and the other readers of my work, Professors Bell Yung and Mary Lewis of the Department of Music and Professor Paula Kane of the Department of Religious Studies.

My thanks also to the American Musicological Society for awarding me an AMS 50 fellowship for the academic year 1991–1992 which enabled me to devote full time and effort to the completion of my dissertation. I also owe a debt of gratitude to the Cushwa Center for the Study of American Catholicism at the University of Notre Dame, which selected my revised manuscript for publication as part of the Irish in America series, and to the staff of the University of Notre Dame Press for their helpful suggestions and assistance in preparing my work for publication.

My profound thanks to the members of the Society of Jesus, especially those of the New York Province, for their support, encouragement, and friendship. Finally, this work is dedicated A.M.D.G.

Introduction

In 1835 Andrew Reed and James Matheson published *A Narrative of the Visit to the American Churches,* recounting their recent experiences in the United States. Reed noted that although "great alarm" was being expressed by many Americans over the power of the Roman Catholic church, there was little to fear. Catholics "do not number, as attendants, more than 550,000 persons; and the influx of Catholics from Germany and Ireland may answer for that amount."[1] The authors had no way of knowing the immensity of the Irish and German Catholic migration to the United States that would take place over the next quarter-century. At the beginning of the 1800s the cities of the Northeast each had one, or in exceptional cases two, Catholic churches; by the outbreak of the Civil War, each urban center would be home to dozens of parishes.

In this study I investigate the musical life and repertory of the Irish Catholic community in the United States between 1830 and 1860. Music historians tend to sum up the Irish contribution to American music in a vague way as a body of Anglo-Celtic oral tradition transmitted to colonial America, and the songs of Thomas Moore, first published in 1808, music that in both cases predated the arrival of the majority of Irish in America. Furthermore, studies of American Catholic church music were often written by musicians connected to the early-twentieth-century Gregorian movement, who found nothing good to say about earlier Catholic musical practice in the country. Thus, the song of hundreds of thousands of Irish immigrants has been muted and largely forgotten.

Yet American Catholic institutions of the 1840s and 1850s employed a large, diverse, and often sophisticated repertory of music. Despite its emphasis on the Catholic religious community, this study is not restricted to religious music. Neither does it limit itself to a study of traditional Irish music in America. Rather it seeks to uncover the evolving musical life of an immigrant group in a new land. The parish was truly a social center, a living institution within the community. The immigrant community managed to raise large sums of money to build impressive churches, schools, convents, and orphanages; music was performed within all these buildings. Parishes were also home (officially and unofficially) to various associations, such as temperance societies, political organizations, brass bands, choirs, singing schools, and devotional societies. And because of the institutional nature of the church, and the continuing existence of many of these institutions, evidence of the musical life of its members has survived. Irish and Catholic newspapers reported the musical events of Irish and Catholic organizations, and bishops recorded their impressions in journals. Financial records were maintained, as well as some music libraries, and personal memoirs were written. Music collections were published under church sponsorship as well as by publishers such as William Cumming Peters and Oliver Ditson, who sought to tap the growing Catholic market. The information contained within these documents allows an enlightening glimpse into the musical life of the Irish immigrant in the antebellum United States.

This view of Irish immigrant musical practice has its limitations. Not all Irish were Catholic, and not all Catholics participated in parish life. Music was clearly employed in the everyday life of the home, the local saloon or "grocery," the dance hall, and other neighborhood locales. Evidence for such musical practice is slight, and is cited whenever possible in the following study. Moreover, the Irish immigrants quickly became involved as performers in minstrel shows and other forms of American popular entertainment, allowing for the easy passage of Irish and American influence back and forth between immigrant and "native." Nevertheless, the parish was a social center for a majority of the Irish immigrants, and the varied musical activity which took place within antebellum Catholic institutions provides an informative view of the largely undocumented music of the Irish in antebellum America.

My study begins with an overview of the socioeconomic separation of the immigrant from mainstream American life. The Irish urban neighborhood of mid-century was usually among the poorest in a city, and frequently the only social services offered to the immigrant were from the church. While the Catholic church was often of assistance to the immigrant community, the immigrants' "Romish" religion was perhaps their greatest liability in dealing with the American establishment. In the second chapter I turn to the journalistic separation of the Irish immigrant. The Anglo-Protestant press was a dominant source of information for nineteenth-century Americans, as well as for the writing of American musical history. An understanding of the attitudes of the press toward the immigrants and their music is vital.

But the mainstream press neither represented nor was interested in the Irish immigrant; thus, an Irish and Catholic press developed in America, represented by such newspapers as the *Boston Pilot,* the *New York Freeman's Journal,* and Philadelphia's *Catholic Herald*. Newspapers such as these represent a previously untapped source of information on immigrant musical life and repertory, which will be investigated in chapters 3 through 6. Chapter 3 looks at the city of Boston in the 1830s, and the musical life of an immigrant community beginning to coalesce. The following three chapters are concerned with the twenty years immediately prior to the onset of the Civil War, each chapter relating a different aspect of the Irish immigrant musical repertory.

Finally, chapter 7 examines the larger musical trends and preferences which the documented repertory displays. This final section also attempts to relate the musical life of the Irish immigrant to the wider American musical life of both the antebellum and post–Civil War years. In this way, I hope that the present study will contribute to the general understanding of mid-nineteenth-century American music, the era perhaps least investigated and least understood in the musical history of the United States.

CHAPTER ONE

The Irish Immigrant and the Catholic Parish

At the beginning of the nineteenth century, Catholics were a curiosity to most Americans, heard about and perhaps feared, but rarely encountered. Organized Catholic communities of more than one parish existed only in the cities of Baltimore and Philadelphia. New York City and Boston had but one Catholic church each. Despite its small size, the public face of the Catholic church in America was a respectable one. Catholic countries had provided aid, support, and military leaders to the colonists during the Revolution, and Anglo-American Catholics had been helpful in sensitive diplomatic negotiations with Canada and France. The Catholics ran three colleges,[1] all highly respected by the contemporary press, including the only college in the new District of Columbia, a college staffed for the most part by English and French Sulpicians or ex-Jesuits, all generally admired for their academic qualifications. American Catholic leadership was genteel, refined, and, perhaps most important, discreet; the wealthy planter Charles Carroll of Carrollton (Maryland), a signer of the Declaration of Independence, was the country's most prominent and wealthiest lay Catholic, and his distant cousin John Carroll, Catholic bishop of the entire country until 1809, and subsequently archbishop of Baltimore, was the ecclesiastical leader of the country. The reputations of some early nineteenth-century bishops went far beyond the Catholic community, most notably those of Bishop Cheverus of Boston and Bishop John England of Charlestown, South Carolina.

With the resumption of immigration to America following the War of 1812, the Catholic population of the United States began to change. Progressively greater numbers of Irish and German immigrants, mostly Catholic, arrived in North America. The federal government began keeping immigration statistics in 1820, reflecting a growing level of governmental concern with the number of immigrants arriving in America. For twenty of the twenty-one years between 1820 and 1840, the Irish were the largest single national group entering the United States.[2] Indeed, it was common during the 1820s for Irish to make up more than half the annual number of those entering the United States. The initial fear of the Irish harbored by the "native" population was not limited to Protestant citizens. Established Catholics were often just as fearful of the poor Irish immigrant as Protestants were.[3] American Catholic leadership, dominated by the coalition of Anglo-American and French clergy, looked with suspicion on the growth of the Irish segment of the church. Nativist sentiment was not intrinsically anti-Catholic, at least initially. But, as Ray Billington has shown, the waning of anti-Catholic feeling in the early years of the new nation was a temporary phenomenon, and in the years following 1820 anti-immigrant, anti-Irish, and anti-Catholic sentiment would forge a powerful and dangerous union.[4] "Irish" and "Catholic" became synonymous in the minds of many Americans, even though Irish Protestants arrived in America in numbers proportionate with the religious division of their homeland.[5]

The population that had revolted against the British empire and successfully launched a new republic was suspicious of any "immigrant." Dale Knobel has shown that the term "immigrant" as used by Anglo-Americans was "a pejorative reference to those who would not 'harmonize' with the mainstream of Anglo-American society."[6] The Irish immigrant was often extremely poor, evicted from his small farm in Ireland by his landlord, and uneducated in both formal learning and urban skills; he faced a difficult process of assimilation in America. The Irishman was suspicious of government and hostile toward the British. A visitor to America in the late 1830s felt that

> The Irish are, by the great majority of Americans, considered an oppressed and injured people, which is sufficient to entitle them to the sympathies of freemen. It is true, the greater number of the Irish who arrive in the United States are poor, and some of them tainted by the vices of poverty, which, in some of the states, have created a prejudice against them.[7]

But perhaps the single most important characteristic of the Irishman, which distinguished him from other immigrants of the time, was his belief that he was an exile, forced from his homeland by tyranny. A European visitor to the United States in the 1830s saw this characteristic clearly manifest:

> But the Irish are desirous of becoming Americans and yet remaining Irish; and this serving of two masters will not do. . . .
>
> What are the reasons that the Irish in this country clan more together than the emigrants of any other nation? I believe they are three-fold. First, more Irish than people of other countries come to the United States, and, as I have observed in a previous letter, they have a predilection for large cities, so that they remain in greater numbers together. Secondly, the Irish feel that they have been wronged in their country; they have, in a degree, been driven from it; the feelings with which they look back to it are, therefore, of a more intense character than they would otherwise be; or, if this be not the case, they feel among themselves the strong tie of bearing one common wrong.[8]

The Irishman's sense of exile in the new world is reflected both in songs popular throughout the nation, such as William Dempster's sentimental "Lament of the Irish Emigrant" (1843), and in lyrics directly addressed to the Irish community in America, such as the opening lines of a newly composed verse of "The Minstrel Boy" published in an Irish-American newspaper: "The Minstrel quits his native land/To awaken friends to save her."[9]

Oscar Handlin, in his masterful study of immigrants in antebellum Boston, suggests an explanation of why an immigrant group would remain in the city, rather than seek out the greater opportunities inland. If the immigrant group was more interested in fleeing Europe than in coming to America, and if "poverty deprived them of the means and despondence of the desire" to face the challenges of the emerging land, Handlin argued, the group would likely remain in a city such as Boston.[10]

In the city of Boston, which was in economic distress through much of the first half of the nineteenth century, the Irish immigrants found a refuge from Ireland but also a social and economic trap from which it was difficult to escape. One Irish immigrant wrote in his journal in 1847, "O! it fails me absolutely to recount the affliction that I felt. I found myself involved in such destitution and misery."[11] Attempts were periodically made to convince the Irish immigrant to move westward. The *Boston Pilot* recommended to immigrants that they "should not for a moment think of settling down in these places [Boston and New York] where want of work, poverty, disease, and death lie in wait," but "without stopping, leave the seaboard . . . to proceed inland."[12] Such suggestions were rarely taken. Handlin holds that the Irish immigrants' "cheap labor and abundant numbers ultimately created a new industrialism in Boston. But for a long time they [the Irish] were fated to remain a massive lump in the community, undigested, undigestible."[13] Most important for our present study is Handlin's observation that "two distinct cultures flourished in Boston with no more contact than if 3,000 miles of ocean rather than a wall of ideas stood between them."[14]

The condition of the Irishman in New York City was no better than in Boston. Concentrated in the fourth, fifth, and sixth wards, the Irish neighborhoods stretched across Manhattan in the area immediately below Canal Street. In the center of the area was the notorious Five Points slum, the worst neighborhood in the city of New York. A visiting Englishwoman, while generally impressed with the city, described Five Points as a place "fertile in crime, fever, and misery, which would scarcely yield the palm for vice and squalor to St. Gile's in London, or the Saltmarket in Glasgow."[15] George Templeton Strong described the Five Points neighborhood in an 1851 diary entry:

> Yet we have our Five Points, our emigrant quarters, our swarms of seamstresses to whom their utmost toil in monotonous daily drudgery gives only bare subsistence, a life barren of hope and enjoyment; our hordes of dock thieves, and of children who live in the streets and by them. No one can walk the length of Broadway without meeting some hideous troop of ragged girls, from twelve years old down, brutalized already almost beyond redemption by premature vice, clad in the filthy refuse of the rag-picker's collections, obscene of speech, the stamp of childhood gone from their faces, hurrying along with harsh laughter and foulness on their lips that some have learned by rote, yet too young to understand it; with thief written in their cunning eyes and whore on their deprived faces. . . .[16]

Crowded into inadequate housing and beset by poverty, the Irish neighborhoods were victimized by disease, crime, and alcoholism. Institutions perceived by the immigrant as friendly to them were few; the saloon was a political, social, and neighborhood center. The parish church was another center, combining these functions with education and religion.[17]

Many factors have been cited as the cause of the distress in Ireland that led to mass emigration: British colonial policies, overpopulation, industrialization, and, of course, the potato blight. Analysis of these factors is outside the scope of the present work. But despite the poverty, hostility, and hard work the Irish encountered in America, the number of Irish fleeing their homeland increased steadily until the peak year of 1851. From 1820 to 1829 the government recorded 51,617 Irish immigrants arriving by ship. From 1830 to 1839 the number totaled 170,672. The decade 1840 to 1849 saw 656,145 Irish arrive. Although Irish immigration crested in 1851, the 1850s saw the arrival of 1,029,486 persons from Ireland.[18] Given the state of transportation at the time, it was a most amazing migration. And given that the Irish immigrants clustered in the urban areas of the east, their presence was impossible for the nation to ignore.

The new arrivals were often exploited by unscrupulous merchants and landlords, some of whom were Irish immigrants themselves; the Irishman could find himself in debt by the end of his first week in America. Untrained in the skills of an urban life, most Irish men worked as day laborers. One European observer of America noted that

> the major portion of them [the Irish] remain labourers and die very little better off than when they went out. Some of them set up groceries (these are the most calculating and intelligent) and by allowing their countrymen to run in debt for liquor, etc., they obtain control over them, and make contracts with the government agents or other speculators (very advantageous to themselves) to supply so many men for public works.[19]

The woman's role in the Irish ghetto must not be overlooked for, unlike in all other national groups migrating to the United States, women made up the majority of the Irish who came to America.[20] Many Irish women worked as seamstresses, often sewing at home for well below a living wage. Prostitution became a temporary alternative for many of these women; a study of New York prostitutes in 1855 found a third of them to be Irish-born.[21] Domestic service became an important source of employment for women, as well as a way of escaping the ghetto.

Nothing could have prepared the population of America's eastern cities for this massive influx. Clustering in the older and poorer parts of the cities, the Irish became an object of fear, scorn, and ridicule for many elements of the American society. Recognition of the inevitable effects that such large numbers of Irish would have on the country led some nativists to violence. The worst cases of anti-Irish rioting took place before the number of Irish immigrants soared as a result of the famines of 1845 to 1849. Perhaps the most violent anti-Irish rioting in American history gripped Philadelphia in the spring and summer of 1844. Catholic churches and institutions were targeted by the nativists; two churches, St. Michael's and St. Augustine's, were set afire and burned to the ground, as did the diocesan seminary. It appears that the Catholic parish church was symbolic for both the nativist and the Irishman; both saw it as an institution at the heart of the Irish community in America.

Several factors combined to make the parish church the most important institution in the ghetto. On the simplest level, the church was a familiar sight in a strange land. The church was, at least externally, the same church the immigrant had known in Ireland. Moreover, the Irish had not experienced either government or Protestantism as benevolent forces in their lives in Ireland. The immigrants' mistrust of government and Protestantism, combined with the nativist sentiments often expressed by those institutions, alienated the Irish immigrant from the two major institutions of America. Centuries of anti-Catholic and anti-Irish treatment by Britain had made the notions Irish and Catholic synonymous for many of the immigrants.

The Catholic church also responded to the immigrants. New churches were built in the neighborhoods in which they settled. Schools were opened and social and devotional societies formed. The church building was a focus for the community and became a source of ethnic pride in the midst of the ghetto. John Neumann, the German-born bishop of Philadelphia, learned the Irish tongue in order to hear confessions from immigrants in northeast Pennsylvania.[22] The Irish-born John Hughes, bishop and later archbishop of New York from 1838 to 1864, became a major force in New York politics. Hughes, and others of his style, preached a ghetto Catholicism, convinced that Catholicism could survive in America only by building up a social order to parallel the one built up by what they saw as a hostile American Protestantism.[23] And Hughes backed up his preaching with action. The parish became the religious and educational center of Catholic immigrant life, with important political, social, and ethnic functions for the community.

The Church and the Immigrant

Studies of the Catholic church in Ireland before the famine have indicated that church attendance and participation varied widely in different areas of the country. The lowest regular attendance at Sunday services, less than 25 percent, was found in rural areas where Irish was still commonly spoken. English-speaking rural areas had attendance figures that ranged from 30 to 60 percent, while in the towns, where the native tongue was largely forgotten, attendance was 70 percent and greater. This is in marked contrast to the universal level of high regular attendance at Sunday mass in Ireland in the late nineteenth century.[24]

Attempts at explaining this phenomenon have centered on the experience of the great famine of 1845–49. Changes in Irish life following the famine led to the practical end of Gaelic culture and to the modernization of Irish society. Traditional beliefs and practices which had supplemented the rituals of Catholicism in the lives of many rural folk quickly came to an end. The part that Celtic rituals had played in people's lives was taken up by the "devotional revolution" in Ireland, which saw the introduction of traditional Catholic devotions that had been rare in Ireland (for example, benediction, stations of the cross, retreats, and sodalities) and the regularization of church discipline in general.[25]

It would appear that American Catholicism served a similar function for the Irish immigrant. Customs that had grown up within a rural society could not survive in the city. Many Celtic rituals were intimately linked with particular sites in Ireland and lost their appeal in a new land. Although a few customs were retained, most notably the "Irish wake," the rituals and societies of the local parish supplanted traditional practices. Thus, within the religious sphere, the Irish immigrant was experiencing changes similar to those affecting the Irish who had remained in their homeland. Events which had often taken place in private homes in rural Ireland—such as weddings, confessions, even Sunday masses—now were centered exclusively in the parish church. Much of Catholic ritual was unfamiliar to the Irishman; one immigrant recalled that "there were doubtless . . . many matters of form and ceremony of which we were, from necessity, ignorant."[26]

Not surprisingly, the large number of immigrants led to the foundation of numerous urban parishes. New York City, for example, had only two Catholic churches before 1825. In the fifteen years from 1825 to 1839, six more parishes were established. In contrast, twelve churches opened in the 1840s and another ten in the 1850s, an amazing feat given the economic position of the Catholic immigrant.

Musical Life in the Immigrant Parish

The parish also became a musical center of immigrant life. In certain parishes there were concerted efforts to develop the fine art of music, often by employing professional musicians. These churches, such as St. Peter's in New York City, were frequently attended by Protestant music-lovers as well as Catholics, and the musical services were at times "reviewed" by the musical press of the day; in some circles the fine arts were viewed as an evangelical tool, while others looked upon them as desecrations of the Catholic liturgy. But churches such as St. Peter's were uncommon and figure only tangentially in the following study. The life of the ordinary parish included many occasions when music was employed, often performed by volunteers from the parish, sometimes coordinated by a paid professional. Some of the occasions were liturgical, many more devotional. But music was employed in social, political, ethnic, and educational parish activities as well.

The parish was certainly not the only place in which the Irish immigrant heard or performed music. Children attending public schools were exposed to both Protestant hymnody and music education. Parades and political rallies employed various forms of music. The saloon and dance hall were also popular social centers within the community. Charles Dickens visited a dance hall in New York's Five Points area in the 1840s:

> ... instantly the fiddler grins, and goes at it tooth and nail, there is new energy in the tambourine; new laughter in the dancers. Single shuffle, double shuffle, cut and cross-cut, snapping his fingers, rolling his eyes, turning in his knees, presenting the backs of his legs in front, spinning about on his toes and heels like nothing but the man's fingers on the tambourine....[27]

A medical doctor offered a long series of suggestions to newly arrived Irish in Boston which included a warning about the local saloons: "above all, do not be found in places of low resort, where the fiddle or the bag-pipes can be heard until 11 or 12 o'clock, and card players in another corner."[28]

While the immigrant undoubtedly encountered music in a number of forums, the Catholic parish appears to provide a cross section of the many types and styles of music popular within the Irish community. Organizations dealing with many aspects of the immigrant's life were connected to a greater or lesser degree with parish life. Moreover, given the institutional nature of the parish, evidence of musical practice has survived and can provide us with a view of the music employed by a substantial segment of the white urban lower-class of the mid-nineteenth century.

Figure 1.1 suggests one model for musical praxis in an urban parish and its relationship to the institution. Liturgical music, that is, the music employed in the official rituals of the church, is placed at the center because it was the music most clearly identified with the Catholic church, as well as the most centrally controlled. Devotional music is music religious in nature

FIGURE 1.1
Musical Organization in the Catholic Parish

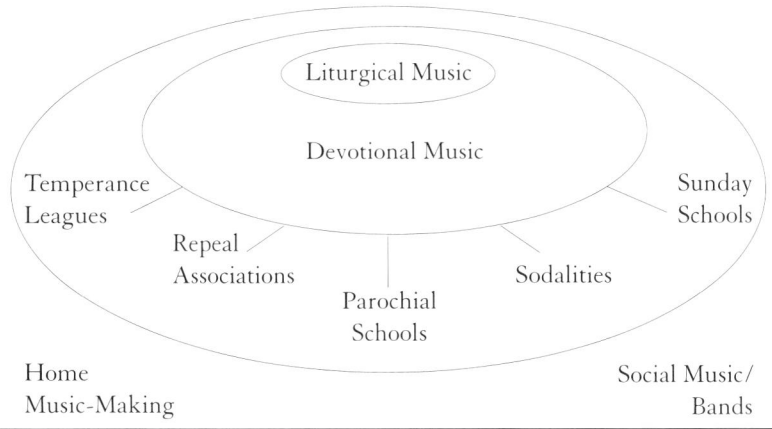

(that is, with religious text and a musical style deemed appropriate for such a text) which could be employed both within and without sacred space, the church building proper. Such music could be sung at "low" masses (while generally avoided at the Sunday "high" mass) as well as at other devotions both inside and outside the parish. These two categories contain most of the music generally associated with church services.

The five groups in the next circle name five types of parish-related associations which often employed music, and for whom new music was being composed in the mid-nineteenth century. Temperance leagues were formed to curb the effects of alcoholism so prevalent within the community. Repeal organizations were political clubs which supported the repeal of the act of union between Great Britain and Ireland. Parochial schools were most often elementary schools, usually founded to counter the perceived anti-Catholicism of the public or common school. Sodalities were religious associations of adults designed to increase the participation of the adult Catholic in his or her faith. Sunday schools were similar to those of the Protestant churches, designed to teach denominational principles and beliefs to the children of the parish.

Finally, the musical activities in the outermost area of figure 1.1 were the activities least controlled by the institution, but still associated with it. Home music-making was encouraged because it was a popular activity in society in general. But the parish encouraged a "Catholic" repertory of music to counterbalance the "Protestant" music taught in the public schools. Social music was employed at parish-related events, such as St. Patrick's Day banquets and summer "pic-nics."

The drawback in viewing the musical life of the parish from the perspective of figure 1.1 is that the classification positions the various musical repertories in an ideal way, in a manner perceived by church authority, rather than as experienced by the people of the parish. For example, devout laborers or domestics, regularly attending the 5:30 A.M. mass each Sunday might rarely if ever encounter "liturgical" music, which in figure 1.1 is at the center of the parish's musical life, but they might encounter music in other parish activities. The schema represented in the diagram grants pride of place, at very least, to liturgical music, yet the repertory of liturgical music was frequently the smallest and most stable of all the repertories encountered in the local immigrant parish.

An overemphasis on the role of liturgical music also presumes that the rituals of parish life are coterminous with the canonical ritual of the church. But many of the organizations that employed music did so in a ritual-like fashion. The ritual nature of liturgical music is obvious. But the opening of a Sunday School class with a hymn, or the use of songs between toasts at a banquet is also ritual. Musical performance itself can be viewed as ritual, or at least as ritualistic; and by analyzing musical performance within a ritual perspective, one automatically contextualizes the music. Music is not an isolated aural phenomenon, or worse yet, a printed page, but the focus of an event which includes performers, listeners, a history, and a significance, both musical and extramusical.

The following categories will be used to analyze the various types of music employed in the average mid-nineteenth-century urban Catholic parish; the categories differentiate musical repertories by their ritual connections, the uses that are made of them, and the authority that sanctions them.

1. *Canonical Music of Ritual*. Styles and types of music mandated for use in official rituals of the church by ecclesiastical authority at a supraparochial level. The category includes the music strictly defined as liturgical, employing only Latin (or occasionally Greek) texts, and mandated by church discipline. The category includes plainchant, composed settings of the mass, and Latin breviary hymns. The limits of the repertory are sanctioned not by the parish but by universal guidelines made in Rome. The actual choice of items for use in a particular place, however, does take place at the local level.

2. *Popular Music of Ritual*. Styles and types of music which spring up in and around a formal ritual, often violating either the spirit or letter of

the laws governing the previous category, and sanctioned either by local ecclesiastical authority or popular approval. The category includes music employed in both liturgical and extraliturgical rituals.[29] The texts of songs are usually in the vernacular, either translations of Latin texts or newly composed. The musical style in which the songs are composed borrows freely from styles popular at the time. The repertory, therefore, reflects the musical preferences of the local community rather than an ideal of proper liturgical music.

3. Music of Popular Ritual. The category embraces the widest range of musical styles and forms because it includes all music employed in parish activities outside of liturgical and extraliturgical worship. The texts are invariably in the vernacular (although occasionally including a phrase in Latin or Irish) and may or may not have a religious content, while the music reflects styles traditional to, or popular with, the congregation. The ritual occasion at which this music is performed is often only implicitly religious (a church-sponsored temperance meeting), or apparently nonreligious (a church social, a fund-raising concert, or political association meeting within the parish). The nature of the event is controlled by the local leadership and participants, rather than by authority outside of the parish community.

Each of the categories of music employed in a mid-nineteenth-century urban Catholic parish will be investigated in a separate chapter here. The categories will be organized according to ritual distinctions, and each chapter will treat not only the music itself but the musical life of the parish membership. The following questions will be asked concerning each type of music employed in the parish, even though sufficient information to properly answer them will not be available in every case.

> Who performed the music—clergy, professional musicians, amateur musicians, or all assembled? Does gender play a part in the differentiation of musical roles?
>
> Who was responsible for the choice of music? Does it reflect an individual's taste, the taste of the congregation, or an authority outside the community?
>
> How was the musical activity financially supported?
>
> In what ritual context(s) was the music employed?
>
> What were the kinds of sources for the music and texts—were they traditional, newly arranged or revised, or newly composed or written? Does any one source predominate within a type of music?

Can the aesthetic, functional, or extramusical values that were attached to the musical compositions be determined?

Not surprisingly, the answers to these questions will be dependent on a number of factors, not least of which are the different traditions that developed in various cities.[30] I believe that by assembling and ordering the various sources of information concerning the Irish immigrant's musical life, I can present a convincing profile, not only of the repertory, but also of the ways in which Catholic immigrants employed, performed, and enjoyed music.

Oscar Handlin, in his study of the Irish in Boston, made an important observation concerning the nature of Catholicism, often assumed to be a monolithic institution.

> In the New World as in the Old, Catholicism assumed a distinctive cast from the background of its adherents. Universal rather than national in organization, and catholic in essential dogma, it nevertheless partook of the quality of the men who professed it; for the nature of the *milieu* modified even religious doctrines, particularly in their application to the problems of secular life.[31]

Handlin's observation is even more valid for the liturgical and musical life of a Catholic church. As catholic as it may profess to be, it is lived by a particular people, acting and reacting within a particular historical period. Two significant areas need to be explored before we examine the music of Catholic immigrants during the twenty years before the Civil War. A group is formed not only by what its members believe about themselves, but by what others believe about them. Chapter 2 looks at the ways in which the dominant culture of the antebellum United States—Anglo-American Protestant—viewed the music and musical life of Catholics. Chapter 3 looks at specific types of changes which were introduced into American Catholic musical life during the 1830s, as immigration intensified but before the massive immigration of the 1840s and 1850s began.

CHAPTER TWO

Music in the Press

Much of our information concerning musical life in antebellum America comes from reports and descriptions found in the musical press of the day. It is important, therefore, to understand the nature of early nineteenth-century musical reporting in order to interpret and analyze the information derived from journalistic sources. An awareness of the preconceptions and assumptions that stand behind the musical reporting of the day is crucial. This chapter will investigate the limited nature of the information one can gather from periodical sources, and suggest three major factors that influenced reporting on the musical life of Catholic immigrants in the mid-nineteenth-century United States: the Transcendental and Unitarian movements, Romanticism, and Nativism.

As shown in chapter 1, the Irish immigrants of the urban northeast maintained a culture and a way of life distinct from that of the majority population. This was partly the result of a conscious choice by powerful segments of the Catholic hierarchy, perhaps most notably Archbishop Hughes of New York. But the isolation of Irish Catholic immigrants was also due to economic conditions and the fear and hostility of segments of the Protestant majority.

The separateness of the new immigrants from the mainstream of American life continued and intensified well into the twentieth century.[1] The separateness would be fostered by the mutual suspicions of the Irish Catholics and the Anglo-American Protestants, and would extend into the musical activities of each group. While the musical life of America in the 1830s and 1840s was growing to include local performing organizations, touring companies from abroad, and public-school and home music-making, as well as a commercial music industry, the local church was still an important musical center. Moreover, the early major performing organizations in the United States, such as Boston's Handel and Haydn Society, often performed music of a religious nature, and had as part of their basic mission the improvement of church music.[2]

The term *church music*, when read in the musical press of the day, inevitably referred to Protestant church music. Indeed, many of these newspapers and magazines were founded precisely for the fostering of Protestant church music. Within their pages, one reads of musical events in Protestant churches and encounters advertisements for numerous publications geared toward the various Protestant denominations. These publications rarely included similar items related to Catholic music. Because so much of the writing of American musical history for the period is based on contemporary musical periodicals, separatism has had a significant effect on our understanding of American musical history. Scholars have assumed that there was little public musical activity taking place within the Catholic immigrant community, but a review of nonmusical periodicals published by or for these various immigrant groups reveals a wealth of information concerning the musical activities.

For example, the *Boston Pilot*, a newspaper produced by and for the Irish Catholic community, often advertised and reported on special musical events within the community.[3] Figure 2.1 lists concerts within the Boston Catholic community advertised in and/or reported on by the *Boston Pilot* in the years 1839 to 1841. These are special musical events, beyond the regular liturgical duties of the choirs, which normally included the Sunday morning high mass, and Sunday evening vesper service.

These years also saw the formation of the Saint Mary's Singing Society and the subsequent controversy that surrounded it, as well as the publication of a large and important Catholic hymnal for the diocese of Boston, *The Morning and Evening Service of the Catholic Church*.[4]

Figure 2.1 reveals a significant concert life within the Boston Catholic community. Particularly notable is the presence of distinguished guest artists at a number of these events. The Rainer Family, a Tyrolean singing family who appeared in benefit concerts for the Catholic community beginning in 1840, was one of the most popular touring groups of its day.[5] They inspired the formation of a number of American singing families, the most famous of which, the Hutchinson Family, admittedly modeled themselves on the Rainers.[6] A rival group of the Rainer Family, the Steyermark Family, appeared together with the Rainers in a Boston concert to benefit

FIGURE 2.1
Concerts in the Boston Catholic Community, 1839–1841

Date	Event	Citation in the *Pilot*[7]
1/20/39	Boston Gregorian Society (hereafter, BGS), with guest artist P. F. White. Public rehearsal.[8]	1:415
2/3/39	BGS. Public rehearsal.	2:15
2/24/39	BGS. Sacred Concert at St. Mary's Church.	2:39
4/21/39	BGS. Grand Miscellaneous Concert.	2:103
12/29/39	Concert of Sacred Music.	2:401
2/2/40	BGS. Complimentary Concert to Madame Brown.	3:15
5/10/40	St. Mary's Singing Society (hereafter, SMSS).	3:127
5/31/40	BGS. Public rehearsal.	3:147
9/20/40	BGS and an "ample orchestra" at Boylston Hall.	3:279
10/25/40	BGS with guests, the Rainer Family, at Boylston Hall.	3:311
11/29/40	"C.T. Young's Concert" at Boylston Hall.	3:361
1/10/41	SMSS (rescheduled from 1/3/1841).	4:7
3/21/41	Rainer Family, "Grand Sacred Concert" for the German Catholic Society.	4:95
3/21/41	SMSS at St. Patrick's Church, South End.	4:95
4/18/41	Rainer Family for Kosmos Ferner (a trustee of the BGS).	4:127
5/9/41	Benefit Concert for R. Garbett, organist of Holy Cross Cathedral.	4:135
5/16/41	BGS. "Grand Concert" at Boylston Hall.	4:159
5/30/41	SMSS, Concert of Sacred Music.	4:167

the German Catholic building fund in December of 1842. The appearances of such groups would have added prestige and general interest to concerts sponsored by the Catholic community.

Nevertheless, the musical press of the day largely ignored Catholic concerts. During the two-and-a-half-year period covered by figure 2.1, three musical journals that commented on the musical life of the city existed in Boston at various times: the *Boston Musical Gazette* (1838–39), edited by Bartholomew Brown; *The Musical Magazine, or Repository of Musical Science, Literature, and Intelligence* (1839–41), edited by H. Theodor Hach; and the *Musical Reporter* (1841), edited by Asa Fitz and E. B. Dearborn.[9] Each of these periodicals carried exactly one item concerning Catholic musical events: *The Musical Magazine* printed a negative review of the Boston Gregorian Society public rehearsal of January 20, 1839, with no specific information on the music presented, but expressing displeasure with the very idea of public rehearsals in general;[10] the *Boston Musical Gazette* mentioned the existence of the Boston Gregorian Society without giving any specifics;[11] and the *Musical Reporter* printed in its music section one hymn from the new Catholic hymnal.[12] It is also notable that almost no Catholic publications are advertised in the mainstream musical press. For example, the Oliver Ditson Company of Boston, while regularly advertising in the mainstream press, never lists any of its music intended for Catholic consumption, including the hymnal *Morning and Evening Services of the Catholic Church*.

This journalistic separatism existed despite the fact that individuals involved in Catholic musical organizations were also involved in the wider musical life of the city. The first musical director of both the Boston Gregorian Society and the St. Mary's Singing Society was the noted violinist Louis Ostinelli, who was also first violinist (and de facto conductor) of the Boston Handel and Haydn Society in its early years.[13] Thomas Comer, conductor of a number of the Catholic concerts, was a Boston opera promoter and later conductor of the Boston Musical Fund Society,[14] as well as a frequent contributor to the *Boston Musical Gazette*.[15] Richard Garbett, British by birth and Anglican by religion, was both organist and director of music at the Catholic Cathedral of the Holy Cross in Boston as well as composer of an oratorio, *The Hymn of the Seasons*, performed in 1839 by the Boston Musical Institute and published the same year in Boston by Crocker and Brewster. It is clear, then, that the musical establishment of Boston could not have been completely unaware of Catholic concert life, for many musicians moved back and forth across the line dividing Protestant and Catholic musical life in Boston.

Although the actual practice of music by Catholics in both church and concert hall was rarely reported in the musical press, there was frequent discussion of the nature of Catholic music. These discussions often served to define issues pertaining to the nature of Protestant church music, such as congregational participation and the use of choirs. Articles dealing with such issues appeared not only in the musical press but in the religious and theological press as well. But the information provided by these articles concerns not so much what Catholics, especially American Catholics, were singing and hearing as what the Protestant establishment *thought* the Catholics were singing and hearing. This distinction has not always been made, and these accounts have been used as reliable indicators of the actual practice of American Catholic church music.

Controversies concerning the proper nature of Protestant church music in the early nineteenth century have been well documented. Reformers such as Thomas Hastings and Lowell Mason spearheaded movements that had a profound effect on both church music and music education. There were great differences among the various musical styles employed by the Methodists for their revivals, the Congregationalists for their psalmody, and the Episcopalians for their choral chant. Each group had clear ideas of what constituted "proper" church music.

The question of what constitutes a "proper" form of music for a religious group is not only a liturgical question but an ethnological one as well. Lois Ibsen al Faruqi argues that the judgment of suitability of a musical style for incorporation in religious rituals is the result of a general consensus within a particular society and is closely linked to that society's belief system:[16]

> As the Western Christian world espoused different national and sectarian bodies of doctrine, some forms of music came to be judged suitable for the Catholic service, others for the Protestant service generally, and still others for particular groups within Protestantism. The religious music of each group varied according to the differences in the correspondent belief system of its participants.[17]

Faruqi's idea of a correspondence between belief systems and forms of religious music has much merit, even though it is more easily applied within cultures that have a common religion. Perhaps never before in recorded musical history, however, had so many different religious denominations, each with its own ideas of "proper" church music, lived in such close proximity. There was neither an official religion, nor government enforcement of particular norms for worship. Indeed, pride in the accomplishment of such freedom may even have fostered suspicion among older Americans of a religious practice that seemed to take its cue from a foreign power—Rome. But many of the Catholic immigrants, notably the Irish, came from countries where religious oppression was the norm; they sought to share in the religious freedom that a largely Protestant society had achieved in the new world. Despite these difficulties, for evidence to support Faruqi's position, even within the diversity of religious culture in nineteenth-century America, one need only turn to the articles concerning the inherent differences between Protestant and Catholic church music found in the musical press of the time.

Many discussions of the characteristics of Protestant and Catholic church music tended to overlook the distinct denominations within Protestantism, and to deal with broader issues. In 1839 Boston's *Musical Magazine* published an overview of that city's musical life, pointing out the fundamental differences between Protestant and Catholic music:

> The Protestant Church stands related to the Roman Catholic very much in the same way in its music as in its religion. The Protestant religion appeals to the heart of man through his understanding; the Catholic through his imagination and feelings. So it is too with their music. The Catholics use but few words, many times repeated; but in a dead language, understood by very few; leaving it to the music to draw forth the feelings and raise the emotions of the congregation. The Protestants, on the other hand, place the chief power of their hymns and psalms in the words, laboring to have the sentiments fully developed, not only poetically but rationally; and then applying them to their simple, but sometimes substantial, and often noble strains. In short, while the Catholics melt in rapture under their *masses*, the Protestants kindle and exalt their devotional feelings by their *chorals*.[18]

Similar sentiments are expressed in a number of articles in the musical press, though not always so evenhandedly. There is often admiration for the quality of music composed for the Catholic Church together with a certain amount of fear of the power of music. The *Musical Reporter* of 1841 published the following:

> The Catholic Church has long known how to avail herself of the services of this potent ally [music]. That church has not been more famous for the gorgeous pomp of her numerous rites, the magnificence of her temples, her painted ceilings, her sculptured marbles, than for the unrivalled excellence of her music,—unrivalled for its power to melt and subdue the heart. Other communions have by no means kept pace with that of the Roman in this department of worship.[19]

Still other articles show a more thorough fear of the power of music in the hands of the Catholic church and its ritual. The *Boston Musical Gazette* of 1848 provides a clear example. Having noted the importance and power of music in the Protestant Reformation, and the power of simplicity in sacred song, the writer looks to practical matters:

> And we ought to learn from these facts, to be satisfied with a chaste simplicity in sacred songs, as an attribute distinctly Protestant and evangelical; and to look with suspicion upon all departures from it, and upon all aping of the Romanizers in their chants and theatrical, musical expedients. Let them have a music which befits their dark design of excluding the gospel of Christ—let them set their mummeries to music if they will, and utter their dark sayings in an unknown tongue. It is ours to sing with the spirit and with the understanding also. And we have probably yet

much to learn of the power which the songs of Zion are to exert in expelling Popery. If their power was so prominent in the reformation which is past, will it not be still more in the reformation that is to come? And is it not time for us to be divising some expedients to bring this power to bear out of the limits of our congregations, and upon the vassals of Popery?[20]

These excerpts reflect the three themes that seem to run through many discussions of music in the musical and religious press, themes best expressed as dialectical pairs: rational/emotive; true worship/idolatry; democratic/hierarchical. These themes are not unrelated to each other and to other intellectual currents existing in the wider context of American life and thought. A more thorough investigation of each of these pairs will show their significance to American musical life.

Rational versus Emotive

The preference for "rational" music was stronger, it seems, in the Boston press than in the New York press. The tendency is not surprising given the Puritan heritage of New England. Although the caricature of Puritan attitudes toward music and dance outside of religious service has been shown to be untrue, church music was strictly controlled and limited. Gretchen Finney has traced attitudes toward music and ecstasy in seventeenth-century England and demonstrates that the concern for "rational" music was strong at the end of that century. She quotes from a 1698 discussion over the propriety of instrumental music in church:

> *Singing of Psalms* with the Voice . . . is a *Rational act*, and exspresseth in a Melodious Manner the *Conceptions* of the Mind. But *Instrumental Musick* is only *Ceremonial*, for it is no *Rational Act*, neither does it *Articulately* express the *Affections*, and Serious *Conceptions* of the Soul.[21]

The use of instrumental music, and the presence of organs in their churches, was never in question for Catholics. St. Joseph's Church in Philadelphia—the first openly Catholic church in British North America—had a small organ by the 1740s, and the first Catholic church in Boston opened in 1803 with an organ already installed.[22] If a church, when erected, could not afford an instrument, provision was made within the design for later installation. The purchase of an organ was a high priority for Catholics and its use as a solo instrument a normal practice. Although a few New

England Protestant churches installed organs in the eighteenth century, it was not until the nineteenth century that any but a handful of churches employed instrumental music. Indeed, the organ was most often employed as an accompaniment to song, congregational or choral. The growth of instrumental music in churches was acknowledged by the Boston-based *Musical Library* in its first issue:

> Music for the organ will be occasionally introduced. This noble instrument is becoming very common in the churches of various denominations of Christians, and the demand for music appropriate to it is constantly increasing. Hitherto very little music has been published in this country for the organ; and many young persons, who officiate as organists, and who play psalmody very acceptably, are often at a loss for an appropriate voluntary, prelude, or interlude.[23]

While instrumental music gradually became accepted in many Protestant churches during the first half of the nineteenth century, the necessary characteristics of "rational" music changed as well. That the texts of church music must be understood by all was a principle retained from Reformation days. But music might also involve devotional *feelings*, which are carefully distinguished from the passions:

> In Protestant worship, sacred songs are used for two purposes—to impress divine truth on the mind, and to excite and express devotional feelings. In Romish churches, music is used, not to impress sentiments, and not to express devotional feeling, but to exert an attraction by mere musical effect. Hence, nothing is lost in that the matter sung or chanted is put into an unknown language. The design which the Romish system seeks in its music, is as well secured in Latin words, as it would be in those of the vernacular tongue. It deals with the taste, imagination and passions. It is no part of its object to aid a rational soul in communion with God.[24]

These sentiments, however, were not limited to either New England or church music. An article on Italian opera appeared in a New York journal of music and dealt with all music in a similar vein:

> Music, in short, is a powerful instrument for good or for evil, and this renders it necessary that in its pursuit and enjoyment we should not give way to a transcendental deification of it, but always preserve our common-sense intact, and ever keep our passional emotions subordinate to religious principles.[25]

The phrase "transcendental deification" of music refers to a threat against "rational" music not stemming from the Romanists or those with Romanizing tendencies; an outgrowth of Protestantism itself—Unitarianism and New England Transcendentalism—would be the greatest challenge. John S. Dwight, founder and editor of the well-known *Dwight's Journal of Music*, the first American musical publication to have a long and established existence (1852–81), was strongly influenced by the Transcendental movement. Irving Lowens noted that Dwight was able to concisely formulate the Transcendentalist's view of music as early as 1835: "if words were to be regarded as the language of thought, then music must be regarded as the language of feeling."[26] Dwight and others influenced by the Transcendentalist movement were in the forefront of advocating the use of the music of Haydn and Mozart written specifically for Catholic ritual. While Mozart's *Requiem* was accepted in some Protestant circles very early, the masses of Mozart and Haydn were found only in occasional rearrangements that disguised their origin.[27] One commentator noted that Haydn was famous for his instrumental music but not his vocal music, a phenomenon simply explained: "But Haydn was a beadsman, and hence these efforts of his genius received the name of *masses;* and here, in *one word,* is the key to all the prevailing indifference, inconstancy and want of knowledge on this subject," while "the *Requiem* of Mozart, being a prayer of intercession for the dead, and thus in its fundamental doctrine exclusively Catholic, the public do not object to listen to."[28]

Dwight's discussion of Viennese orchestral masses expresses a view of music almost completely opposite that of the supporters of "rational" music:

> For music, fortunately, is of no sectarian persuasion, and come from whatever source it may, if it be genuine, great music, it goes to the very inmost heart of all men, and becomes a blending, reconciling influence.... Such music is too beautiful, too vital, too human, too universal and eternal in its meanings to be monopolized by any church. They belong to humanity.[29]

A theme common to many Unitarian articles concerning church music emphasized the religious values intimately tied to aesthetic value. In a review of a church music collection entitled *Cantus Ecclesiæ*, which included a number of psalm tunes adapted from instrumental themes of the Viennese classicists, one staunchly Unitarian journal wrote that "there is more religion in the instrumental Quartettes and Sonatas from which these classic Psalm tunes are derived, than the so called *Sacred* music of any but the Catholic church has ever manifested."[30] For many of the Unitarian denomination, the music written for the Catholic ritual—especially the masses of Mozart and Haydn—evinced the finest aspects of an ideal church music.

From the vantage of the more conservative denominations of Protestantism, Catholic music was viewed as nonrational, as mere musical stimulus for the passions, and incapable of expressing worship. But according to the viewpoint of the other end of the Protestant spectrum—the Transcendentalists and Unitarians—the music of Catholicism was a treasure that belonged to all humanity, that transcended even the oppressive doctrine and empty ritual of the Catholic church. It should be remembered, however, that this view of Catholic music was not postulated on American Catholic musical practice, but on an aesthetic judgment of a European Catholic repertory.

True Worship versus Idolatry

The second theme running through the treatment of Catholic music in the musical press is the tension between true worship and idolatry, not unrelated, of course, to the first theme. One of the leading Unitarian journals described Catholic services as nothing more than pagan:

> All the most prominent and characteristic features of the Roman ceremonial are of Pagan origin. Enter one of their churches here or elsewhere, observe the rites and functions there exhibited, attend the high Mass, or the low Mass, and what do you witness? You witness the same Pagan rites which were practiced in Rome before the coming of Christ.[31]

A number of years earlier, the same journal doubted the antiquity of the music of Catholicism. Reviewing a publication containing "hymns of the primitive church,"[32] the author called the book a "tasteless selection of hymns from Roman Catholic sources, written, nobody knows when, or by whom, but none of them having the least claim to a primitive antiquity."[33] The *Musical Magazine* accepted the idea that "fragments of melody which was used in the days of Ambrose and Gregory, are still extant among the specimens of ancient music," but noted that "all the *musical* interest now attached to them has been furnished by the *modern* composer," and that "the specimens in their present dress, have just about as much resemblance to the ancient originals, as modern relics do to the cross of St. Peter—all being made of wood."[34]

Histories of music, which appear frequently in the musical press of the day, treat the Middle Ages as symbolic of all things Catholic. C. M. Cady related medieval religion and musical practice:

> A century or two later, as the dark ages set in, the congregational hymn singing was overthrown by the hierarchical system which then became thoroughly organized, and has since characterized the Romish church. The choir, or chancel, which separated the singers from the general assembly, was an invention of medieval architecture, corresponding with this change. Choir music has ever since been a favorite in great ecclesiastical establishments.[35]

The Reformation, however, was perceived as freeing music from these prisons: "Congregational singing was introduced shortly after the Reformation, and distinguishes Protestants from Romanists, where the laity never join the singing during divine service. *Not* singing *congregationally at all*, then, is *anti-Protestant*."[36] Some writers went even further in their claims.

> Music is essentially Protestant. The pope has spared no money in order to Romanize it; but music is not the property of the pope, or the possession of the devil, or the monopoly of either, but the creature of God, and meant to be, and yet destined to be, the utterer of his praise. . . . Unison is popery, harmony is Protestantism.[37]

The writer clearly conceived of Catholic music as being limited to the chant, while Protestant music was characterized by four-part chorales. Unlike many other articles of the time, it overlooks the polyphonic and orchestral masses composed from Palestrina through composers of the nineteenth century.

An enlightening article appeared in the *Western Messenger*, a Unitarian journal, commenting on a letter which appeared in the *Cincinnati Journal*.[38] At a concert held in a Presbyterian church in Cincinnati, a song was sung which included both English and Latin words, including the lines "Ave Sanctissima" (Hail Most Holy Woman) and "Ora pro nobis" (Pray for us).[39] A furious concert-goer wrote to the journal that "It is *idolatry*, naked and undisguised—a hymn, a *prayer* to the Virgin Mary. . ." and that "if papists ever succeed in duping the people of this community to embrace Romanism, it will be by disguising its bloated and hideous form in the garments of poetry and music."[40]

After giving the full text of the original letter, the author comments that one must draw a distinction between worship and a concert. "We grant, that if such a hymn were sung for public *worship*" it would be idolatry. But the context in which it was performed altered the situation. "It is sung at a concert— It is sung as an expression of art, of beauty, of poetry, of music— not as a *hymn* or *prayer*."[41]

The tension between true worship and idolatry became all the more confusing as the influence of Romanticism spread throughout much of the musical establishment in America. Over and over again one finds comments about Catholic ritual and music that reflect the tension between the romantic interest in the medieval period and the Protestant rejection of such ritual and its music:

> At length the grand cathedral arose, and the stately spire; courts and arches echoed, and pillars shook with the thunder of the majestic organ, and choirs, sweetly attuned, joined their voices in all the moods and measures of the religious heart, in its most exalted, most profound, most intense experience put into lyrical expression. I know that piety may reject, may repel this form of expression, still these sublime ritual harmonies cannot but give the spirit that sympathizes with them, the sense of a mightier being. But sacred music has power without a ritual.[42]

Once again the writer distinguishes between the music itself and the rites that gave birth to it. One can admire the beauty of the music while rejecting the objectionable ritual. Another author employed an analogy to another art form to provide a strong argument against the use of Catholic music within Protestant worship, while not denying its value in a purely aesthetic context:

> A Christian may visit a gallery of prints with pleasure and with profit; but what Protestant would consent to have even the most beautiful and unexceptionable pictures hung upon the walls of our churches, as help to our devotion? Such productions excite the imagination, and chain the feelings to the earth; they do not help, they rather injure true devotion.[43]

Other articles exhibited an even more tolerant attitude toward the product, while not excusing the creator: "May not a wicked carpenter construct a very good pulpit, from which the word of God may be faithfully delivered?"[44]

Romantic tendencies were, of course, not a phenomenon unknown to Unitarianism. A letter to the editor of a Unitarian journal describes the author's reactions to attending a Catholic mass on Christmas morning in Philadelphia:

> I shall not attempt to describe the sublime effect of the service, in which the heavens seemed to be descending to the earth on the wings of har-

mony, and the awful traditions of the Christian history, of the advent of God to humanity, reproduced in the elaborate creations of the inspired artist. I cannot deny that there is something inspiring and grand in the Catholic ritual, even perhaps to my ultra Protestant disposition. It is to me the embodiment of that instinctive aspiration for unity, which the heart clings to so fondly. . . . I love to regard it as an anticipation of the choral harmonies of a better day.[45]

But the faithful Unitarian adds that he "may be permitted to interpret the solemn and beautiful services of the Church in a different sense from that in which they are received by the devout Catholic."[46]

The effect of Romanticism on perceptions of "ideal" Catholic music is most evident in the treatment of Allegri's *Miserere*. The seventeenth-century Italian composer Gregorio Allegri had composed his setting of the *Miserere*, a text sung during the Catholic Tenebrae service in Holy Week, for the papal chapel and it had remained the sole property of the papal choir until the late eighteenth century. Charles Burney heard it during his travels in Italy and spoke of it with high praise, as did, later, Goethe and Mendelssohn. As early as 1825 it was described in the most romantic of terms in a staunchly Congregationalist journal:

> The shadows of evening had now closed in; and we should have been left almost in total darkness, but for the dull red glare which proceeded from the hidden lights of the unseen choristers, and which, mingling with the deepening twilight, produced a most melancholy gloom. After a deep and most impressive pause of silence, the solemn Miserere commenced; and never by mortal ear was heard a strain of such powerful, such heart-moving pathos. The accordant tones of a hundred human voices—and one which seemed more than human—ascended together to heaven for mercy to mankind—for pardon to a guilty and sinning world. It had nothing in it of this earth—nothing that breathed the ordinary feelings of our nature. . . . It was the music of another state of being.[47]

A similar description was printed twenty years later by *The Boston Musical Gazette:*

> The silence at length became too painful. I thought I should shriek out in agony; when suddenly a wail, so desolate, so sweet, so despairing, and yet so tender, like the last strain of a broken heart, stole slowly out from the distant darkness and swelled over the throng, that the tears rushed unbidden to my eyes, and I could have wept like a child in sympathy.[48]

A somewhat tamer article from 1854 described the history of the famed composition, noted both Emperor Leopold's and Mozart's admiration of it, and included the question, "Is it wonderful that, in such circumstances, such music as that famed *Miserere*, sung by such a choir, should shake the soul of even a Calvinist?"[49] It is interesting, then, to note that the work was included in the Catholic hymnal of 1833, of which only a few copies were printed before the plates were destroyed by a fire, but was omitted from the revision of that work that finally appeared in 1840.[50] The reason for the omission may be that "the composition, however fine, is nothing without the voices which perform it here [Rome]. It is only the singers of the papal chapel who can execute the Miserere."[51]

Thus, the interest which the Romantic movement found in things medieval, beautiful, and Catholic tempered the tension between the notion of true worship and that of idolatry. The idealized history of Catholic music and worship became for many a fascinating topic, a fact that was not lost on a number of Catholic apologists and defenders of the time. The aesthetic dimensions of Catholicism, the defenders discovered, could be used to create more favorable views of the Roman church, and perhaps even lead to conversions to the church.

Democracy versus Hierarchy

Protestant writers were aware of the threat from the aesthetic dimensions of Catholicism, as can be seen in many of the citations already quoted. In the first two themes we have focused on—reason/emotion and true worship/idolatry—the tension was tempered by Unitarianism, Transcendentalism, and Romanticism; in the third dialectic, democracy/hierarchy, the tension between the theological need for a simple, "rational" church music and the growing popular interest in more elaborate Catholic styles was fueled by an external movement, Nativism. The growth of anti-Catholic feeling throughout the thirty years following 1820 was punctuated by such violent outbursts as the burning of the Ursuline Convent and school in Charlestown, Massachusetts, in 1833, and the anti-Catholic riots and church-burning in Philadelphia in 1844. To this day, Old St. Patrick's Church in New York City is surrounded by a wall built to defend the church against such mob violence. The Catholic immigrants and their religion were seen as a very real and present danger, not merely a philosophical problem.[52]

There were many styles of warnings presented to the Protestant readership concerning the lure of Catholicism. "The [Catholic] Church has most powerful influences to address to the eye, the imagination, and the feelings," wrote one Unitarian author. "These are susceptibilities which are akin to the religious sentiment in many breasts." Other publications warned against attending Catholic services, even if just to hear the musical performances, as appears to have been the custom in a number of urban areas. "No musical attractions, however excellent, must draw you to join in a worship that is idolatrous, or to unite with company ungodly and profane."[54]

The intrinsic link between American democracy and Protestantism was expressed strongly by even those of such liberal bent as the Unitarians. In 1854, Frederick H. Hedge, a leading journalist in the Unitarian movement, gave one explanation of that link, in an article dealing with Catholic worship:

> It was Luther who laid the corner-stone of the mighty fabric of these United States. Without the Protestant Reformation, the Constitution of these States would be as impossible, as the Christian Church would be without Christ, the corner-stone. Every conversion which takes place from the Protestant faith to that of Rome, is a blow aimed at that Constitution.[55]

The press was filled with stories, sometimes quite lurid stories, about the evils and dangers of Catholicism. They often warned of the particular dangers of Jesuitism. The musical press was no exception. Some provided examples from other countries:

> Nolrega [sic] (a Jesuit) had a school where he instructed the native children . . . they were trained to assist at mass, and *to sing* the church service. . . . He set the catechism, creed, and ordinary prayers to *sol fa;* and the pleasure of learning to sing was such a temptation, that the little Tupis sometimes ran away from their parents to put themselves under the care of the Jesuit.[56]

Other threats existed closer to home:

> At this moment the Jesuits, driven by late revolutionists from the Continent, are watching with lynx eyes for every and any plank on which to float into power, and one of the means they are usurping is music in Popish worship. Numbers of Jesuits have become teachers of music ostensibly—teachers of Popery really. You must resist the devil in whatever shape he comes—whether building grand Cathedrals, or writing sublime oratorios—whether with trowel or trumpet.[57]

It was not uncommon to read of Catholic plots against Protestant America:

> While losing its hold on the common mind in the old Catholic countries, it grasps elsewhere with the strength of a young giant.... There is to be a long and severe struggle in this land between it and Protestantism.... Its attention to the fine arts is proverbial, and is included in its policy. It has studied their effects on the human mind, and on man as a religious being. And thus it seeks to propitiate the enlightened by affording gratification to a refined taste.[58]

The public perceptions of Catholic music in antebellum United States clearly were related to larger societal movements current in mid-nineteenth-century America. These perceptions form part of the context in which actual Catholic musical practice existed, yet they tell us perhaps more about Protestant than Catholic culture. The views of the American press often were not based on the actual experience of American Catholic musical life, but rather reflect a biased, intellectualized, or romanticized picture of Catholicism.

The material presented in this chapter also points out how closely linked religion and music still were in mid-nineteenth-century America. Certainly there was a growing audience for musical events outside of the church, yet there was often a religious dimension as well as an aesthetic one in the reception and perception of these events. Musical journals regularly carried articles of purely religious interest.[59] Interest in the subject of church music was lively. The value of the music of Beethoven or Italian opera was considered within an aesthetic, moral, and religious framework. And just as Frederick Hedge could see no distinction between America and Protestant America, so the musical press was a Protestant estate.

CHAPTER THREE

Change and Adaptation in the 1830s, Boston

Historians view the year 1828 as a pivotal date in American history. The election of Andrew Jackson to the presidency meant the inauguration of a new style of American government, and a recognition of the expansion of the country into the West. Work was commenced on the Baltimore and Ohio Railroad that same year, the first of many railroad systems that would change the shape, economics, and history of the developing nation. The massive railroad-building projects also called for massive numbers of physical laborers, a need that thousands of Irishmen would arrive to fill in the coming years.

As the makeup of Catholic communities of the United States became more and more heavily Irish, significant changes occurred in the nature of American Catholic life. The First Provincial Council of Baltimore, a meeting of all the Catholic bishops of the United States, took place in 1829, and marked the beginning of a more centralized regulation of the Catholic church in America. It has been suggested by Patrick Carey that the First Provincial Council marked the beginning of "shifts in patterns of thought . . . that reflected what could be called the romantic impulse."[1] Carey includes among these romantic tendencies the idea that the church (particularly the papacy) was the protector of the poor against political and economic forces that could enslave them, and the notion that the greatest art and literature of Western civilization was a product of the "Catholic spirit."[2] The former idea would help fashion the way in which the church dealt with the growing number of Catholic immigrants arriving in America; the latter would influence the styles of music employed by the church as well as the way in which the music was used.

The present chapter will examine the musical changes that took place among the Catholic communities of Boston during the 1830s. During that decade the Catholic church of the Boston area became predominantly Irish, both in its leadership and membership. There are a number of reasons for studying the Boston Irish. First, Irish immigration to Boston in the 1830s was proportionately greater than in any American city. Second, the Irish of Boston were more organized and centralized than in other places. Third, beginning in 1829 the news of the Irish community was regularly reported by a weekly newspaper, whose editors were interested in musical matters.[3] Finally, throughout the 1830s, the Catholic community of Boston attempted to publish a music collection for its use, finally succeeding in 1840. The revisions of the collection between 1833 and 1840 document the change of musical preferences in a community becoming more and more Irish-dominated in the intervening years.

Official government statistics concerning the number of Irish arriving in Boston are deceptive. Large numbers of Irish were not counted because they did not arrive in Boston directly from Ireland or England but came by land or sea from New Brunswick; from 1830 to 1835 the indirect route was the cheapest way for an Irishman to come to the United States, and most of these immigrants arrived and remained in Boston and environs.[4] Thus in the early 1830s, Boston received not only the largest number of Irish immigrants, but also a disproportionate number of the poorest Irishmen who came to America. Such conditions may offer a partial explanation of why Boston saw the rise of violent anti-Irish and anti-Catholic sentiment earlier than other urban areas. Events such as the burning of the Ursuline Convent in 1834 and the Broad Street riots of 1837 further galvanized the identity and separateness of the Irish Catholic community in the Boston area.

In 1830, the Catholic community in Boston was served by a single parish, the Cathedral of the Holy Cross, which had sufficed since 1802. The rise in immigrant arrivals in Boston is reflected in the sudden growth in the number of Catholic parishes: St. Augustine's in 1831, St. Mary's in 1836, and St. Patrick's later the same year. Other institutions sprang up, including the Charitable Irish Society and Patrick Mooney's Catholic Book Store, both of which became centers of Irish life in Boston. The "room over Mr. Mooney's Bookstore" and the "schoolroom" beneath the Cathedral were important social centers. The former was the site of the Catholic singing school, begun by Francis Mallet and continued by Charles T. Young;[5] the latter was employed as a rehearsal and performance space by various Catholic musical organizations.

Much of the character and organization of Boston Irish life, as well as our knowledge of it, was due to the existence of the newspaper which eventually became known as the *Boston Pilot*. Although started by Bishop Benedict Fenwick in 1829 as a purely religious newspaper, it was taken over by the Irishman Patrick Donahoe in 1834 and emerged as the leading Irish-American newspaper of the decade. Not only did the *Pilot* report on musical events within the community, it also featured articles on Irish music, and later printed sheet music for the Irish community of Boston. Donahoe, who would be a major force in Boston Irish life over the next forty years, involved himself with the musical life of the Irish community, serving as president of the St. Mary's Singing Society in 1838.[6]

In late 1833, the publication of *The Catholic Church Service Book* was eagerly awaited by the Catholic musical community.[7] There was a first printing, but only a few copies remained from it after fire destroyed the printing establishment, S. H. Parker. Fortunately, a copy used at St. Mary's Church has survived in the collection of the Boston Public Library. Unsuccessful attempts were made to publish the collection over the next few years until finally in 1840 a revised edition was produced with success. A comparison of the two versions will help to show the evolution of musical preferences within the Boston Irish community during the 1830s.

We begin with the growth of musical organizations among the Catholic parishes of Boston. Then we will turn to the types of repertory employed by the immigrant community in Boston, following the categories explained in chapter 1.

Catholic Musical Organizations

The Church, later Cathedral, of the Holy Cross employed music and musicians from its earliest years. Francis Mallet, said to have been the organist at the dedication of the new building in 1802, was active in Catholic musical affairs as late as 1832, a year before his death, running the singing school mentioned above. The Hogan sisters appear to have been prominent musicians at the cathedral until about 1835, and Mrs. D. L. Brown also served as cathedral organist throughout the 1830s.[8] There was a children's choir at the cathedral in the early 1830s which was made up of students in the free school run in the basement of the church.[9] Sophia Hewitt Ostinelli, daughter of the musician James Hewitt and wife of the violinist Louis Ostinelli, was cathedral organist on a number of occasions.

The greatest influence on music in Catholic Boston in the early years of the decade was undoubtedly the attempt to publish the music collection *The Catholic Church Service Book.* The leading force behind the collection of church music was the bishop of Boston, Benedict Fenwick. Born in Maryland and educated at Georgetown, Fenwick was himself an amateur musician. Numerous accounts refer to his fine singing voice; he appears to have been a pianist as well.[10] The first public mention of the proposed collection was in Fenwick's newspaper, *The Jesuit,* and noted the need for "a cheap collection of easy music, adapted to the Catholic church service"; the notice stated that a "gentleman has lately offered to print such a collection, the music to be furnished by the Bishop, if a sufficient number of subscribers be obtained."[11] Response must have been swift and sufficient, for less than a month later it was reported to be in preparation.[12] Subscribers could obtain the book for two dollars.

Advertisements noted that it consists "almost entirely, that is, with very few exceptions, of GREGORIAN Music, harmonized and arranged for the Organ or Piano."[13]

> The Gregorian Music, however excellent, is understood, comparatively by few musicians of this country. Hence the difficulty they experience generally in a Catholic Choir, and especially when invited to become Organists in a Catholic Church. To obviate this want of knowledge, this book has been chiefly compiled. The Gregorian chant has everywhere been transposed in it [from four to five line staves]; and the modern musician will be delighted to see that the ancient music, so venerable for its antiquity, and at the same time so beautiful and solemn, arrayed before his eyes, scientifically harmonized with the *Soprani, Tenor,* and *Base,* and seldom without the *Alto,* and never without the accompaniment for the Organ and Piano.—He will in fact find himself perfectly at home.[14]

The description provides a number of clues to musical practice of the time. It suggests that non-Catholic organists, unfamiliar with chant and the Catholic service, were regularly hired. But it also suggests that the music employed was something of a compromise: the Gregorian tunes, but harmonized and performed in a contemporary style, the welding of "tradition" with "science."

The promised hymnal gave impetus to other musical activities. In September of 1833, Charles T. Young announced the opening of his singing school, the "object of which is, to form a society of young singers, and to use the Music Book published under the direction of the Rt. Rev. Dr. Fenwick." It is impossible to ascertain if Young's singing school obtained an advance copy of the music collection; nevertheless, the school must have been somewhat successful. Just two months later, Young advertised a "Concert of Sacred Music, at the Masonic Temple, on Sunday evening, Nov. 24th to consist of selections from the services of the Catholic Church, and other pieces from the Handel and Haydn Society's works, etc."[15] The day before the concert the *Daily Evening Transcript* printed the program:[16]

I

Psalm 109: Dixit Dominus	Chant
Kyrie eleison and Gloria	Mass by DeMonti
Solo and chorus: Ave Maris Stella	Rev. M. F. W.
Hymn: Daughter of Zion	Carr
Solo and chorus: Jerusalem, my happy home	Clifton
Anthem: O praise ye the Lord	

II

Mottet: The voice of angels	Clark
Duett: Ave Maria Gratia Plena	
Solo and Chorus: Great God, What do I see and hear	Judgment Hymn
Duett: Ave Sanctissima	Mrs. Hemans
Song: Pilgrim Fathers	Mrs. Hemans
Duett and Chorus: There is a stream	
Finale: Ecce Quam Bonum	Chant

The concert was clearly a success:

> We feel a very great pleasure in publishing, that the first Catholic Concert, which ever took place in New-England, (and, for aught we know, in the United States of America)—was held on Sunday evening last, in the Masonic Temple, in this City. It being an entirely unprecedented thing and almost a momentary thought, the interest which it excited seemed not very intense; but the result was astonishing. Never was the Masonic Temple more densely crowded; and great were the numbers who could not gain admittance.[17]

The very next issue of *The Jesuit* carried the sorry news that the hymnal, all the plates, as well as a manuscript of sacred music which was to make up the second part of the new hymnal, had been destroyed in a fire. "But a small number of copies had been taken from the plates, previous to their entire destruction."[18] Bishop Fenwick, writing to Bishop Rosati of St. Louis, provides greater detail:

> The Gregorian music book, which you request me to forward to Mr. Dinnies [a St. Louis bookseller], is no more. I have in all but four copies remaining, out of 1,000 which I had sent to the bookbinder. All have been consumed in a fire, which destroyed not only my printed copies but also my plates. Thus I have incurred a loss of about $600. Am I not very fortunate in my undertakings?[19]

The loss of the hymnal was certainly a blow to Catholic musical life in Boston, but the success of the concert, and its repetition a few weeks later, ensured the further development of musical activities among the Catholics of Boston. Not only did they enjoy the music, but perhaps more important, they had discovered a new way to raise money.

Indeed, if any one characteristic united almost every Catholic endeavor in Boston during the 1830s, it was lack of money. The sudden need for new churches, an orphan asylum, and schools strained the resources of the largely immigrant community. Concerts were a way in which a group of people could raise money without incurring great expense, and more and more concerts would be used for fund-raising purposes. An "Oratorio" at the Masonic Temple, February 15, 1835, benefited the Sisters of Charity Orphanage. A "Concert of Sacred Music" was held in the same location on April 10, 1836, to "create means for establishing an efficient choir in the new Catholic Church in Pond Street [St. Mary's], and to institute in connection with it, a free singing-school."[20]

An "Oratorio of Sacred Music" was held at St. Mary's Church on May 8, 1836, to meet the debt on the building of the church. The "conductor of the oratorio" was Thomas Comer, a professional musician involved at various times with the Handel and Haydn Society, the Boston Musical Institute, and the promotion of opera in Boston. The "Leader of the Orchestra" was Louis Ostinelli, a professional violinist involved with many aspects of Boston musical life. At least in financial terms the concert was a great success. The *Boston Pilot* reported the proceeds as $1,735.[21] The program was as follows:

Part I

Sacred Overture	Winter
Grand Chorus—Kyrie—from the Mass of Haydn	

Solo—"Holy, Holy, Lord."	Handel
Grand Chorus—Gloria in Excelsis—from the Mass of Haydn	
Trio—O Salutaris Hostia	Gossec
Anthem—Hear My Prayer	Kent
Solo—Domine Deus—(from Mss. Mass)	Comer
Trio—Domine Filii	Comer
Duett—Quoniam tu Solus Sanctus	Comer
Grand Chorus—Cum Sancto Spiritu	Comer

Part II

Overture, from the Oratorio Occasional	Handel
Song—How Cheerful	Arne
Chorus—Gloria in Excelsis Deo	Pergolesi
Song—When from the Sacred Garden Driven	G. J. Webbe
Song—When I think upon thy goodness	Handel
Song—Great Source of Day	Comer
Grand Chorus—Credo—from the Mass of Haydn	
Solo—Gratias Agimus Tibi	Gulielmi
Quartette—Agnus Dei—from the Mass of Haydn	
Grand Chorus—Dona nobis pacem—from the Mass of Haydn	

Perhaps the most remarkable aspect of the program is its similarity to programs of the Handel and Haydn Society. The Haydn Mass, most probably the "Harmoniemesse," was frequently sung by the society and Comer's "Great Source of Day" was written for them.[22] Perhaps the only piece unimaginable on a Handel and Haydn Society program was the Gossec "O Salutaris Hostia." It is certainly possible that members of the Handel and Haydn Society assisted at this and other similar concerts.

Having modeled their programs after those of the Handel and Haydn Society, it is no surprise that eventually the singers of Catholic Boston sought to form their own organization similar to it. Late in 1836 the following notice appeared in the *Pilot:*

> Agreeable to a notice given, the Young Men composing the different Choirs in the Catholic Churches of Boston and vicinity met at Montgomery Hall on Sunday evening, Nov. 13th. The meeting being called to order, an interesting and animated discussion on the object of the meeting took place, after which the following resolution was read and accepted unanimously. Resolved, That the state of Musical science among

our various choirs in the city and vicinity render it absolutely necessary for us to form a Singing Society for the improvement of ourselves in that most delightful of all sciences—Music; knowing that the correct performance of our own unrivaled Church Music adds greatly to the splendor and sublimity which attends the worship of God, therefore, we, the Catholics composing the different choirs, do form ourselves into a society, to be governed by such rules and regulations as may be adopted hereafter... under the name of the BOSTON GREGORIAN SOCIETY.[23]

If there were any doubts that most of Boston's Catholics were Irish, the surnames of the new society's leadership would dispel them: O'Neill, Carver, Madigan, O'Brien, Cassidy, McDonald, Mooney, and Kelly. Only one surname suggests a non-Irishman: Kosmus Sirner.

The Gregorian Society quickly became an important force in the musical life of the Catholic community. While the society was modeled on the original aims of the Handel and Haydn Society—a city-wide organization for the improvement of church music—the repertory of the Gregorian Society became less and less similar to the repertory of the Handel and Haydn Society. Gregorian Society concerts programmed music that parish choirs could use in liturgical contexts. An 1838 concert included the following:[24]

Part First

Chaunt	Gregorian
Mass in G	DeMonti

Part Second

Requiem	Gregorian
Ode	T. Power
Adoramus in aeternam	Webbe
Sacred Song	
Regina Caeli	Walter
Ave Regina	Haydn
Sanctus Dominus	DeMonti

All of these pieces were suitable for use by parish choirs within a liturgical situation. Indeed, the setting of the Mass in G by DeMonti, along with DeMonti's other settings of the Mass, became staples of Catholic parish choirs throughout much of the century.[25]

The concentration on liturgical music did not endure however, and soon the concert programs of the Gregorian Society were largely made up of devotional rather than liturgical music. The following program was performed by the society on April 20, 1839:[26]

Part I

Chant—Laudate Pueri Dominum	
Song—You Abbey Bells	
Solo & Chorus—Almighty God, when round thy shrine	(Mozart)
Duett—Arrayed in clouds of golden light	(O. Shaw)
Chorus—The Storm	(Whitaker)
Song—The Star of Bethlehem	(F. Granger)
Sanctus	DeMonti
Duett—Far o'er hill and dell	(Sola?)
Chorus—Strike the Cymbal	Pucitta

Part II

Chorus—Glory to God in the Highest	(Handel?)
Song—He Shall Feed His Flock	(Handel?)
Hymn—Break Forth, O Sion, thy sweet Savior sing	
Song—Grant we beseech thee	
Anthem—Sound the loud timbrel	(Avison)
Song—Pilot on the Deep	(Nelson)
Anthem—There were shepherds abiding	(B. Carr, arr.)
Solo & Chorus—But who shall see the glorious day	(Webb)
Song—The Polar Star	(O. Shaw)
Finale—Doxology Gloria Patri	(B. Carr?)

The inclusion of Benjamin Carr's anthem "There were shepherds abiding," an arrangement of melodic materials borrowed from Handel, Corelli, and Haydn, was not surprising. A new edition of the anthem was the first music published by the Gregorian Society as part of an ambitious project to become a major supplier of Catholic church music.[27] The *Pilot* printed the prospectus for "Periodical Publications of Catholic Church Music by the Boston Gregorian Society" in August of 1838:[28]

> The great want of cheap Music for the use of Catholic Churches has long been felt in the U. States. The high cost of occasional publications in Philadelphia, Baltimore and New York, has hitherto placed it beyond the means of most Catholic Choirs. . . . the Boston Gregorian Society, instituted about two years ago for the cultivation of Catholic Church Music, proposes to establish in this city a Music Press, for the sole and specific

purpose of publishing, periodically, cheap Catholic Church Music in all its branches, ancient as well as modern.... The Society propose to publish, in successive numbers of 40 pages each, or thereabouts, a collection of choice Catholic Music.... These numbers will be issued every two months... and will be delivered to subscribers at the moderate rate of TWO CENTS PER PAGE.... The Society will commence printing as soon as 500 copies of the intended work shall have been subscribed for.... Proposals to print any original or previously published Music, not secured by copyright, will be taken into consideration whenever the publication of such Music shall be recommended by any three subscribing Choirs, Societies, or Congregations.... The Rt. Rev. Bp. Fenwick has kindly tendered to it [the Society] his collection of some of the most beautiful compositions from Rome and other places.... [The Society] have it also in contemplation to print a *cheap book of Music Instruction* both in the Gregorian and modern style of sacred singing, for the Catholic Youth of this country, who hither to have been almost entirely dependent on elementary works of Protestant compositions.[29]

Although even more ambitious than Fenwick's collection of 1833, the initial numbers proposed in the series were probably very similar to the earlier collection. The rather democratic method of "nominating" music to be published in the series would have produced interesting data concerning the types and styles of music popular among Catholics of the time. Unfortunately nothing seems to have come of the plan; the only music published by the society was the previously mentioned work by Benjamin Carr, which also included Carr's setting of the "Gloria Patri," a hymn "My God, My Life" by Massi, and a setting of the "Veni Creator."[30]

The Boston Gregorian Society, however, soon found itself in severe financial difficulties; whether the publishing venture was the cause of the problem, or the abandonment of the publishing venture was the result of the problem, is unclear. It is clear, however, that the society was not funded by the Catholic church but needed to raise its own funds, even though it was in effect the choir of the Cathedral: "the singers have always borne the expense attendant upon it."[31] On December 1, 1838, an announcement was made: "Male members of the different Congregations are requested to meet in the School Room under the Cathedral... immediately after Vespers, to devise means for the permanent support of the choirs belonging to the Churches, as now conducted by the Gregorian Society."[32]

Shortly before Christmas of 1838, a plan was proposed by a member of the congregation of Holy Cross Cathedral that would have raised a regular source of funding for each parish's choir and music program:

> Let every pew holder place an assessment of 12 1/2 cents per quarter, upon each seat in his pew,—this sum is trifling in itself, yet by everyone doing it, it will be found sufficient to answer all the calls, and at the same time, the expense will not come upon a few, but will be equally borne by all.[33]

The plan does not seem to have been taken up by the congregation, because the financial difficulties of the Gregorian Society continued. The *Pilot* printed a number of appeals for attendance at the society's concerts to help them resolve their financial woes.[34]

A second city-wide Catholic musical organization was founded in 1839, the St. Mary's Singing Society. Centered on the new St. Mary's Church, as the Gregorian Society was on the cathedral, the new singing society advertised itself not as a competitor with the older organization but rather as an auxiliary to it:

> For it must be apparent to any reflecting mind, that the Gregorian Society cannot be benefited by new members, unless they have been previously instructed in the rudiments of vocal music; and as that Society confines itself principally to performances of a higher order, by joining the St. Mary's Society persons could qualify themselves in musical *taste*, as well as practice for more difficult performances; and thus qualified, many would be induced to join the Gregorian Society who would otherwise feel no inclination to study music, imagining themselves incapacitated.[35]

Despite its protestations, "the St. Mary's Singing Society is looked upon by some as in opposition to the Gregorian Society."[36] The tension between the two organizations most likely reflected the fact that, once St. Mary's opened, it quickly became larger than the parish of the cathedral. The latter's neighborhood was becoming less residential and more commercial, a fact that would lead to the sale of the cathedral property in 1860. The two organizations did in fact coexist, giving concerts in their own churches and visiting others.[37]

In 1857, a letter, addressed to Patrick Donahoe—publisher of the *Pilot* and one-time president of the St. Mary's Singing Society—and signed "Psallite Domino," was published in the *Pilot*. The author recounts his recollections of Catholic church music of the time:

> You remember what the singing was twenty-five years ago. You and I sang in the choir,—we thought the music to be good, so did the people. Then came the first concert of Catholic music given in Boston within my recollection,—it was given at the Masonic Temple by our old friend,

C. T. Young, who did more than any ten men of his day to make our church singing good. He would have given us Mozart, Haydn and Beethoven, if he could, but he had very raw material for such a purpose. Then came the concerts of the Misses Hogan, and, in 1837, those of the Gregorian Society, the last of which was given in 1842.

During all this time the music performed was not above the level of Webbe and DeMonti. Nearly all the singers sang by rote,—few could read. A few classical pieces, not well executed, were occasionally thrown in. But a steady improvement was quite evident from year to year. The singers were satisfied, and the people generally thought that the performances were grand. They were good enough for the time, but their chief merit was, they created a taste for music, and a want for something better than we could have then. That want is satisfied now.[38]

"Psallite Domino's" recollections suggest that the view of music held by the Protestant musical establishment, men such as Lowell Mason, George Webb, and later John Dwight, was also found in the Catholic community. The concern for the improvement of musical execution and the development of musical "taste"—both understood in terms of the European art-music tradition—was found within both groups. Yet at the same time, the Irish manifested a sense of special ownership over "Catholic" music, particularly the sacred music of Haydn, Mozart, and Beethoven: Protestants may perform the music, they may enjoy the music, they may esteem the music, but they will never truly understand the music—unless they experience it as a Catholic.

A Music Book for Catholic Boston

The ill-fated collection of church music which burned on the press in 1833, and which was again attempted in serial form by the Gregorian Society, was successfully issued in a revised edition by the Boston printer Oliver Ditson and the New York printer D. J. Sadlier in 1840. The 1840 version—edited by Richard Garbett, the cathedral organist—was a clear success; an expanded edition was issued by Kidder & Wright in 1842, and was reprinted as late as 1910 by P. J. Kennedy. A comparison of the 1833 and 1840 editions sheds light on the changing musical preferences of the Irish community in Boston and elsewhere.

The preface to the 1833 edition begins: "We are at liberty to state, that the present work has been compiled under the immediate direction and inspection of the Rt. Rev. Dr. Fenwick, Bishop of Boston."[39] The preface of

1840 begins in almost the same fashion.[40] Fenwick's interest in and concern for musical practice has already been noted, and the bishop manifested a clear preference for the use of Latin in liturgical singing.[41] Fenwick's newspaper noted that in the basement chapel of the cathedral, where the children worshiped, "No other music is there allowed than that of the *Gregorian,* which is chanted by the children with considerable effect."[42] The 1833 collection consisted "purely of Gregorian Masses, Anthems, Psalms, Hymns and Canticles, as they are sung in almost every part of the Catholic world."[43] But the contemporary understanding of "Gregorian music" was quite different from modern conceptions of it.

The Latin language is used throughout the collection with only two exceptions: one piece has Italian lyrics with a singable English translation, and one piece—Benjamin Carr's "Spirit Creator of Mankind"—has both Latin and English lyrics. Many of the melodies provided are in accord with Gregorian melodies as known at the time. But "harmony has also been added, which will be found a great improvement, together with the accompaniment for Organ or Piano."[44]

The index gives attributions for most of the sixty-nine musical pieces and three masses contained in the volume (fig. 3.1). But the attributions are somewhat confusing. There are three basic types of attribution: a name following "comp. by," a name following "arr. by," and a name standing alone. The first of these obviously stands for the composer of the music and such familiar names in Catholic circles as Carr, Webbe, DeMonti, and Novello are found. The second style of attribution clearly stands for the arranger of a previously existing piece, most often a Latin hymn. The two names most cited in this context are Mallet and the Ursuline Convent. Francis Mallet (1750?–1834), a well-known musician and teacher in New England, is known to have worked at the Boston cathedral as noted earlier. The fact that he arranged some of the old chants is not surprising.

The Ursuline Convent, as mentioned above, is perhaps most famous for being burned to the ground by an anti-Catholic mob in 1834, but a few words of background are in order here. In 1820 the Ursuline nuns had established a convent and day school next to the cathedral. In 1826 both the convent and the school were moved across the river to a ten-acre farm in Charlestown and named Mount Benedict.[45] The school became a boarding school for girls, attracting students from Canada and all parts of the United States. Few Boston Catholics could afford the tuition of $125, but the reputation of the school became so good that many Unitarians of Boston sent their daughters to Mount Benedict. Musical instruction was provided, for an additional fee, by Elizabeth Harrison (Sister Mary John), a native of

FIGURE 3.1
Index of the 1833 *Catholic Church Service Book*

Adeste Fideles	Arr. by Webbe		80
Alma Redemptoris	Ursuline Convent		66
Ave Regina	Ursuline Convent		67
Adoremus	Author unknown		75
Audi Benigne	Mallet		88
Alleluia	Ursuline Convent		98
Asperges	Webbe		3
Ave Verum, No. 1	Comp. by Kozelbuch		55
Ave Verum, No. 2	Comp. by Novello		107
Ad Regias Agni Dapes	Arr. by Mallet		102
Ave Maria	Author unknown		108
Ave Maris Stella	Arr. by the Ursuline Convent		115
Creator Alme	Mallet		79
Crudelis Herodes	Mallet		84
Coelestis Urbs	Mallet		122
Deus Tuorum	Mallet		118
Ecce Quam Bonum	Ursuline Convent		19
Exultet Orbis	Mrs. Cecilia Brown		116
Gloria, Laus, et Honor	Mallet		92
Gaude Virgo	Comp. by Novello		110
Hosanna Filio David	Arr. by Mallet		91
Hoec Dies	Comp. by Webbe		99
Inviolata	Arr. by Mallet		112
Iste Confessor, No. 1	Mallet		120
Iste Confessor, No. 2	Ursuline Convent		120
Jesu Redemptor	Mallet		82
Jesu Dulcis Memoria	Ursuline Convent		86
Jam Sol Recedit	Mallet		104
Jesu Corona Virginum	Mallet		121
Litany of B.Virgin, No. 1	Ursuline Convent		1
No. 2	Ursuline Convent		2
No. 3	Comp. by Demonti		3
No. 4	Author unknown		3
Libera Me	Novello		52
Lucis Creator	Arr. by Ursuline Convent		60
Mass No. I Missa Regia, or The Royal Mass, with the different parts.			
Kyrie	Novello	5	Sanctus	Novello	14
Gloria	Novello	6	Agnus Dei	Novello	16
Credo	Novello	9			
Mass No. II Missa de Angelis, with the different parts.			
Kyrie	Novello	20	Credo No. 2	Ursuline Convent	28
Gloria	Novello	21	Sanctus	Novello	32
Credo No. 1	Novello	23	Agnus Dei	Novello	33
Mass for the Dead, with the different parts.			
Requiem	Novello	34	O Meritum	Novello	48
Absolve	Novello	36	De Profundis	Novello	49
Dies Irae	Novello	38	Agnus Dei	Novello	51
Domine Jesu	Novello	44	Lux Oeterna [sic]	Novello	51
Sanctus	Novello	47	Libera Me	Novello	52

FIGURE 3.1 — *Continued*

Magnificat, No. 1	Arr. by the Ursuline Convent	63
No. 2	Author unknown	84
Miserere, w/out the Parce	Author unknown	88
Miserere, as sung in Rome	Allegri	125
O Jesu Deus	Webbe	13
O Salutaris	Arr. by Ursuline Convent	15
O Sanctissima	Author unknown	75
O Filii et Filiae	Arr. by Webbe	101
O Sacrum Convivium	Comp. by Webbe	105
O Interiora Sancta	Arr. by Ursuline Convent	106
O Bella Speranza	Comp. by Tiorananti	114
Parce Domine	Arr. by Ursuline Convent	87
Pueri Haebreorum [*sic*]	Mallet	92
Pange Lingua	Ursuline Convent	95
Popule Meus	Ursuline Convent	96
Placare Christe	Mallet	116
Responses		
after the Gloria		8
at the Preface		14
at the Pater Noster		16
after the Communion		18
Regina Coeli	Ursuline Convent	68
Rorate Coeli	Ursuline Convent	76
Rex Gloriose	Mallet	119
Sacris Solemnis	Ursuline Convent	17
Salve Regina	Arr. by the Ursuline Convent	70
Stabat Mater	Webbe	89
Salutis Humanae	Mallet	103
Subtuum Proesidium	Mallet	109
Sanctorum Meritis	Mallet	118
Tantum Ergo, No. 1	Ursuline Convent	72
No. 2	Novello	73
Tota Pulchra	Ursuline Convent	111
Tristes Erant Apostoli	Mallet	117
Te Deum	Ursuline Convent	122

Vespers				
Deus in Adjutorium	56			
Beatus Vir	57	Laudate Dominum	59	
Beati Omnes	107	Laudate Pueri	58	
Confitebor Tibi Domine	57	Loetatus sum	82	
Credidi Propter Quod	85	Lauda Jerusalem	83	
De Profundis	49	Memento Domine David	81	
Dixit Dominus	56	Nisi Dominus	83	
In Exitu Israel	58			

Vidi Aquam	Arr. by Webbe	4
Veni Creator, No. 1	Ursuline Convent	8
No. 2	Comp. by B. Carr	64
Vexilla Regis	Arr. by the Ursuline Convent	99

Philadelphia.[46] The preface of the 1833 collection speaks of the musical accomplishments of the nuns:

> Their extensive knowledge of Music, as well ancient as modern, has been of essential service to us in the arrangement of very many of the prominent pieces which appear in this work, and which we were under the necessity of getting transposed from the original Gregorian; and also, in the adjustment of the proper harmonies necessary for the several accompaniments.[47]

Fenwick's journal records that the choir at the convent was "conducted by the Nuns, with the aid of harp and piano."[48] Harrison herself described her teaching schedule at the trial of one of the accused rioters: "I was a teacher of music in the establishment.... I gave 14 lessons per day, and of 35, 40, and 45 minutes each."[49] As the community was a small one, with only five sisters in 1834, it is probable that Harrison was responsible for most of the musical activities at the convent, including the arrangements of the chant melodies attributed to the Ursulines.

The third type of attribution in the *Catholic Church Service Book,* a name standing alone, is somewhat confusing. All three styles of attribution are found with Webbe's name. Novello is given for all three masses: the "Missa Regia," a pseudo-chant mass composed by Henri Dumont, the "Missa de Angelis," a Gregorian composition, and the chant Requiem. Obviously none of these were composed by Novello, but Novello, the English musician and publisher, was the foremost printer of Catholic music in the English-speaking world. The two names most often used in the third style of attribution are, like the second, Mallet and the Ursuline Convent, and most of these pieces are ancient Latin hymns. Thus it would appear that the attribution provides us not with a composer or arranger, but either the source through which the publisher obtained the music or the editor who "transposed" the music from Gregorian notation to modern.

The preface also provides a few indications of the "proper" execution of church music:

> [It] should be sung slowly and solemnly; taking care that every word and every syllable be distinctly pronounced. This mode of execution should be observed in Gregorian Music generally, whose beauty and excellence mainly depend upon it. It should be well also,—indeed such is the spirit of the Catholic Church,—that the people in the body of the Church should join in, and mingle their voices with the Choir, during the service, especially while chanting the Credo, which is a solemn profession of faith; they should likewise, when sufficiently drilled, sing, too, on

some occasions, alternately with the Choir; but in all such cases, great care must be taken by them to keep always together.[50]

The *Catholic Church Service Book* was exactly what its title indicated—a collection of ecclesiastically sanctioned music for use within the official ritual of the Catholic Church. As such it falls clearly within the first category of music suggested in chapter 1: canonical music of ritual. But the revision of the collection, issued in 1840, will be less simple to classify.

The Third Provincial Council of Baltimore was held in 1837, bringing together all the Catholic bishops of the United States. Among the decrees issued by the council was one concerned with church music. Two major concerns were voiced: the liturgy must not be made into a mere vehicle for a musical entertainment and the use of song in the vernacular must not be allowed during solemn worship.[51] It is certain that such a decree would not have been issued unless such irregularities were actually taking place. Fenwick himself was clearly interested in controlling the music used in Catholic worship; both the 1833 and 1840 collections' prefaces note Fenwick's desire that the collection serve as "a standard work for the regulation of Music in the Choirs of all the Catholic Churches" of the Boston diocese. But while the 1833 edition is in full conformity with the council's decree, that of 1840 contains a far broader spectrum of music, including many works with English texts and melodies borrowed from both Protestant and popular sources.

The editor of *The Morning and Evening Service of the Catholic Church,* was Richard Garbett.[52] Born in Exeter, England, in 1789, Garbett served as organist of St. David's (Anglican) Church in his native city. In 1818 he published a hymnal: *Sacred Harmony: A Selection of Psalms and Hymns in Score.* Between 1818 and the mid-1830s, Garbett published a number of short piano and vocal pieces. He appears to have emigrated to the United States in the late 1830s; he first appears in the Boston city directory of 1839. In 1839 his *Hymn of the Seasons* was performed by the Boston Musical Institute and published by the Boston firm of Crocker and Brewster. Other than the collection under discussion, only one other musical publication by Garbett can be found: *Nursery Melodies for Little Voices, to be Played with Little Hands* published by the author around 1864. He died at the age of 91 in 1881.

Much of the music contained in the 1833 edition is found in the 1840 edition as well, often with minor changes in the harmonization (see fig. 3.2 for the 1840 contents). The breviary hymns, however, now appear with both Latin and English texts, usually employing the primer translations used by Bishop Cheverus, a predecessor of Fenwick as bishop of Boston, in his text-only hymnal of 1802, the *Roman Catholic Manual*. Allegri's "Miserere," so admired by Protestant writers and contained in the 1833 edition, is replaced in Garbett's book by an unaccompanied chant setting of the "Lamentations."

Other additions in the later version are taken directly from earlier collections of Catholic music published in America: John Aitken's 1787 hymnal, Benjamin Carr's 1805 collection (both published in Philadelphia), Walter's 1825 collection (Baltimore), and the *Vesper Book* of 1836 (Philadephia). In short, Garbett consulted all of the major music collections published for Catholics in America. Whether the items included from these other works represent Garbett's taste or the popularity of the selections themselves is difficult to determine. But once again, many of these selections contained English lyrics.

FIGURE 3.2
Index of the 1840 *Morning and Evening Service of the Catholic Church*

Adeste Fideles		100
Adoremus in aeternum		93
Ad regias Agni dapes		141
Alma Redemptoris	Gregorian	79
Alma Redemptoris	Webbe	87
All is but vanity		176
Asperges	Gregorian	2
Asperges	Carr	4
Ave Maria		150
Ave Maris Stella	Gregorian	152
Ave Regina	Gregorian	81
Ave Regina	Carr	88
Ave Verum, No. 1	Novello	147
Ave Verum, No. 2	Kozeluch	194
Audi benigne conditor		112
Ave Sanctissima	Mrs. Hemans	193
Adoro te		226
Behold the royal ensigns fly	Gregorian	115
Bright Maker of the Starry Poles		99
Bright Mother of our Maker		200
Coelestis urbs Jerusalem		161
Children of the Heavenly King	Pleyel	182
Come all devout harmonious tongues		143
Come Holy Ghost		185
Come let us lift our joyful eyes		174
Come sound his praise abroad		172
Creator alme siderum	Gregorian	99
Crudelis Herodes		107
Deus tuorum militum		156

FIGURE 3.2—*Continued*

Exultet orbis gaudiis		155
Fading, still fading	Mrs. Hemans	196
Gaude Virgo	Novello	151
Good Friday [service music]		129
Graces from my Jesus flowing		178
Grateful Notes		163
Gustate	Corelli	199
Guardian Angels		205
Hail Heavenly Queen		198
Haec dies	Webbe	138
Holy Thursday [service music]		123
Holy Saturday [service music]		136
Have mercy on me, O God	Psalm	111
Hosanna Filio David		116
In this unfathom'd mystery		188
Iste Confessor	Gregorian	159
Jesu dulcis memoria	Gregorian	109
Jerusalem, my happy home		175
Jerusalem, whose name		161
Jesu, corona Virginum	Walter	160
Jesus, the only thought of thee		109
Jesu Redemptor omnium		103
Jesus the Ransomer of man		103
Jesus, Savior of my soul		191
King of Kings		167
Lamentations in Holy Week	Gregorian	119
Litany of the Blessed Virgin, No. 1		1
Litany of the Blessed Virgin, No. 2		2
Litany of the Blessed Virgin, No. 3		2
Mass in A	Webbe	8
Mass in C Major	Webbe	22
Missa Regia	Gregorian	40
Mass for the Dead	Gregorian	50
My soul thy great Creator praise	Haydn	162
My God, My life, My love	Bishop David	189
O bountiful Creator, No. 1		112
O bountiful Creator, No. 2	Eman. Bach	179
O come, loud anthems	R. Taylor	206
O Deus ego amo te		204
O Filii et Filiae	Gregorian	139
O great Creator of the light		70
O God in whom thy servants find		156
O Jesu Deus magne	Webbe	17
O let our fervor glow		173
O Power divine	J.M. of P.T.	177
O praise ye the Lord		165
O Salutaris, No. 1		192
O Salutaris, No. 2		192
O Salutaris, No. 3		193
O Sanctissima		194
Parce Domine	Gregorian	111

FIGURE 3.2—*Continued*

Pange Lingua	Gregorian	124
Placare Christi		153
Pueri Hebraeorum	Gregorian	117
Regina Coeli	Gregorian	82
Regina Coeli	Webbe	90
Regard our Vows		160
Rorate Coeli	Gregorian	95
Sacris Solemnis	Gregorian	149
Salve Regina	Gregorian	84
Salve Regina	Carr	91
Sanctorum meritis	Garbett	158
Saving Host	Bishop David	186
See the Paraclete descending		184
Sion rejoice		105
Sitivit anima mea		193
Spare, O Lord	Gregorian	111
Spirit Creator of Mankind, No. 1	Carr	11
Spirit Creator of Mankind, No. 2	Carr	145
Stabat Mater	Gregorian	114
St. Aloysius (Hymn to)	Rev. E. Fenwick	201
St. Francis Xaverius (Hymn to)	Rev. E. Fenwick	203
St. Joseph (Hymn to)		201
Tantum Ergo	Gregorian	91
Te Deum	Gregorian	207
The fiery sun now rolls		146
The Red Sea's dangers		142
This Christ's Confessor	Gregorian	159
Throughout the World		155
To-day he is risen		182
Vespers [psalms and responses]		63
Veni Creator, No. 1	Gregorian	144
Veni Creator, No. 2		145
Vexilla Regis	Gregorian	115
Vidi Aquam	Gregorian	6
Vital spark		179
What Happiness	Bishop David	190
What makes thee, cruel Herod		107
Young Men and Maids	Gregorian	141

The second edition [1842] added the following items:

Adoro Te	Plain Chant	226
Christmas Canticle [in French]		253
Hymn to St. Joseph	Bishop David	225
Le Souvenir De La Presence De Dieu		256
Mass in C	H. Demonti	211
Mass in F	Demonti	227
Misericorde De Dieu Envers Le Pecheur		256
O Salutaris, No. 4		226
Passion Canticle [in French]		254
Veni Creator Spiritus	Bishop David	225

The work of at least two American clerics finds its way into Garbett's collection. The first hymns of Bishop David of Bardstown, Kentucky, to be printed with both text and music appear. Two hymns composed by Edward Fenwick, Benedict Fenwick's brother, are included: "Hymn to St. Aloysius," and "Hymn to St. Francis Xavierius" (fig. 3.3). Neither of the hymns is of high quality, both having rather awkward melodic lines and convoluted texts. But they do represent a new genre in Catholic music of the period—songs dealing with canonized saints. In earlier collections saints were generally ignored; the contents included liturgical texts, hymns addressed to God, or Marian hymnody. The growth of hymns to saints was rapid; an 1843 hymnal contains dozens of such hymns.

Benedict Fenwick's correspondence with Bishop Rosati of St. Louis makes it clear that Fenwick took a pragmatic view of the musical situation in his diocese. Rosati informed Fenwick that the St. Louis diocese would have no use for the book because it was insufficiently "gregorianized." Fenwick, stung perhaps by Rosati's criticism, argued against the practicality of teaching Gregorian chant in America:

> But to attempt to introduce it [the chant] all over the United States, in which the greater part of the congregations consist of Americans or Irish, who know as much about music of any kind, as they do about Greek, and the greater part of the clergy, too, have neither voices nor ears for music, would be to attempt an impossibility. . . . What then was to be done? I saw, with the population I have to deal with, that nothing could be done with any probability of success, but what I am now doing. I shall soon have a book which will be perfectly intelligible to all musicians and from which the poor and uninformed can learn. The Masses in it are plain and beautiful and easily learned. . . . I am persuaded it will do good, and an immense good somewhere, both in and out of my diocese.[53]

Perhaps the most significant addition Garbett made to the collection of 1840 was a number of songs which were clearly not liturgical in character. Some of these were songs that had become popular in sheet-music editions, songs such as Mrs. Hemans' "Evening Hymn to the Virgin at Sea," T. V. Wiesenthal's "Fading, Still Fading" (1826) (incorrectly attributed to Mrs. Hemans), and the anonymous "Jerusalem My Happy Home" (c. 1835). Sir John Stevenson's "Hark the Vesper Hymn," based on a Russian folk song, became "See the Paraclete Descending." The opening theme of Mozart's A Major Piano Sonata accompanied the text "Graces from my Jesus Flowing" (fig. 3.4).

FIGURE 3.3
Edward Fenwick's "Hymn to St. Francis Xavierius"
Courtesy The Music Division, New York Public Library for the Performing Arts, Astor, Lenox, and Tilden Foundations.

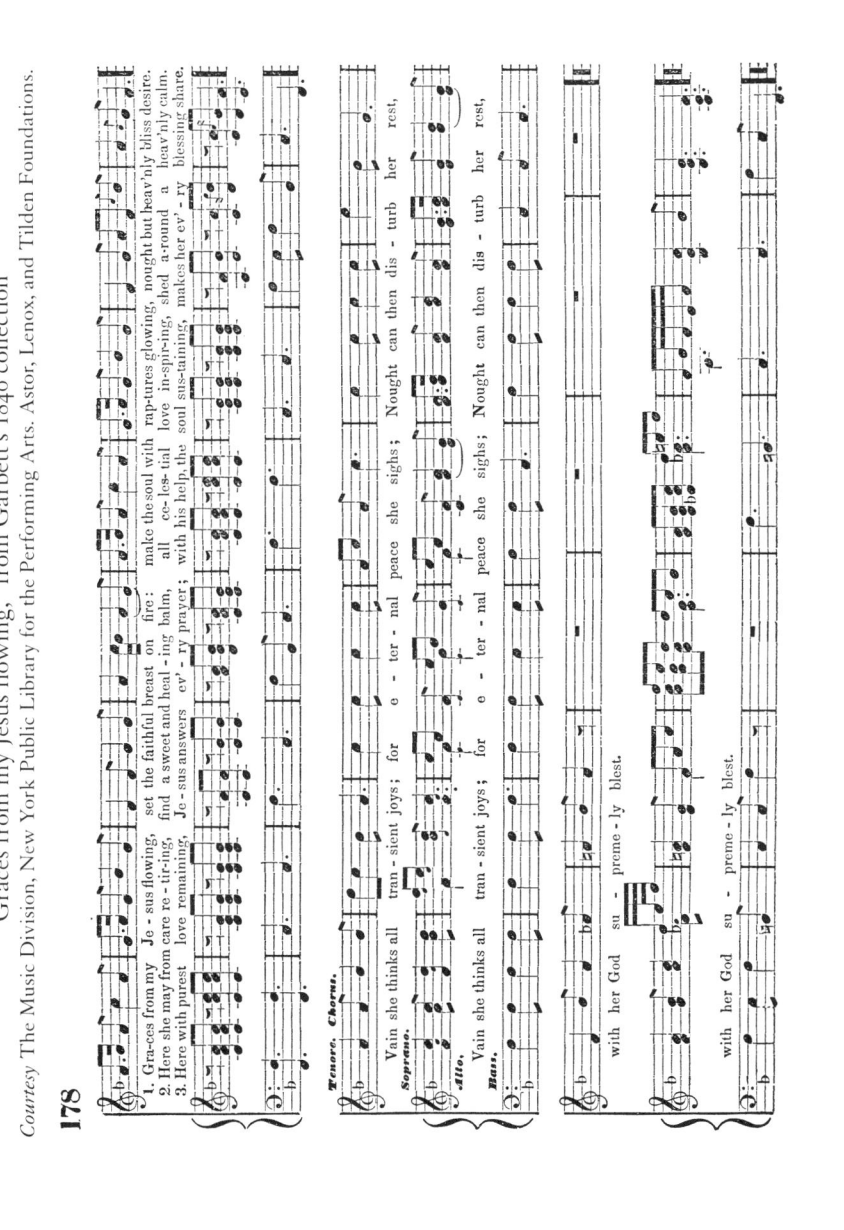

FIGURE 3.4
"Graces from my Jesus flowing," from Garbett's 1840 collection
Courtesy The Music Division, New York Public Library for the Performing Arts. Astor, Lenox, and Tilden Foundations.

Garbett's collection was not the first to include such music. The *Vesper Book* of 1836 included even more of this music than Garbett's book had. But the *Vesper Book*, although beautifully printed, does not appear to have been much of a success. It had but one printing and only one copy is known to have survived.[54] Lists of Catholic hymnals compiled in the late nineteenth century do not include it. Garbett's *Morning and Evening Services*, on the other hand, went through numerous printings over sixty years, up to 1910. Perhaps even more significant, it was identified by a noted ecclesiastical leader, Bishop Fenwick, as a "standard" for the regulation of Catholic church music. Advertisements for the collection, which appeared throughout the American Catholic press, included the testimonial from "a Rt. Rev. Prelate, universally allowed to be the best judge of sacred music in this country":

> I have no hesitation in saying, and all who are acquainted with church music will agree with me after examining it, that it is the most useful, correct and comprehensive collection of choir music, that has ever been printed in this country for the Catholic Church. . . . In short, it has only to be examined to be approved of.[55]

The standard set by Garbett's work proved to be far more powerful than the instructions of the Third Provincial Council of Baltimore. The first printing of Garbett's collection sold out in less than a year, and in January of 1842 an expanded edition was aggressively, and successfully, marketed.[56] The printer delivered a third edition in October of 1843.[57] A number of music collections printed over the next twenty years would draw upon the collection of 1840, both for specific musical selections and for the general format.

Morning and Evening Services is not exactly what its title suggests. While there is a great deal of music sanctioned for use within the formal liturgy of the church, there are also many selections that reflect the emergence of a repertory that can best be classified as popular music of ritual. The music is similar to styles popular outside of ecclesiastical institutions, and is in forms which make inclusion of these pieces within the official church ritual difficult, if not impossible. But by freeing itself from church ritual restrictions, the music takes new shape. It is difficult to imagine Mallet's arrangement of "Ad regias Agni dapes" being sung anywhere other than within a vespers service; "Jerusalem My Happy Home," composed by a "young lady," might be found within a church service, at a social gathering, or even within the home.

Irish Music in Boston

There was obviously more to the musical life of the Boston Irish than church and devotional music. The emigrants did not abandon the musical culture of their homeland. On board ships bound for America, the Irish passengers considered themselves fortunate to have a musician amongst their number. One emigrant wrote back home that on board his ship "were two fiddlers and a piper. We were all agreeable and happy together, keeping the time in dancing, howling and other amusements."[58]

As the number of Irish in Boston grew, there was a natural growth of interest in, and performance of, Irish music. Articles in the *Boston Pilot* attest to this interest; the actual performance of Irish music in the 1830s is somewhat more difficult to document, although some evidence can be found.

The musical traditions of Ireland were presented as important to the immigrant for two reasons. First, according to a Boston newspaper, the splendid history of Irish music reflected upon the very nature of the Irish people:

> we have shown, that in the early ages the Irish were unrivalled in the art of vocal and instrumental harmony. The great degree of perfection which the charming science attained in our country, and the widespread fame of its professors, furnish indubitable criterions of the learning and refinement of the ancient Irish, and must, in the opinion of all intelligent and candid men, serve to refute the unfounded calumnies which English and Scottish writers have endeavoired [sic] to propagate against our primitive character.[59]

Second, and on a more individual level, Irish music is strength and comfort for the unhappy exile:

> When the Irish exile, in a far distant clime, hears the music of his native land, his heart feels transport; the image of his country floats on every note, and its voice speaks audibly in every sound. Music has an assuasive charm for the desponding lover, and its sounds, when borne on the wing of the breeze to the depth of the captive's dungeon, alleviate his painful agony of feeling, and light up, in his languishing hopes, the bright torch of imaginative liberty. . . . It is music that fires the soul of the hero and the minstrel.[60]

Within the Irish-American press, the songs of Thomas Moore were held in the highest esteem:

> In Moore's soul subduing songs, we hear the touching melody of our native land—the personified voice of the genius of Ireland, invoking our sympathies and remembrances;—and surely there is not, in America, an Irish bosom so frigid and frozen, as not to be warmed by the vivid strain—as not to leap with joy—and not to catch a patriotic spark from the glowing verse, in which the spirit of the ancient Tara still lives.[61]

Moore's songs, already popular with the general American public, perform both the functions mentioned above; the songs show the value of Irish culture, and comfort the exiled Irishman in America. But while they were certainly a product of Irish culture, the songs were not first brought to America by the Irish immigrant of the 1830s; many had been popular in America years before the immigration began.

Even today, the amount of Irish music performed in America increases in early March, leading up to the celebration of St. Patrick's Day; the same appears to have been the case in the decade under discussion. "On the approaching festival, the national songs of the Irish Anacreon will, no doubt, enliven the hilarity and social pleasure of every circle within which the memory of St. Patrick will be hallowed and enshrined," a Boston newspaper noted on March 14, 1835.[62] A few weeks later the same newspaper reported the toasts offered at a Boston St. Patrick's Day dinner, toasts separated by the playing of such tunes as "Patrick's Day," "Garry Owen," "Blame not the Bard," "Exile of Erin," "Erin Go Bragh," and "The Irishman."[63] These titles are found in accounts of many such dinners during the period. The toast to Thomas Moore leaves no doubt that the immigrants considered the poet one of their own.

> Thomas Moore, the unrivalled Poet, and ardent Patriot, he has caused the wrongs and woes of his native land to be sung all over the Globe. May he soon tune his Harp to the Hymn of her Freedom.[64]

The feast of Ireland's patron was celebrated in the church as well as in the banquet hall. In 1833 a hymn to St. Patrick, "Hail Glorious Apostle," was first printed for Patrick Donahoe. With words composed by one of the nuns of the Ursuline convent in Charlestown, the hymn was *"harmonized and arranged by* Thos. Comer, to the justly celebrated National air of good old Ireland."⁶⁵ In his *Journal of the Diocese of Boston*, Fenwick indicates the author was the late Sister Mary Austin; the tune is the traditional air "St. Patrick's Day."

> Hail glorious Apostle selected by God
> To enlarge the bless'd pale of Christ's faithful believers
> Accept our weak efforts to honor thy virtues
> And chiefly thy wonderful Charity.
> For twas thy bright flame of love seraphic
> Which moved thee thy Country and kindred to leave
> All earthly enjoyment and comforts to part with.
> Hail glorious Aspostle selected by God
> To enlarge the bless'd pale of Christ's faithful believers
> Accept our weak efforts to honor thy virtues
> And chiefly thy wonderful Charity.

The debut of the hymn, on St. Patrick's Day, 1833 at the Boston cathedral, was an apparent success:

> although the weather was exceedingly warm, and the great body of people, then present, had been pent up for the space of two hours almost to suffocation, yet not an individual offered to stir from his place, to retire after divine service was over, until the whole Hymn, which is of considerable length, was concluded by the Choir. Even those who stood without, and whose ears had caught some of the exhilarating sounds, as they issued from the Choir, used every effort to get within complete hearing, to the great annoyance of those who were within, near to the doors of the church, so highly captivated were they with what they had heard.⁶⁶

The initial popularity of the hymn continued undiminished for years; it was often found on concert programs and sung at church services. Advertisements for the sheet-music edition of the song appeared regularly throughout the 1830s, 1840s, and 1850s; Ditson also issued the song as a text-only broadside. The technique Comer employed—wedding a new religious text to an existing Irish tune—would be used by other musicians over the next thirty years.⁶⁷

Concerts and occasional lectures on Irish music were given by touring Irish musicians. P. F. White, billed as a friend of Thomas Moore, was performing with great success in the United States during 1839. The following is a representative program performed by White.⁶⁸

Part I

Lecture on Music—Its Origin, Rise and Progress
The Troubadours, their Poetry—Remarks on
Irish Music, Tara—The Ancient Palace of the Kings of Ireland
Irish Bards—Remarks on
Beranger, Moore, and other Lyric Writers of the present age.

Part II

Song—This Heart of Thine; Words and Music by Mr. White. Piano Accompaniment.
Song—Oh! Yes I Remember; Words and Music by Mr. White. Guitar Accompaniment.
Fantasia on the Guitar.
Song—Oh! The Days are Gone; Words by Mr. Moore. Music arranged by Sir J. Stevenson—Piano.
Song—Nora Creina; Words by Mr. Moore, arrangement by Mr. Moore. Piano.
Song—When he who Adores Thee; Words by Mr. Moore. Music arranged by Sir J. Stevenson. Piano.
Glee—Come, Come Away. A popular Serenade, Written and Composed by Mr. White.

Perhaps the most revealing words on the program are "the above Songs from Moore Mr. White will sing as Mr. Moore himself sings his melodies." The *Boston Musical Gazette* printed both a favorable review of White's concert and, in the next column, the following quote from Thomas Moore:

> It has always been a subject of some mortification to me, that my songs, as they are set, give such an imperfect notion of the manner in which I wish them to be performed, and that the most of that peculiarity of character, which I believe, they possess as I sing them myself, is lost in the process they must undergo for publication . . . and, as it but too often happens that they are indebted for their originality to the violation of some established law, the hand that corrects their errors is almost sure to destroy their character, and the few little flowers they may boast of are generally pulled away with the weeds. In singing them myself however, I pay no such deference to criticism, but usually give both air and harmony, according to my own first conception of them, with all their original faults, but at the same time, all their original freshness.[69]

It would appear that Moore, as well as White, sang these songs closer to the style of traditional Irish song than printed arrangements (such as Stevenson's) would imply.[70]

The music the immigrant brought from Ireland serves as an example of our third category: music of popular ritual. The rituals which sustained a sense of identity for the poor and often despised Irishman made use of traditional Irish music and did so for a conscious reason. The music employed in "Irish Evenings," St. Patrick's Day parades and banquets, and various parish organizations was both a clear link to the home from which they had been forced and a validation of the worth of their native culture.

In this chapter I have tried to show some examples of the changes in musical preferences among the Boston Irish during the 1830s, a decade in which their numbers began to swell. The number of Irish arriving in the United States during the 1840s and 1850s would help to make the Irish the largest European ethnic group in America. But the assimilation of such a large immigrant group would not be an easy task. Given the social upheaval which accompanied such an immigration, there is little surprise that musical change occurred as well. The immigrants were faced with internal tensions. The majority of Irish immigrants considered themselves exiles, but exiles in a land of opportunity. They faced bias, even violent discrimination, yet never lost faith in American freedom. They were Irish, and would always be Irish, but they were becoming American as well. The music of the immigrant community reflected these tensions. They formed singing societies in imitation of "native Americans," yet they sang the "music of the Catholic Church" and the songs of Thomas Moore, Samuel Lover, and the "national airs of Ireland." They attended churches which prayed in a "foreign tongue" and sang their Latin Masses and Gregorian hymns; yet they sang English lyrics as well, to both Protestant tunes and familiar melodies of their native land.

The 1840s experienced a tremendous increase in the amount of music published and marketed for the Irish Catholic community. Music publishers certainly do not ignore a growing market, and the success of Garbett's collection of music may have made publishers aware of the potential for music sales among the new Irish-Americans. Major music publishers, perhaps most notably William Cumming Peters, developed entire series of publications directed specifically toward Irish Catholics. Many Catholic publications began including the music for a hymn, a devotional song, or a secular song with each issue; the *Catholic Expositor* and the *U. S. Catholic Magazine* are notable examples. Many of the composers and lyricists were not Irish themselves, but the consumers of these products were, to a great extent, sons and daughters of Eire.

It is worthy of note that, although provincial councils of Baltimore were held by the Roman Catholic hierarchy in 1840, 1843, 1846, 1849, and 1852, the issue of music in the parish churches did not arise.[71] The councils faced a host of pressing issues—immigration, poverty, schools, and anti-Catholic sentiment, among others—and it is generally assumed that music was not important enough for consideration on a national level. In the reform of liturgical music which began, at least officially, with the Plenary Council of Baltimore in 1884, music was clearly employed as both a symbol of ultramontanist ecclesiology and a tool of Roman theology. In the antebellum United States, music in Catholic parishes was not directed by a central authority but developed according to the interest and taste of members of the local community. The next three chapters will survey the types of music that emerged within the growing immigrant church.

Chapter 4 focuses on the canonical music of ritual in Irish Catholic parishes from 1840 to the start of the Civil War. Because the repertory includes not only Gregorian chant as performed at the time, but also the orchestral masses composed by European masters, the chapter will touch on the relationship between the growing American interest in European art music and the cultural life of the Irish immigrant.

Chapter 5 surveys the vast repertory I have called the popular music of ritual. The years 1840 through 1860 were marked by the publication of dozens of collections of religious and devotional music for the "ordinary Catholic." During the same years, the parish mission, a form of Catholic revivalism, took shape, creating an emotionalism within the adherents of the church that was previously unknown. In the years just prior to the Civil War a number of hymns were introduced to American Catholics that endured for a hundred years as staples of the Irish Catholic repertory.

Chapter 6 looks at the even less homogeneous repertory designated as the music of popular rituals. As Irish Catholicism in America became more and more established in a ghetto mentality, the group required more and more institutions and organizations parallel to the Protestant establishment. Many of these groups—schools, temperance societies, sodalities, ethnic societies, orphanages—employed music, and sought a repertory distinctively their own.

CHAPTER FOUR

Canonical Music of Ritual: Art Music and the Immigrant

Studies of American Catholic Church music often cite the antebellum years as a low point in musical taste. John Grady, in an article in the recent *New Grove Dictionary of American Music,* refers to this period as one of "general decline in church music ... hastened by the large number of English and Irish immigrants."[1] What music did the Catholic immigrants hear in church? What music did they sing? This chapter investigates the canonical music of Catholic ritual, that is, music that adhered to the liturgical traditions of Roman Catholicism, in the twenty years before the outbreak of the Civil War. It must not be assumed that the "universal" rules governing music in Catholic worship were monolithic. Catholicism in the middle years of the nineteenth century did not yet have a codified canon law, and would not until the beginning of the next century. The rules governing musical worship came from a variety of sources; the teachings of the sixteenth-century Council of Trent were perhaps dominant at the time, but local usages and traditions, directives from the diocesan bishops, and the taste and interest of the local pastor, musicians, and congregation were all significant forces shaping the repertory of a particular church.[2] Although certain general principles were followed everywhere—the use of the unchanging Latin texts in the mass, for example—the liturgical music of the period was not isolated from shifts in public preferences and the larger musical culture of the country.

Chapter 2 surveyed the impressions of Catholic music held by the largely Protestant musical establishment, a view that may be summed up as wary admiration. Yet much of what appears in the musical press concerning Catholic musical practice deals with either abstract ideas or works of composers, both viewed outside of the ritual context. Did the Boston musician know Mozart's *Requiem* from its use in Catholic churches of Massachusetts, or from performances by the Handel and Haydn Society? Quite often one is left with the impression that the writer had never entered a Catholic church; was this the result of fear or distaste for the perceived ritualism or superstition associated with Catholicism, or was the fact simply that the admired music was not being performed in American Catholic churches, but in reality belonged solely to European Catholicism? If so, what was the music performed at the high mass each Sunday in the Catholic churches that were spreading across the urban northeastern United States?

It is clear that the musical establishment's admiration for "Catholic music" was not lost on Catholic leadership in America. Especially in the larger cities, Catholic churches were concerned about the quality of the music performed. John Carroll, once he was appointed the first bishop of Baltimore, lost no time in obtaining an organ from England for his new cathedral; twenty-five years later it would be replaced by an American instrument, built by Thomas Hall of Baltimore, and heralded in the press as the largest organ in the country: three manuals and pedal, thirty-six stops (including a 32' sub-bass) and 2,213 pipes.[3] Sacred concerts in Catholic churches also drew wide public attention as well as occasional footnotes in music history: for example, in 1837 New York's Catholic Chapel (a temporary facility located at 716 Broadway) was the site of the first American performance of Pergolesi's *Stabat Mater;*[4] in 1834 St. John's Church in Philadelphia hosted the first complete performance of Mozart's *Requiem* in America.[5] Although not held in a Catholic church, the first American performance of Mozart's *Magic Flute*, in Philadelphia, 1841, was a benefit for the Catholic orphanage.[6] As the number of Catholic churches rapidly increased in the 1840s and 1850s, so too did the amount of music needed for the now largely immigrant church.

Music for the Mass

While certainly not representative of all American Catholic parishes, St. Peter's on Barclay Street in New York City provides an interesting musical history for our purposes. After damage to the original structure by fire in the 1830s, a larger and more impressive building opened in 1838 and was clearly the highest-profile Catholic church in New York. To protest Catholic and immigrant political influence, mobs would go to the city's cathedral, St. Patrick's; to hear "Catholic" music, New Yorkers mobbed St. Peter's. Two major sources provide information on the music at St. Peter's: newspaper reviews and the diary of George Templeton Strong.

At the February 25, 1838, dedication, the orchestra of the National Theatre, under the direction of Urelli Corelli Hill, performed the so-called Twelfth Mass of Mozart (K. anh. 232). George Templeton Strong was in the congregation and wrote that "the choir was very effective; choir and band together might amount to about fifty, and with the organ aiding them, the music was such as I never heard before. No wonder the Catholic faith has so many votaries."[7] Strong, an Episcopalian and parishioner of Trinity Church on Wall Street, often stopped at St. Peter's on his way home from Trinity. After Christmas services at his own church in 1839, Strong

> then went up to St. Peter's and heard the last act of High Mass. All the National [Theatre] Band was in full blast upon that Mass of Mozart's that they performed at the Consecration, and the clangor of the trumpet blended with the torrent-like roar of their organ went forth really in a very glorious manner. . . . The music was well worth being a little overcrowded.[8]

While Strong clearly enjoyed the music at St. Peter's, his sarcastic reference to the "last act of High Mass" seems to indicate disapproval of such music in church services; it was entertainment, even inspirational, but not the music of Christian worship. Yet at St. Peter's on Christmas day two years later, it was not the music but the people, presumably the Irish immigrants—often stereotyped as "rowdy"—who annoyed Strong:

> church jammed—squeeze terrific. . . . They had a choir of fifty or sixty, well drilled, and the effect with which the choir and full organ came out with the Hallelujah chorus at the end of the services was great. . . . It's a shame that the Church can't—or doesn't—have such music as is thrown away on those rowdies at St. Peter's![9]

Mozart's *Requiem* had been performed at a solemn Mass celebrated by Bishop Dubois at St. Peter's. Strong was present on that occasion and described the service and his reaction to Mozart's music:

> They had a very full band and choir—any quantity of bassoons and trumpets and several immense articles which I took to be kettledrums, and which added greatly to the effect of some parts of the performance.

... Some parts of the *Dies Irae* are certainly very splendid indeed, but I think on the whole I'd rather hear the "twelfth Mass." The whole affair today was first-rate, but if it had not been for the splendid style in which it was got up, I shouldn't have thought much of it.[10]

It is significant that the parishioners of St. Peter's knew the *Requiem* and settings of the Mass not from concert performances but from actual ritual use of Mozart's composition; in ritual use the various musical movements are separated in time by either nonmusical rituals or musical ritual not set by the composer, either by preference or rubrical necessity. For example, the "Kyrie" and "Dies Irae" of Mozart's *Requiem* would be separated by the singing of the Gradual and Tract, not set by Mozart; the "Hostias et Preces" and "Sanctus" would be separated by the chanting of the preface. In settings of the ordinary of the mass, there would be many more such "interpolations" into the work of Mozart or Haydn, including the proper of the mass and "motets" at the offertory and communion. But at concert performances—as was the first New York City performance of the *Requiem,* February 22, 1835, at the City Hotel—a musical setting of the mass would be performed as an uninterrupted series of movements. But the parish choir of St. Peter's did not think it improper to insert other musical compositions between movements of Mozart's *Requiem,* even in concert. On June 22, 1841, the parish choir, under the direction of Signor Maroncelli, performed the following program:[11]

Part I

1. Introduction, Organ, Mr. Timms
2. Dies Irae, Chorus (from the celebrated Requiem) — Mozart
3. Ove tu sei mio Dio, Aria di Soprano — Bellini
4. Tuba Mirum, Quartett (from the Requiem) — Mozart
5. Der Friede Gottes, Aria di Basso — Kalliwoda
6. Ave Maria, Aria di Tenore — Schubert
7. Rest Spirit, Rest, Hymn, Chorus — Mozart

Part II

1. Confutatis Maledictus, Chorus (from the Requiem) — Mozart
2. Lachrymosa
3. Angels ever bright and fair, Aria di Soprano — Handel
4. Benedictus, Quartett (from the Requiem) — Mozart
5. Come tremenda l'Alma, Duo Soprano e Tenore — Mercadante
6. Recordare Jesu Pie, Quartetto — Bellini
7. Come all come ogni cosa, Chorus — Bellini

As in Boston, the parish choir often performed sacred concerts to raise money for particular needs within the community. Maroncelli's performance was billed as a "concert by amateurs" to raise money for the Catholic orphanage.

But professional concerts took place at St. Peter's as well, none receiving more acclaim than a series of performances of Rossini's *Stabat Mater* the week of October 9, 1842. The world premiere of the revised version of Rossini's work had taken place in Paris earlier the same year; the New York premiere took place May 5, 1842, at the Broadway Tabernacle. The premiere performance in New York must have stirred up interest in the Rossini composition, for the performance at St. Peter's was eagerly awaited by both public and press. The concert was conducted by a Mr. Pearson, with a "powerful orchestra," a chorus of twenty-seven (including the five soloists), and a Mr. Beames as organist. And, of course, George Templeton Strong in the audience:

> Went to St. Peter's and heard Rossini's *Stabat Mater*. The crowd was intense; all the aisles were jammed. The Pope made money and roasted the heretics at the same time, for it was as hot as the *Limbus Patrum*. Didn't know but that there was going to be another *Strages Ugonottem*. As it was, the whole church was one great battlefield. Music splendid.... This is a pretty way to spend a Sunday, isn't it?[12]

New York's newspapers, including the *Herald*, the *Mirror*, and the *Daily Tribune* all reported on the event:

> All that was hoped and anticipated of the Grand Concert at St. Peters Church last evening has been fully realized. It was a performance of the most impressive perfection and of a most brilliant artistical finish in every one of its parts—all replete with expressive *motive* of the composer. It was attended by over three thousand persons, and will be repeated on next Wednesday and Friday evenings by the desire of numbers who could not gain admission.[13]

Strong was impressed enough with the first performance that he attended the second as well, noting that the church was barely half full on Wednesday evening.

That the musical traditions of St. Peter's in Barclay Street continued throughout the antebellum years is attested to by an enthusiastic and descriptive article reprinted in *Dwight's Journal of Music* in 1862:

> St. Peter's Roman Catholic Church, in Barclay street, has, for years, maintained the reputation of engaging one of the choirs *par excellence* of the city of New York. Where is the lover or patron of fine music, either

sacred or secular, who cannot bear testimony to this assertion. . . . it has been celebrated among fine art critics and church-goers for the sublimity of its sacred music. . . . we have never known St. Peter's to be afflicted with a poor choir.[14]

The correspondent proceeded to describe the musical life of the church in a way which Dwight found somewhat humorous.

A few short years ago it was, bona fide, a sensation church. People flocked there from various parts of the city. . . . Why was this? . . . Who could resist the inducement? George Loder was organist: Mary Taylor (our own seraphic Mary) was prima donna; Salvi was tenor, and Masset was basso. Think of it! What an array of talent was there! And when Haydn's or Mozart's Kyrie Eleison was begun, Loder (more enthusiastic at the organ than he ever was in the orchestra) made that grandest of organs vibrate until it shook the edifice, until it burst through the windows, and filled the air without with seraphic tones from heaven. No wonder there was a rush and excitement in the crowd.[15]

In equally enthusiastic tones, the reporter speaks of the high mass as a "grand carnival, mingled with sacred and profane devotion. The devout, it is hoped, came to pay homage to the shrine of the Savior, the profane to pay homage to the interpreters of the sacred service, in divine song."[16] The attendance of non-Catholics at high mass, while usually welcomed, also caused some resentment among parishioners. A letter to the editor of an Irish newspaper in New York City noted that on a recent Sunday when

a large number of Protestants were present I was shocked at the amount of insulting disrespect and indelicate conduct which is tolerated by some members of our over good natured Catholic community. . . . During the interesting part of the performance, they stand on tip-toe on the kneeling board to obtain a good view; when the music pleases them they listen in silent admiration; when the interest of either Mass or music flags, conversation, not always confined to an under tone, beguiles the time.[17]

One reason church leadership permitted such attendance was mentioned by the letter's author—"I am one of those, Mr. Editor, who, perhaps, owes my salvation to the courtesy of those who admitted me as a stranger and non-Catholic inquirer to their seats"; the reason, of course, was the hope of conversions to Catholicism. But many Protestants who attended, such as George Templeton Strong, had no such inclination and perceived Catholic services as purely aesthetic occasions. As such, however, Catholic churches had a significant impact upon the musical life of a number of American cities. As the Catholic embassy chapels of London had introduced the choral music of the Viennese classicists to the British public, so Catholic churches often introduced new European music to American cities: Baltimore first heard Rossini's *Stabat Mater*[18] and Haydn's *Creation* from a Catholic choir, Boston Beethoven's *Mass in C*, Chicago Mozart's *Requiem*, and Philadelphia Gounod's *Messe Solennelle de St. Cécile*.[19]

St. Peter's in New York City may be regarded as exceptional among Catholic churches of the time only by the amount and quality of European sacred art music performed. Smaller parishes, with fewer resources than the premier Catholic church of the country's largest city, employed the music of Mozart and Haydn in both worship and concert whenever the occasion warranted and the resources were available. At the dedication of St. Andrew's Church in New York, Haydn's Mass No. 1 (Hoboken no. 10) was performed with "an inefficient substitute for an organ put up *'pro tem,'*. . . with the aid of a few string instruments."[20] The *New York Freeman's Journal* noted that

> This unique and inspired work of the immortal master, although so frequently performed, *appears still to be a stock mass with most of our choirs*, and, truly, whether we consider its beauties in the light of a work of art, or as an appendage to the awful ceremony for which it was composed, it is equally entitled to our admiration.[21]

The same work was performed for the dedication of Holy Trinity Church, in Boston's first German Catholic parish, and advertised as the first performance of the work in Boston.[22] The masses of Hummel, especially his Opus 80, were heard; George Templeton Strong described a Hummel mass he heard at St. Peter's as "transcendent music, and well chosen for Easter Sunday."[23] The music at St. Augustine's in Philadelphia, where Benjamin Carr had led the musical life for thirty years early in the century, was described in the *New-York Musical Review* as "of superior quality." But, the correspondent added, the choices of music, "being in many instances from operas or secular authors, do not under any circumstances meet my approbation in the church, no matter what argument may be used to justify the practice."[24] Unfortunately, the author gives no specific examples of inappropriate music. But the repertory of St. Augustine's is suggested by the works contained in the musical library of William Augustine Newland, an organist at the church; the collection will be discussed later.

In the Boston diocese choirs performed the masses of Mozart and Haydn, even outside of the city itself. The volunteer choir of St. Peter's in Lowell performed "Mozart's magnificent mass," probably the "Twelfth."[25] Sacred concerts including the works of the classical composers abounded. Mozart's *Requiem* was popular, as in New York. Although the first complete Boston performance of the *Requiem* is attributed to the Handel and Haydn Society in 1857, the *Boston Musical Gazette* reported that the

> choir of the Church of the Holy Cross, (catholic) assisted by the children of the Blind Asylum, gave a concert for the benefit of the suffering Irish, in the Melodeon, Feb. 23 [1847]. The principal passages from Mozart's Requiem were among the performances.[26]

The choirs of the Catholic churches of Boston were sufficiently confident to unite to perform the complete Mozart *Requiem* in the same season as the Handel and Haydn Society's first performance, and in the same concert hall.[27] The *Boston Pilot* billed the concert as Mozart's *Requiem* "performed for the first time in Boston by a Catholic choir" and notes that

> Catholic music sounds strange to us when performed by performers who are not Catholics. Such performers, be they ever so accomplished, can scarcely do more than give the bare music just as it is written, each note given with correctness. Catholic singers—baptized vocal organs—infuse a life, a soul into the otherwise lifeless body of musical notes. They bid the dry bones live.[28]

A long review of the performance in *Dwight's Journal of Music* attests to the success of the concert. Surprisingly, the reviewer—probably Dwight himself—appears to agree with the *Boston Pilot* concerning Catholic singers and their music:

> Yet the effect was far greater than we could have anticipated; indeed at times the sublimity of the music was fully realized and felt. And this was owing partly to the earnestness and heartiness with which the choral duty was discharged by those believers in such music as a part of their religion.[29]

While enjoying the performance, the audience proved bothersome to the reviewer:

> An unwonted crowd that, for the Music Hall! composed of course very largely of the Irish Catholic population, who listened to not a little with

reverence and wonder, but who had a singularly naive and frank way of showing when they were interested and when they were weary.[30]

The reviewer concluded by expressing his hope for further concerts, since "opportunities of hearing the noble compositions in the Mass form are entirely too few."[31]

Vocal scores for the masses of Mozart, Haydn, and other European composers had been available in the United States since the 1820s. Originally they were imported from the English Catholic publisher Novello. By the 1840s, American publishers—Oliver Ditson in Boston, for example—were producing reprints of the Novello editions. The numbering system for these masses reflects not the composer's order but the order in which Novello published them. Novello also marketed masses under the names of Haydn and Mozart that later were discovered to be spurious; the most outstanding example is the Mozart Twelfth Mass (K. anh. 232), often held by the musical press of the day to be the finest work of the composer. The editions published after 1840 invariably contained both the original Latin and an English text, either a singable translation or newly composed lyrics. Thus the publisher could attract both Catholic choirs and Protestant music lovers.

Especially in the 1850s, there appears to have been a growing interest in the mass form. John S. Dwight wrote a long article in 1851 on Mozart's Twelfth Mass and mentioned a popular musical activity of the day:

> The depth and beauty of the Masses grow upon the hearer with every repetition; and the little musical groups who study them together, singing such portions as they can, by way of practice, or holding social "readings" of them for the edification of themselves and listening friends, soon become partial to them, before all other vocal music. And well it may be! For in their composition the rarest genius, the profoundest musical learning and science, the most inspiring texts, and the most solemn occasions conspired.[32]

In many places "Mass clubs" were formed by musical amateurs. Dwight's *Journal* reported that "'Mass Clubs' have become almost as common as 'Glee Clubs' in and around Boston."[33] In New York the *Musical World* reported that

> the singing of masses, of which mention was made about this time last year, has been resumed during the past Lent season by accomplished amateurs in our New York society. There is great charm in this music

and an unusual satisfaction in singing it during this graver season of the churchly year.³⁴

The demand for mass music produced by the combination of "mass clubs" and new and swiftly growing Catholic parishes insured that music publishers would provide the product.

Especially in New York City and Philadelphia, there was a second source of European musical settings of the Catholic liturgy: manuscripts of contemporary masses. St. Stephen's Parish on East 28th Street was founded in 1848 to meet the needs of immigrants who were settling in the then northern reaches of the city. The first pastor, Dr. Jeremiah Cummings, was educated in Rome and was well known throughout the city; the *Musical World and Times* described him as "a gentleman of great refinement and cultivation, particularly in music, which he has made his especial study."³⁵ He first erected a combination school and (temporary) church, and began a singing school for the children of the parish, under the direction of Professor Loretz.³⁶ For the dedication of the permanent church a setting of the mass by the Italian opera composer Saverio Mercadante was performed, a setting brought from Italy by Cummings himself. A flair for public relations was also in evidence; Cummings had prepared a "reporter's table within the chancel" from which the gentlemen of the press could observe the dedicatory mass.³⁷ The popularity of the Italian operatic style is also evidenced by the desire for new music; the church of St. Francis Xavier on West 16th Street, with "a choir capable of executing the most difficult compositions extant . . . receive[s] every month manuscript masses from the pen of Mercadante."³⁸

The leading Catholic musician in Philadelphia in the mid-nineteenth century was William Augustine Newland. The Library of Congress purchased Newland's music library in 1929, and its contents reveal the importance of manuscripts for the dissemination of nineteenth-century Catholic church music. Although many of the printed books in Newland's library have been dispersed to the general collection of the Library of Congress, the manuscript masses remain intact.³⁹ Newland possessed an extensive array of masses in manuscript, including works by European composers such as Beethoven, Hummel, and the French Jesuit Louis Lambillotte, as well as by composers working in the United States. Works by the latter include two masses and a Kyrie by Henry Dielman (professor of music at Mount St. Mary's College in Emmitsburg), a mass in G by A. F. Dos Santos, and two masses by Pedro Daunas, *Missa Espagnola* and *Missa Pastorelle* (both composers were Philadelphia organists).⁴⁰

While it is clear that there was significant interest in and use of the masses of the Viennese classicists and even of contemporary Italian composers, the average parish on the average Sunday certainly would not have had the resources to employ such difficult and sophisticated music. Most parishes did not have extensive libraries of sacred music, but rather worked out of one or more collections of Catholic music designed for average churches, supplemented by a limited amount of sheet music. Figure 4.1 lists the collections of music compiled for Catholic parishes that were in print in the years before the Civil War and indicates the masses included in each volume.

The list shows a clear trend in the selection of mass settings contained in the collections. Jacob Walter's collection of 1825 (which was reissued in 1834 and 1856 with the same contents) is an interesting link between the earliest repertory of American Catholics and the later antebellum repertory of masses.[41] Published in Baltimore, it likely reflects the tastes of the aristocratic "old-guard" Catholicism of the Federalist age. The "Ancient Mass, arranged for this work" is the same Gregorian-based mass as the one contained in the first collections of Catholic music issued in the United States, John Aitken's collections of 1787, 1791, and 1814, with the instrumental "symphonies" left to the organist's discretion. Samuel Webbe's "Grand Mass" is a legacy of the British Catholic tradition of the Embassy chapels. The text and music of the Gregorian Requiem Mass is a constant that appears both in Aitken's first publication for American Catholics and in collections published in the twentieth century.[42] Yet the inclusion of DeMonti's "Favorite Mass for Three Voices," which appears to be the first publication of a DeMonti work in the United States, looks forward to the dominant role DeMonti's masses would have throughout much of the period under consideration.

The Fenwick collection burned on the press, and therefore had little influence on the repertory; but it reflects a conservative attitude toward the choice of mass settings.[43] Garbett's 1840 work, the heir of the Fenwick, offers no surprises, relying on Webbe, the Requiem, and the Missa Regia. Samuel Webbe's daughter, Mrs. Brown, was a predecessor of Garbett as organist at the Boston cathedral;[44] the Missa Regia had been employed extensively in the Boston area by both European and Native American Catholics.[45] Garbett's collection of 1840 was successful enough that a new and expanded edition was offered to the public the following year. The major additions were the two masses by H. DeMonti. An advertisement for the second edition referred specifically to the two DeMonti works as "so very popular at the South and West."[46] The success of Kirk's 1844

FIGURE 4.1
Masses in American Collections of Catholic Music, 1825–1860

Walter	Grand Mass for Three Voices	S. Webbe, Sr.
1825	Favorite Mass for Three Voices	DeMonti
	Ancient Mass, arranged for this work	
	Requiem	Gregorian
[Fenwick]	Missa Regia	Dumont
1833	Missa de Angelis	Gregorian
	Mass for the Dead	Gregorian
Garbett	Mass in A	Webbe
1840	Mass in C	Webbe
	Missa Regia	Dumont
	Mass for the Dead	Gregorian
Garbett	Mass in A	Webbe
1842	Mass in C	Webbe
	Missa Regia	Dumont
	Mass for the Dead	Gregorian
	Mass in C	H. DeMonti
	Mass in F	H. DeMonti
Kirk	Missa de Angelis	Gregorian
1844	Mass in C	H. DeMonti
	Mass for Sundays of the year	Gregorian
	Missa Regia	Dumont
Kirk	Missa de Angelis	Gregorian
1845	Mass in C	H. DeMonti
	Mass for Sundays of the year	Gregorian
	Missa Regia	Dumont
	Favorite Mass in Three Voices	DeMonti
Lloyd	Mass in G	Webbe
1850	Mass in F	Natividad
	Mass for the Dead	Gregorian
	Missa Regia	Dumont
Peters	Mass No. 1 in Four Voices	Tauman
1851	Requiem	D. Müller
Werner	Mass for Soprano, Alto, and Bass	F. H. Schmid
1853		
Lloyd	Mass in G	Webbe
1855	Mass in F	Natividad
	Requiem	Gregorian
	Missa Regia	Dumont
Elliott	Missa de Angelis	Gregorian[47]
1855		
Werner	Missa Brevis	Palestrina
1857	Mass in B-flat	M. Stoeclin
	Mass in C	A. Werner
	Mass in D	Zing
	Mass in E-flat	F. X. Schmidt
	Mass in G	Witzka
	Requiem	F. X. Schmidt

music book led to its expanded republication the following year—adding "DeMonti's Favorite Mass for Three Voices [in B-flat]" to the DeMonti Mass in C contained in the original edition. The three DeMonti masses do not appear in any later collections, probably reflecting the fact that the masses began to appear as separate editions from both Oliver Ditson of Boston and A. C. Peters of Cincinnati.[48] The "Kyrie eleison" from DeMonti's Mass in C is reproduced in figure 4.2.

It is clear that DeMonti's masses continued to be performed. Bishop Benedict Fenwick heard DeMonti's Mass in G sung at a small church in rural Maryland to "tolerable effect."[49] Both the Boston Gregorian Society and the St. Mary's Singing Society had DeMonti masses in their repertories.[50] When a newly composed mass was sung at a Boston concert, one reviewer called the various movements "very splendid—parts of them equal to the finest pages of DeMonti."[51] *Dwight's Journal of Music* reviewed a DeMonti mass sung at St. Bridget's in New York City as late as 1862.[52]

Not a great deal is known about the composer Henri DeMonti. Eitner provides the following biographical data. Born in 1758 at Padua, Italy, DeMonti went to Vienna and Prague, and eventually to Scotland, where he died in 1830.[53] An essay on music by DeMonti, "The Self-taught Musician," was published at Edinburgh in 1796, so we may assume he arrived in Scotland some time before that date. His reputation seems to have been primarily as a music teacher, and the British Library holds eight publications for piano composed by DeMonti. Surprisingly, that same library has only one of his masses, the "favorite mass" in B-flat in the 1856 Oliver Ditson edition.[54]

Dwight's Journal reviewed the B-flat Mass when the Ditson edition was released. The reviewer was obviously not familiar with the composer or his work:

> Of the composer we know nothing save what here appears. It seems to be one of those light, easy, warbling, almost secular masses, which are much in use here in our Catholic churches. You are constantly reminded of the lighter moments in Haydn's masses; but it is a weak dilution of Haydn; Haydn has ideas, musical invention, richness of modulation, and occasional passages of imposing depth and grandeur; here it is all one level of sweet commonplace, with solos of a warbling and popular character, the charm being altogether melodic. Doubtless most congregations would feel that they could better spare a better mass.[55]

FIGURE 4.2
"Kyrie eleison" from H. DeMonti's Mass in C
Courtesy The Music Division, New York Public Library for the Performing Arts. Astor, Lenox, and Tilden Foundations.

The critic's low opinion of DeMonti's mass was beginning to be shared by others in the late 1850s. A letter to the editor of the *Boston Pilot* in 1857 reflected upon the musical changes in Boston Catholicism. The writer noted that in 1840 "the music performed was not above the level of Webbe and De Monti" although it satisfied the singers and congregations of the time. Indeed, when first exposed to a Haydn mass, the "hearers would have listened more gladly to DeMonti, altho' they had heard him often. Their taste was not educated then quite up to the classical standard." But following the success of the Mozart *Requiem* performed by the Catholic choirs of Boston (mentioned above), "it will not do . . . for our choir to sing any other than universally acknowledged classical music before such critics [e.g., John S. Dwight] as they are now sure to be at every concert." But the writer makes a clear distinction between music presented at concerts and music used in worship: one should trust the taste of the choir director, Mr. Werner, rather than the "not thoroughly formed taste of us, old fogies, to whom the old strains are very dear. Moreover, we can have them in church."[56]

The Mr. Werner in question was Anthony Werner, a German immigrant and the organist at the Cathedral of the Holy Cross in Boston. The two music collections Werner published before 1860 (see fig. 4.1) contain masses that stand in stark contrast to those contained in other collections of the time. Werner was clearly trying to lead the Boston Catholics away from the English tradition and toward a Germanic one.

The preference for German music, coupled with the concern for "educating" the taste of Boston Catholics toward "classical" music, seems to indicate that the ideas of that part of the Boston musical establishment led by John S. Dwight were making inroads with the immigrant community in at least one area. Yet in New York, the Italian operatic composers seemed to be held in the highest esteem, as evidenced by the importation of Mercadante masses, and performances of Rossini and Donizetti scores in Catholic churches of the city. While Dwight certainly had influence in New York, William Henry Fry, the composer and the critic for Horace Greeley's *New York Tribune*, exerted a strong anti-Dwight influence. Although Fry argued strongly for the development of an "American" music, his own music looked to the Italian school of Rossini, Bellini, and Donizetti for musical models. As isolated from the Protestant establishment as the Catholic immigrant community was, the evolution of musical styles employed in immigrant parishes appears to bear some relationship to the currents of musical thought going on around them, although a direct link would be hard to substantiate.[57]

While European compositions formed the bulk of the repertory of masses employed in Catholic parishes, it must be noted that American composers provided settings of the Catholic liturgy as well. The masses written by Benjamin Carr for the Catholics of Philadelphia did not lose currency; two of Carr's settings of the mass were still in print in 1871. William Cumming Peters, who would compose, adapt and publish a large amount of music for Catholic choirs during his lifetime, saw his first mass (in C) published by George Willig, Jr., in 1841.[58] The *Board of Music Trade Catalogue* of 1871 lists three masses composed by Peters (masses in G and D, and a "jubilee mass" in G) and his arrangements of two Gregorian masses (the "Missa de Angelis" and the Requiem). Figure 4.3 shows the opening of Peters' "Mass in G."[59] Dr. Henry Dielman, professor of music at Mount St. Mary's College throughout the 1840s and 1850s, published his own mass setting for three voices in 1854.[60]

Louis Selle, the music director of Assumption Church in Brooklyn, New York, published a mass of his own composition in 1848. Selle explained the need for his setting of the Catholic liturgy:

> The scarcity of masses, particularly adapted to the use of the Catholic church choirs of this country, has induced me to write an easy and melodious mass in modern style, for three voices and organ, which, I hope, is well calculated to please. I take the liberty of soliciting the Rev. Pastors and the leaders of choirs for their friendly support of this publication by subscribing to a supply for their churches.[61]

Selle also called upon the most well known New York musicians associated with Catholic music to provide testimonials: Henry Timm, George Loder, organist of St. Peter's, Barclay St., and D. R. Harrison, organist of St. Patrick's Cathedral, Mott St. All three stress the suitability of the mass for "small choirs."

The two most surprising aspects of the mass repertory of antebellum American Catholics are its smallness and its durability. Few church choirs had either the ability or the desire to perform Beethoven's Mass in C. Most parish choirs appear to have learned to sing one, perhaps two masses, and to have used them again and again. Few masses that achieved any popularity went out of print; the *Board of Music Trade Catalogue* reads like a synopsis of almost fifty years of American Catholic mass settings. Mozart and Haydn masses predominate in numbers, to be sure, but they are joined by the work of Peters, Selle, Dielman, DeMonti, Carr, and Webbe—masses that were probably performed far more often than most of the Viennese masses.

FIGURE 4.3
"Kyrie eleison" from Peters' Mass in G

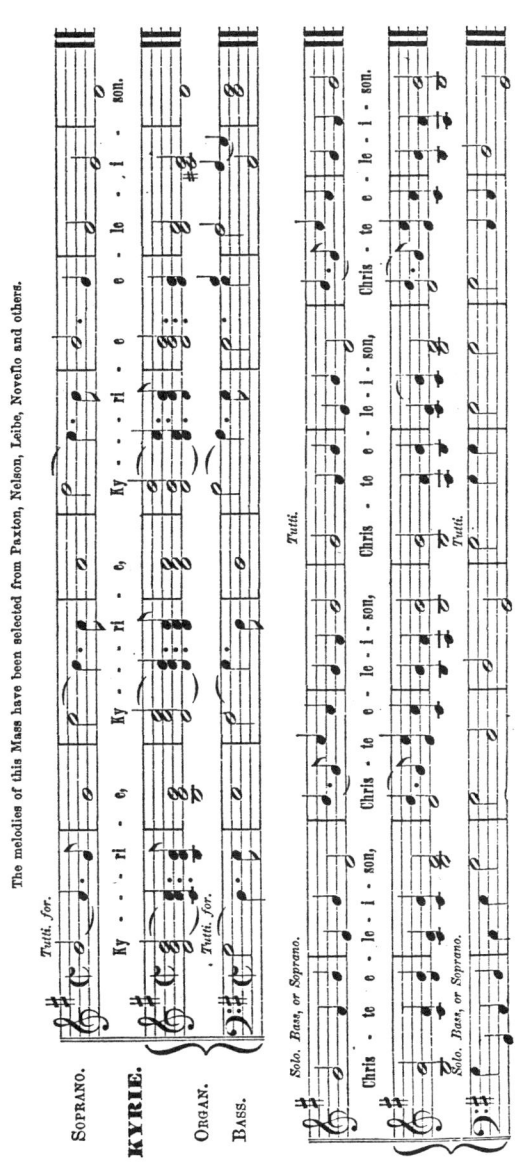

Music for Vespers

While the repertory of masses appears to have been relatively small, the music available for Sunday vespers and benediction (which were invariably paired on Sunday afternoon in urban American Catholic churches of the time) was quite extensive. Charles C. Pise wrote the following description of the "ideal" vespers service in his novel, *Father Rowland, A North American Tale*:[62]

> [Father Rowland] entoned the *Deus in adjutorium*, or "Incline unto my aid, O God." He was answered by full choir, who continued the anthem; after which the Father and the whole congregation sat. The Psalms 109, 110, 111, and 116 were then chanted without interruption, in a plain, noble and solemn tone. The verses were sung alternately by male and female voices. The effect of the evening service is truly delightful.... After the psalms were concluded, the Father arose and chanted the lesson of the day. A hymn was then sung by the choir, and then followed the beautiful canticle of the Virgin Mary, *Magnificat*....

Numerous settings of psalms, antiphons, and hymns for Vespers were published; William Cumming Peters appears to have been the most prolific publisher of such pieces. The complete catalogue of W. C. Peters' publications for Catholic parishes is reproduced in figure 4.4. The catalogue, which appeared on the cover page of George Onslow's *Ave Maria* (copyright 1845) represents Peters' catalogue from sometime between 1854 and 1858: the *Young Catholic's Vocal Class Book*, the last item listed, was published in 1853, and the listing does not include *Peters' Evening Service*, a major work of W. C. Peters, published in 1858, which certainly would have been included if available. Many of the other works listed, even when a copy is located, do not provide a publication date.

If one looks carefully at the selections in Peters' catalogue, one finds but a single major difference between the mass repertory we have looked at, and the vesper/benediction repertory: the latter is far larger. But once again the London Catholic Embassy tradition is represented in composers such as Novello and Webbe, classicism in Mozart, and the older American Catholic tradition in Carr, Taylor, Cross and Wiesenthal. Mid-nineteenth-century American Catholic composers are represented by George Loder, William Newland, and W. C. Peters himself. The Italian operatic tradition is represented by Rossini, Mercadante, and Donizetti, and the growing influence of German musicians is reflected in the significant number of German surnames.

FIGURE 4.4
W. C. Peters' Catholic Publications, circa 1854–1858

Select Sacred Music Suitable for the Catholic Church Service.
Published by W. C. Peters and Sons, Cincinnati

1059	Adeste Fideles and Responses			15cts
2216	Ag. Dei Duett for Bassi	Marcello		25cts
2638	Adoremus	Lambillotte	4v.	85cts
120	Alma Redemptoris	Pleyel	4v.	15cts
1701	Alma Redemptoris	Stadler	4v.	25cts
2370	Alma Redemptoris	Lambillotte	4v.	35cts
1772	Alma Redemptoris	Zimmers	2v.	25cts
1704	A solis ortus, and Litany B. V.			25cts
1762	Asperges (No. 1)	Hummel	4v.	35cts
1763	Asperges (No. 2)	Zimmers	3v.	35cts
1764	Asperges (No. 3)	Himmel	4v.	35cts
1765	Asperges (No. 4)	Himmel	4v.	35cts
1766	Asperges (No. 5)	Novello	3v.	25cts
1768	Asperges (see Laudate)	Cross		15cts
1691	Audi benigna, and Lucis Creator			15cts
1653	Ave Maris Stella	Donizetti	3v.	25cts
75	Ave Maria	Onslow	4v.	25cts
1434	Ave Maria	Schwing	solo	25cts
1965	Ave Maria	Winter	3v.	25cts
1737	Ave Maria	Italian	solo	25cts
1738	Ave Maria, or O Queen	Marliani	solo	15cts
1741	Ave Maria, or Ave Regina	Cherubini	solo	25cts
2626	Ave Regina	Novello	solo & ch.	25cts
1740	Ave Regina; or, Gaude Virgo	Novello		25cts
1742	Ave Regina, and Ave Maria	Mercadante		25cts
1757	Ave Verum	Novello	solo	15cts
1758	Ave Verum	Himmel	solo	15cts
1700	Ave Verum	Mozart	4v.	25cts
1759	Ave Verum	King & Cook	solo	25cts
1825	Ave Verum	Rossini	4v.	25cts
2633	Catholic Harmonist; a collection of Masses, Hymns, Vespers, etc., for the Principal Feasts of the year, by W. C Peters			1.50cts
1654	Carr's Chant Mass	B. Carr		25cts
1647	Carr's Christmas Hy. (See "There were," etc.)			25cts
1656	Carr's easy Mass (for Low Mass)		3v.	50cts
1646	Carr's Te Deum	Carr	3v.	50cts
2361	Christmas Anthem (Pastores)	Lambillotte		60cts
2237	Credo (Semi chant)		4v.	35cts
1684	Domine exaudi, Beautiful soprano solo	Schwing		25cts
1729	Ecce Panis	Himmel	solo	25cts
1730	Ecce Panis	Herold	solo	15cts
1731	Ecce Panis	Himmel	duett	25cts

FIGURE 4.4—*Continued*

1697	Ecce Panis	D'Hollander	duett	25cts
1702	Ecce Panis	D'Hollander	duett	35cts
1854	Ecce Panis	Donizetti	duett	25cts
1486	Ecce Panis	Verhayden	solo, ch.	35cts
1625	Fading, still fading	Wiesenthal		25cts
1740	Gaude Virgo (See Ave Regina)			25cts
67	Hail to the Lord's Anointed		solo & ch.	25cts
1445	Hymn for Easter	Schwing	4v.	15cts
1434	Hymn to the B. V. (See Ave)	Schwing	solo	25cts
1695	Inclina Domine	Schneidermeyer	4v.	25cts
2214	In violata (Who Can Compare)	Colliere		35cts
1703	Iste Confessor		3v.	25cts
1650	Italian Litany, and Miserere, in English			25cts
1699	Jesu dulcis memoria	Baumgarten	bass solo	35cts
1124	Jesu Fili Dei	Winter	3v.	25cts
1675	Jesu Mater Ave	Mozart	solo & ch.	25cts
1768	Laudate Dominum; or Asperges	Cross		15cts
1735	Laudate Dominum	Himmel	4v.	25cts
107	Litany of the Blessed Virgin	Peters		25cts
2630	Loder's Vespers, with O Salutaris	Loder		30cts
2164	Magnificat (from a Gloria)	Mozart		35cts
2629	Magnificat	Loder		35cts
1654	Mass, (chant Mass)	Carr		25cts
1656	Mass (For Low Mass)	Carr	3v.	50cts
1376	Mass in C	Schneidermeyer	4v.	1.50cts
2325	Mass in E Flat	Buhler	4v.	1.50cts
1667	Mass (easy)	Stark	3v.	1.00cts
1607	Mass Pastoral in G	Knitze	4v.	1.50cts
2217	Mass-selected	Dietsch	3v.	1.50cts
2631	Mass in D, for one voice	Gregorian		1.00cts
2632	Mass for 3 voices. Selected			1.50cts
74	Memorare	Lambillotte	solo & ch.	50cts
1732	Miserere nostri	Martini	duett	25cts
1733	Miserere-Gregorian chant			15cts
1649	Newland's collection of sacred music, containing:			
	No. 1–Alma, by Webbe			
	No. 2–Ave No. 1 by Carr			
	No. 3–Ave No. 2 by Carr			
	No. 4–Regina Coeli, by Purcell			
	No. 5–Salve Regina by Handel			35cts
952	O Benigna (Blessed be thou)	Novello		25cts
1626	O Cor Amoris		solo, duett & ch.	85cts
1777	O Gloriosa Domina	Lambillotte	4v.	75cts
1733	O Maria; or, Ave Maria		duett	15cts
1487	O Quam dilecta	Lambillotte	solo & ch.	50cts
1115	O Salutaris	D'Hollander	duett	25cts
1696	O Salutaris	D'Hollander	duett	15cts
1753	O Salutaris		treble solo	25cts
1754	O Salutaris		trio	
1755	O Salutaris		solo	15cts
1652	O Salutaris	Dufort		15cts
2215	O Salutaris	Stradella	solo	25cts

FIGURE 4.4—*Continued*

1448	Parce Domine, and Miserere	Schwartz		15cts
2361	Pastores (See Christmas H.)	Lambillotte		60cts
1648	Prayer for the Commonwealth	Taylor		15cts
1375	Quid Retribuam	Lambillotte	solo & ch.	50cts
2202	Regina Coeli	Lambillotte	duett & ch.	85cts
1438	Regina Coeli	Gansbacher	4v.	15cts
2627	Regina Coeli	Winter	3v.	25cts
1743	Regina Coeli	Herold	solo & ch.	15cts
1687	Regina Coeli and Ave Maria	Stark		15cts
1644	Requiem for 3 or 4 voices	Ohnewald		1.50cts
1760	Responses at High Mass			15cts
1769	Riposa in pace	Martini	duett	25cts
1693	Salve Regina	Baumgartner	4v.	25cts
1744	Salve Regina	Himmel	solo	25cts
1745	Salve Regina	Manners	solo	25cts
1746	Salve Regina	Cooke	solo	15cts
2628	Salve Regina	Loder	trio	25cts
2635	Sancta Maria	Buhler	solo, chorus	65cts
1686	Stabat Mater	Baini	3v.	35cts
1761	Stabat, Jerusalem and Miserere			15cts
1747	Tantum Ergo	Novello	3v.	25cts
1748	Tantum Ergo	Cooke	3v.	15cts
1749	Tantum Ergo	Winter	3v.	25cts
1750	Tantum Ergo	Giardini	3v.	25cts
1751	Tantum Ergo	Carusi	3v.	15cts
1752	Tantum Ergo	Webbe	3v.	15cts
1451	Tantum Ergo	Schwartz	4v.	15cts
1689	Tantum Ergo	Terziani	4v.	35cts
1698	Tantum Ergo	Stark	4v.	15cts
2324	Tantum Ergo (grand)	Lambillotte	4v.	40cts
1966	Tantum Ergo	Lambillotte	5v.	25cts
1645	Te Deum	Newland	3v.	1.00cts
1646	Te Deum	B. Carr	3v.	50cts
1647	There were shepherds	B. Carr		25cts
1771	Thirteen Hymns for Vespers	Loder		50cts
1734	Tu Rex Gloriae	Novello	bass solo	25cts
2162	Veni Creator	Sofge	4v.	25cts
1690	Veni Creator			35cts
1855	Veni Creator	Himmel	solo & ch.	25cts
1736	Veni Sancte Spiritus	Handel	solo	15cts
1933	Veni Sancte Spiritus	Dietsch	4v.	75cts
1694	Venite Filii	Baini	3v.	15cts
49	Vesper Hymn to B. V.		solo & ch.	25cts
112	Vespers for the Assumption	Peters		35cts
2630	Vespers, with O Salutaris	Loder		30cts
1770	Vespera and Magnificat	Novello		35cts
1655	Vespers (10 settings for various F'ts)	Newland		1.25cts
1767	Vidi Aquam	Novello	3v.	25cts
2634	Young Catholic's Vocal Class Book, containing a practical course of vocal instruction, and a series of Catholic Hymns			50cts

Peters was but one of a number of publishers who supplied music for the Catholic churches of the United States: S. T. Gordon of New York published an entire line of Catholic masses, C. G. Christman, 404 Pearl St., New York, billed himself as "publisher of Music proper to the Catholic Choir." It has already been noted that Ditson of Boston and Willig of Baltimore, by all accounts major American music publishers of the time, did not ignore the growing Catholic market. Figure 4.5 reproduces the first movement of the 1855 "Tantum Ergo" composed by William Berge, organist of St. Francis Xavier Church in New York City. The work was published by William A. Pond in New York, Ditson in Boston, and A. C. Peters in Cincinnati.

One of the selections listed in Peters' catalogue reflects a trend that began during the 1840s, and became a common occurrence in American Catholic music after the Civil War—the adaptation of operatic melodies to Latin words for use in church services. The *Jesu Mater Ave* by Mozart will not be found in any catalogue of Mozart's works. It first appeared in a Catholic music periodical, *The Catholic Choralist*. No copy of the periodical has been located, although two reviews of the first issue provide a sense of the general flavor. It was to "be issued regularly every Two Months" by W. J. Ashe of Philadelphia and would "contain a Choice Collection of Catholic Music, viz. Litanies, Hymns, Masses, &c., designed for choirs."[63] From a review in the *United States Catholic Magazine* we learn that in the initial issue the

> first hymn, "Jesu Mater," the words from the gifted pen of the Rev. E. J. Sourin, arranged from the gifted pen of Professor André from Mozart's Zauberflotte [sic], is of itself an acquisition to our church music, and would well compensate the purchaser of No. 1 of "the Catholic Choralist."[64]

Not all critics held the arrangement in high esteem. Orestes Brownson, one of the major forces in Catholic intellectual life of the period, noted

> if Mozart were here, he would be not a little surprised to find the passage taken from his *Magic Flute*—originally composed, if we recollect aright, to be sung by a half-idiot with a bell accompaniment—arranged as a sacred piece to be sung by our choirs. Are the singers in our choirs expected to accompany themselves with bells, or to personate half-idiots, when singing the praises of God, or a hymn to the Blessed Virgin?[65]

FIGURE 4.5
William Berge's "Tantum Ergo" (first movement) (transcription)

FIGURE 4.5 (cont.)

82   HOW SHALL WE SING?

FIGURE 4.5 (cont.)

Brownson continues by encouraging the idea behind such a publication, but expresses his hope that future issues will provide *"religious* choral music from Catholic masters, either of the German or Italian school."[66] The division of opinion on the practice of adapting operatic tunes to church services continued to be a heated battle until the adaptations fell out of use in the early twentieth century.

Mention should also be made of the Frenchman Louis Lambillotte, one of the first reformers of church music in nineteenth-century France. His edition of St. Gall Codex 339, published in 1856, was an important step in the growth of the Gregorian revival which would drastically change Catholic musical practice in America during the first decades of the twentieth century. But Lambillotte was also a composer in his own right, represented by nine compositions in Peters' catalogue.

Plainchant in America

We have ignored the use of Gregorian chant by American Catholics, except for a few references to the Requiem mass. Indeed, the later Gregorian reformers of the early twentieth century felt that the chant employed was so "corrupt" as not to be called chant at all. Yet there clearly was use of chant, not in a "purist" or "archaeological" form, but as a living tradition—melodies passed on and employed as the musicians of the time saw fit.

Two very different chant traditions existed in the eighteenth century as sources for American Catholics: the English and the French. What little music was sung in the worship of English Catholics appears to have been the chant; the masses of Samuel Webbe are described as "the first to supersede the use of the Gregorian chaunt in Catholic choirs."[67] The English tradition employed the chant melody in the upper voice and added a second, bass voice as accompaniment. This style was represented in some of the chant contained in John Aitken's hymnal of 1787. The second tradition of chant performance, the French style, called for the chant to be sung by basses. A 1793 instruction noted "it is preferable that the chanters be basses, for when chant is sung by tenors and countertenors, it does not fill the church."[68] The speed of the chant was regulated by the solemnity of the feast celebrated; the more important the feast, the slower the chants were sung. A description of the French style of chant around 1800 appeared in a Boston newspaper in 1834:

> I am well aware of the miserable cawing that used to be heard in our London chapels, some thirty years since, when the tremulous prolongation of the "gregorian" note *a la Francoise aided the distraction* of the assembled faithful. Old Webbe has been seen more than once peeping out from the curtains of the organ loft, at Lincoln's Inn Fields, in a state of petrifaction, at the poor French emigrants, (sancti confessores!) as they astounded the walls with their "canto fermo." But this was not the Gregorian chant as it should be sung.[69]

The French also retained the practice of choral improvisation by the upper voices. One writer described the waning practice as it existed in 1838:

France . . . has never abandoned its mania of improvising on a plainsong . . . and if today the combat has come to an end, it is only for lack of contestants. I say "combat" and for good reason; for it was indeed a perpetual battle, in which all the combatants appeared to butcher each other. The cathedral chancels were real battlefields, where one heard the cantors droning hoarsely in their lower register, then the counter-tenors shouting at the top of their lungs, and the tenors fitting in as best they could. For this, all these good men had no rule other than habit: they tried to start off on one of the notes of the harmony, and, for the rest, they abandoned themselves to Providence.[70]

The French *chant sur le livre*, as it was known, does not appear to have been practiced in America. The unpublished memoirs of John Mondesir describe the style of chant favored in Baltimore around 1800. Mondesir himself preferred the simple style of chant: "I very much agree with his excellency the Archbishop of Lyon, who wants to restore the Gregorian chant in all its noble, grand, and majestic simplicity." Mondesir also explains the manner of chanting the psalms at the Baltimore cathedral:

> In Baltimore they sang the psalms as in the Greek church; a fine singer, positioned by the organ which accompanies throughout, intones the first verse; the whole congregation chants the second verse and the choir takes over for the third, and so on until the end.[71]

Musicians who employed the chant in America felt the need to adapt and arrange it. The extent of the use of chant varies from region to region. Philadelphia Catholics, for example, who for many years were under the musical influence of Benjamin Carr, do not appear to have employed the chant tradition extensively until it was reintroduced by Bishop Neumann in the 1850s. Boston, in particular, seems to have always stressed the importance of the chant, probably due to the influence of Bishop Fenwick. Fenwick's hymnal of 1833 contained a good number of chants, arranged by different musicians. Richard Garbett's collection of 1840 was the first successful collection of music for American Catholics that included a large selection of chants, often harmonized by Garbett himself.

Figure 4.6 is Garbett's arrangement of the Gregorian hymn "Veni Creator Spiritus" as it appears in the *Morning and Evening Service of the Catholic Church*. As in all of the arrangements in the collection, the top staff indicates the tenor voice, which is doubled (occasionally displaced an octave) in small notes on the grand staff below, for the convenience of the organist. Although the hymn is actually in the eighth (hypomixolydian)

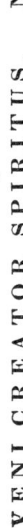

Figure 4.6

Richard Garbett's arrangement of "Veni Creator Spiritus"

Courtesy The Music Division, New York Public Library for the Performing Arts. Astor, Lenox, and Tilden Foundations.

144

WHITSUNDAY, OR PENTECOST

Vespers :—Psalms, the same as on Sundays ; also, the following day.

HYMN.

VENI CREATOR SPIRITUS. No. 1.

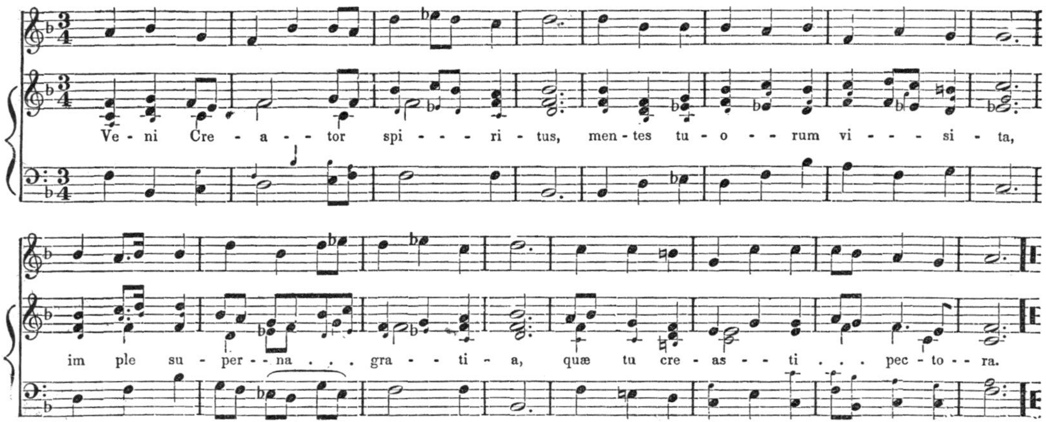

2
Qui diceris Paraclitus,
Altissimi donum Dei,
Fons vivus, ignis, caritas,
Et spiritalis unctio.

3
Tu septiformis munere,
Digitus Paternæ dexteræ,
Tu rite promissum Patris,
Sermone ditans guttura :

4
Accende lumen sensibus,
Infund' amorem cordibus,
Infirma nostri corporis
Virtute firmans perpeti.

5
Hostem repellas longius
Pacemque dones protinus :
Ductore sic te prævio,
Vitemus omne noxium.

6
Per te sciamus da Patrem,
Noscamus atque Filium ;
Te utriusque Spiritum
Credamus omni tempore.

7
Deo Patri sit gloria,
Et Filio qu' a mortuis
Surrexit, ac Paraclito
In seculorum secula. Amen.

mode, Garbett sets the melody firmly in F major. It was common practice of the period to raise the seventh degree to the leading tone even when it was not so marked. One organist noted that "very few editions of the plain chant mark or print the naturals, and less so the accidental sharps; they are to be supplied by the good taste of the performer; and if they are judiciously used, the plain chant will not differ so widely from modern music, as it is generally imagined."[72]

It is interesting, however, that Garbett has tried to provide some "flavor" of the mode by employing the E-flat in the accompaniment of the first three phrases. But Garbett's use of the flatted seventh always fits into the major mode; the E-flat in measure three, for example, makes the F major chord sound more like a V7/IV-IV than simply a I-IV progression. But the same concern for leading tones forces Garbett into altering the melody at the end of measure 7 to produce the V chord of C minor on which he will cadence at the end of phrase two; the B-natural in measure 7 is the only change in the melody of the hymn inconsistent with other mid-nineteenth-century editions of the "Veni Creator Spiritus." Only in the final phrase of the hymn do we find E-natural, as the arrangement leads us to a clear and final resting place in F major.

Figure 4.7 provides the arrangement of "Veni Creator" as it appeared in Fenwick's ill-fated music book of 1833. Melodically, this version is identical to Garbett's, including the B-natural, suggesting that Garbett used the 1833 version as a melodic model. Rhythmically, however, it is extremely different, retaining the freer flow of the chant; bar lines separate phrases and beams connect notes sung on one syllable. The harmonization also differs from Garbett's arrangement, although it does employ the modal E-flat, which Garbett may have borrowed for his harmonization of the tune.[73]

Although the chant was employed in at least a small way in most churches, there were continuing calls for both its reestablishment and reform. Bishop Fenwick, ever a supporter of the chant, had an article from a British publication reprinted in his diocesan newspaper in 1834, an article that looks at Catholic music from the standpoint of the ritual involved:

> It may seem Paradoxical to give the preference to the Gregorian chant, in these times, when the faultless and most exquisite compositions of Haydn, Mozart, &c., are so well performed, and attract such crowds of strangers to our chapels. . . . But is religion promoted by this—is one convert made by it? or is the devout Catholic helped in his prayer? are the purposes of religion fulfilled? How often is it, (is it not always so?)

FIGURE 4.7
"Veni Creator" from Fenwick's 1833 Music Book (transcription)

that the sacrifice is interrupted by this novel music? The priest has become the second person in the church, the Maestra di Cappella is the first—the priest waits until the choral gentry think it prudent to stop—the Mass is regulated by the choir now, and not the choir by the Mass.[74]

The somewhat romantic concept of discovering and restoring the "primitive simplicity" of church music was looked upon with interest from many parties. The *Boston Musical Gazette* noted in 1847 that

> the pope [Pius IX] is about to revive a project conceived by his predecessor, Gregory XVI, to reduce the church music to its primitive simplicity. He has appointed the Abbe Manni, and M Alessandro Moraldi, chapel masters to St. Peters, to undertake a mission to search in the libraries of

> Italy, and also foreign countries, for the early manuscripts of church music, and to prepare an edition as correct as possible, in modern notes, which will be published at the expense of the government, and under the auspices of Puisy.[75]

The interest in the music of "primitive" Christianity was strong enough even in non-Roman circles to warrant a two-part article on "The Old Church Modes or 'Tones'" from John S. Dwight in early issues of his new journal:

> There has been manifested of late more or less of a tendency, in the sphere of Sacred Music, to go back for models even to times earlier than Art itself. The severity, solemnity and grand simplicity of the old ecclesiastical chants has won many to the belief, that here was the only *sacred* music; that in those old traditional tunes, plain, yet inimitable, the prayers and pious aspirations of Christendom once for all were inspired with a form of utterance, to be forevermore repeated in all public worship.[76]

The author goes on to say that the peculiar nature of the chants is the result of the "*imperfect*, half-developed scale in which they were written." Indeed, the whole history of music is viewed as the process of discovering the true Art of music which we now possess. "We must regard then all this musical development before the 17th century, all from Ambrosian *plain chant* to Sebastian Bach . . . as mere preparation for the modern Art of music proper."[77] Dwight looked with suspicion on the medieval church that he believed held music captive, and implied that the revival of interest in the chant was something to be feared, perhaps even an attempt to impose restraints on the free development of music:

> As the priests took the conscience and the thinking of men into their own keeping, so they became the keepers of the infancy of Music; and closely was the child kept to its cradle, as if it had no destiny beyond,—rocked by certain rules and theories out of the brains of bookish monks and pedants, who allowed it only *that* expression and no airing in the secular and growing world of nature and genius.[78]

It should be noted that the interest in chant was increasing in both the Roman and the Anglican churches, particularly those parishes influenced by the Oxford movement.

Due to the rapid increase in the number of Catholics in the United States, the various bishops of the country looked to ways of bringing some order to their vast new flock. In the late 1840s and especially in the 1850s many dioceses worked to standardize parish practices; the manner of worship and the music employed were important targets of the new reforms. There was, in addition, a growing ultramontanism among much of the American Catholic hierarchy—invoking Roman authority as the standard of Catholic practice. These two factors created a need for a new and complete edition of plainchant for use in American parishes. The need was fulfilled by the publication in 1857 of two volumes: a *Kyriale* and a *Vesperal*.[79]

The Preface to the *Vesperal* leaves no doubt that the book is intended to be a tool to help bring American Catholic practice in line with that of Rome:

> It is now presented to the Catholics of the United States to meet the want that has always been felt in this country, both by the Clergy and Laity; for both it is published. The clergy will find it the Liturgical book required in every church. To the laity it will be a *vade-mecum*, by which they may assist at the services of the Church, and take part in the same.... The Chants of the Church should be familiar to all. It will take time, in our new country, to effect this. Yet, if this work is introduced into our parochial schools, academies, colleges, &c., a few years will effect a great change....
>
> As a proof of the imperfect manner in which the afternoon services or Vespers is sung in our churches, one long accustomed to hear it need only to cast a glance over these pages and he will find many things strange.[80]

Both works were issued in two versions, square notation and modern round notation. An identical set of directions included with both works indicates that the chants were to be sung in unison, and that there should be no regular pulse:

> The unequal value of the notes will produce the beautiful effect which we allude to; but it must be remembered that the value is not so much of mathematical exactness as of good taste and proper training in matters of Liturgy. Then the spirit of modern music must be banished from our choirs; for it is unbecoming to the simplicity of our chants, and also to the majesty of God.[81]

These directions imply a growing concern for understanding Catholic church music within its ritual context; but they also betray a growing mistrust of the "modern" world and its music.

Figure 4.8 shows the hymn "Veni Creator Spiritus" as published in the 1857 *Kyriale*. The beams connecting the groups of notes do not affect the

FIGURE 4.8
"Veni Creator" from the 1857 *Kyriale* (transcription)

value of the notes; they indicate syllabic groupings. The hymn is correctly designated in the eighth mode; the small asterisk after the clef correctly identifies the final. But by beginning on the note C, rather than G, the edition destroys the mode—but manages to include the favored "leading tone," B-natural. Melodically, the edition is identical to Garbett's, save for Garbett's characteristic penultimate raised note in the second phrase. Rhythmically the two editions are far apart, in terms of both the length of individual pitches and the use or absence of a regular meter.

Ultimately these two collections of plainchant do not appear to have had any great effect on the music of Catholic parishes in America. Other editions of the chant, published with similar ambitions, would appear in later years, but it would not be until the twentieth century that plainchant became standard practice in American churches. These early reformed volumes, however, did provide easy access to chant, and began to be used more and more within theological seminaries and colleges, perhaps making the church leadership of a later day more receptive to the Gregorian repertory in its "Roman" form.

Summary

Clearly performers of various kinds were involved in supplying the canonical music of Catholic ritual. In prestigious urban churches, such as St. Peter's in New York, professional opera singers were often hired. Yet even St. Peter's organized an amateur choir. Indeed, it appears that such a choir was the most common performing organization of the antebellum period. Almost no mention was found concerning professional quartet choirs in Catholic churches before the Civil War. Children's singing schools and the choirs formed out of them appear to have been a relatively common phenomenon as well.

Organists and choir directors were often paid professional musicians, not infrequently Protestant. Men such as George Loder and Charles M. King appear to have been organists simultaneously at Catholic and Episcopal churches. In the years before 1840 women organists in Catholic churches were neither the rule nor uncommon; the cathedral of the Boston diocese employed two women organists in the 1830s: Mrs. D. L. Brown and Mrs. Ostinelli. Between 1840 and 1860 almost no mention of women organists is found, except for churches where the members of a convent provided the music of the parish.[82]

Before 1840, church music was a matter often left to interested parishioners or the parish trustees. As bishops' concern for liturgical uniformity increased, local pastors appear to have taken a more active role in the selection of repertory; certainly a pastor such as Jeremiah Cummings at St. Stephen's in New York was intimately involved in such choices. It was perhaps more common that a professional music director, whether Catholic or not, chose the music to be sung. But ultimately, a great many of such choices rested with the editors of the various collections of Catholic music published during the period. Many parishes relied on a single collection throughout the era. Not only were the parish music libraries often quite small, the repertories of amateur choirs were often small as well.

With the tremendous influx of mostly poor immigrants, Catholic parishes, even the largest of them, were often economically strapped. Construction costs for churches, schools, and orphanages—and their attendant mortgages—often severely burdened the local church. Consequently, parish music programs were generally forced to be self-sustaining; the large number of benefit concerts sung by parish choirs, many of a more secular than sacred nature, attest to the practice. Parishes do not appear to have been shy in requesting professional musicians, especially Catholic ones, to donate their services for concerts. Benefit concerts usually had one of three beneficiaries: the choir itself, the organist or choir director, or a building fund for a church, school, or orphanage. The Boston Mozart *Requiem* of 1857, for example, was performed for the benefit of the Catholic boys' orphanage in Boston, the House of the Angel Guardian.

The ritual context of the music we have discussed is almost self-evident: the ritual of the Catholic liturgy, particularly the mass and vespers. At the same time, it must be noted that the American church had to instill a new concept of the nature of Catholic ritual to the Irish immigrant. A letter to the editor of the *New York Freeman's Journal* requested information concerning the proper conduct of the congregation at mass. The author recalled that

> In my childhood I was accustomed to assist at the Divine Sacrifice in such lowly chapels as our fathers, then lately emerging from the dark period of the penal proscription could erect in the rural districts of Ireland. There were doubtless under such circumstances many matters of form and ceremony of which we were, from necessity, ignorant.[83]

George Templeton Strong, visiting Old St. Patrick's Cathedral in New York, encountered "a crazy, or tipsy, Irishwoman in front of us who created quite a sensation while the Bishop was busy with the chalice. She sung out at the top of her voice: 'Jest pass the brandy and water along here, will you?'"[84] The *Boston Pilot* found it necessary to print an article entitled "The Gentleman at Church May Be Known By the Following Rules" which included: "Never thinks of defiling the house of God with tobacco spittle, or annoying those who sit near by chewing that nauseous weed in church. . . . Does not whisper, or laugh, or eat fruit in the house of God, or lounge in that holy place."[85] The conduct of a Catholic congregation of the 1840s may have been quite different than that which we imagine.

While much of the music employed by the antebellum church was not newly composed, it was often newly arranged. Plainchant was made tonal and harmonized; DeMonti's three-voice masses were rearranged as four-voice compositions. Yet new music was both acquired from Europe and composed in America, by both Catholic and Protestant musicians. Some names are familiar in American music history but for other reasons: W. C. Peters and George Loder, for example. Others are all but forgotten, such as A. F. Dos Santos and Louis Selle.

Finally, there appear to have been three basic factors governing the choice of music in American Catholic ritual before the Civil War. The first was prestige, the prestige of being able to claim the respected genius of a Mozart or Haydn as both Catholic and servant of the Catholic liturgy. It gave the church a respectable face to present before a society that had little respect for Catholicism or Ireland. The second factor was accessibility; the masses of Mozart were far more difficult to perform than those of DeMonti. The music had to correspond to the availability and ability of the musicians. Third, the inherent nature of Catholic ritual, as well as the particular manifestation of that ritual that the institutional church sought to foster, helped determine the repertory. The language, of course, was Latin, and the texts preexisting. The way in which the nature of the ritual was viewed exerted influences—sometimes subtle, sometimes overt—on the repertory of canonical music. The tension can be seen most clearly in the music we turn our attention to in the next chapter: the popular music of ritual.

Michael Broyles has suggested that Americans in the 1830s and 1840s, and particularly Lowell Mason—perhaps the most influential musician of the day—viewed themselves as part of an Anglo-American culture with London as its capital.[86] Much that is found in the practice of canonical ritual music in Catholic parishes of the period supports Broyles' ideas. The popularity of the compositions of Samuel Webbe and Henri DeMonti, and the music and publications of Vincent Novello (who introduced the masses of Haydn and Mozart to both England and the United States), indicate the high level of British influence. But in later years, as the musical establishment of both England and America turned its attention toward the music of Germany, American Catholicism began to look elsewhere. Even the arrival of massive numbers of German Catholics in America in the late 1850s prompted American Catholicism to look less to German Romanticism than to Palestrina and the polyphonic tradition, the so-called Caecilian reform of Catholic music.

In a later article, Broyles suggests that the gradual separation of music in America into "cultivated and vernacular" traditions stems largely from antebellum Boston.[87] The development of Boston musical life, according to Broyles, led to the idea of high musical culture in America and the belief that appreciation of such music reflected a high socioeconomic status. Yet as most writers before him, Broyles entirely ignores the Catholic immigrant community in Boston, which by 1860 was clearly the largest population group in the city. Under the leadership of John S. Dwight, music became a part of the "sacralization of culture," a term coined by Lawrence Levine.[88] But especially in its canonical ritual music, American Catholicism would reject such a sacralization of the secular. Although the Catholic "masters" Haydn and Mozart would continue to be employed in worship, Catholicism turned more and more to either Italian operatic composers, or German composers who imitated sixteenth-century polyphonic practice, before the reform in the early years of the twentieth century led to the widespread use of plainchant.

The turn toward Italian opera by American Catholics was not only an aesthetic preference. It was support for their coreligionists. The *Boston Pilot* noted that the appearance of a touring opera troupe in Boston "only affords us another evidence of what Catholic Europe has achieved in the science of Music; it proves to us incontestably that there are no musicians like the children of the Catholic faith."[89]

In 1856 the *New York Freeman's Journal* published an anonymous article which boldly called for the conversion of all of America to Roman Catholicism. The article noted that "The Catholic Church speaks not from the pulpit alone. She speaks through all her solemn ceremonies. The music, the incense, the processions, of her festivals, all speak,—and, when rightly performed, these speak with power and effect."[90] As the nineteenth century moved into its last decades, the canonical music of American Catholic ritual more and more spoke a message of separatism and difference; separateness from Protestant America and differentiation from secular culture. Yet the Catholic immigrant was both Catholic and American, and much of the tension would be expressed in the popular music of Catholic ritual.

CHAPTER FIVE

𝔓opular 𝔐usic of 𝔐itual: 𝔗he 𝔗radition of 𝔙ernacular 𝔖ong

The Irish-Catholic newspaper of Boston, the *Boston Pilot*, carried an announcement in the issue of May 3, 1856, of the publication of the fourth edition in five years of *Rohr's Collection of Favorite Catholic Music*. The advertisement stood out prominently, for it carried a boldface headline: Music for the Millions! By the mid-1850s, American Catholics could reasonably speak of such numbers, for the waves of Irish immigrants which were beginning to ebb, and the waves of German Catholic immigrants which were just beginning, had profoundly altered the makeup of the American population.

The phrase "Music for the Millions" became a catch phrase to describe the most popular style of song marketed in America during the years preceding the Civil War. Often published as sheet music, it included instrumental and vocal compositions which were readily accessible to the general listener and within the abilities of the amateur performer. Such music may be labeled "popular" in the sense that both composer and publisher were aiming at the largest possible market—the "millions" who now made up America. James H. Stone has suggested that American music in the years preceding the Civil War was a result of the marriage of the muse and merchant, in the unique circumstances of the years from 1840 to 1860; the rapid increase in population, technological developments in the field of publishing, and the increasing urbanization of America were all contributing factors.[1]

Within the present study, popular music of ritual refers to song or hymnody employed within the religious rituals of the Catholic parish, but not conforming to the ritual prescriptions fixed by an external authority.[2] On the most obvious level this includes the use of vernacular lyrics in place of Latin, either in new compositions or paraphrased translations of ritual texts. But we also include within the category music designed to be employed in devotional or educative organizations, specifically sodalities and singing schools. Both of these organizations endeavored to improve the music of the ritual life of American Catholicism, as well as to strengthen the membership's link to the church. In efforts to do so, the leaders of these organizations sought to attract the largest audience possible, much as did the creators and marketers of "popular music"; with a tremendous increase in the Catholic population—and always with a view toward enlarging membership through the conversion of Protestant Americans—Catholic leaders welcomed the products of American music publishers as prominent as William Cumming Peters and C. G. Christman, who marketed lines of music specifically aimed at the Catholic population.

As the Civil War approached, American Catholics were on the verge of obtaining the limited repertory of song that would be known and sung by every American Catholic for the next hundred years, a repertory best exemplified by the hymns "Holy God, We Praise Thy Name" and "Mother Dear, O Pray For Me." As with much of antebellum Catholic song, the lyrics and melodies of each of these pieces evolved separately, finally combining into hugely successful "hits." The evolution of these two hymns provides an overview of the development of Catholic popular music in antebellum America.

"Holy God, We Praise Thy Name" is an English paraphrase of the Latin "Te Deum," translated by a Redemptorist priest, Clarence Walworth. Walworth was one of the first priests in America to preach "missions," the Catholic equivalent of the Protestant revival.[3] The translation first appears in a Redemptorist mission manual assembled about 1850 and in two other collections printed in the same decade.[4] The "Holy God" text was not, however, associated in print with the tune "Grosser Gott," a late-eighteenth-century Austrian hymn tune. The tune did, however, become current in America during the 1850s as well, associated in Rohr's above-mentioned collection with the text "Thee, sovereign God, we grateful praise," and in a W. C. Peters collection of 1860 with the text "God of Might! We Sing Thy Praise."[5] Finally, in a sodality collection of 1863, an

American translation of an ancient Latin hymn was wedded in print to the Austrian melody; it became perhaps the most popular Catholic hymn in American life (fig. 5.1).[6]

"Mother Dear, O Pray For Me," our second example, began as a parlor song composed by Isaac Baker Woodbury and published by G. P. Reed of Boston in 1850. As composed, Woodbury's song portrays a son speaking to his earthly mother. But with a few changes of wording, the text, combined with a new melody of unknown origin, appeared in the W. C. Peters collection *Peters' Catholic Harp* of 1863, as a hymn addressed to the Virgin Mary.[7] The compiler (possibly Peters himself) found the sentiment of Woodbury's third verse so suitable for Marian devotion that he changed not a single word:

> Mother dear O pray for me,
> When all looks bright and fair,
> That I may all my danger see,
> For surely then 'tis near;
> A mother's prayer how much we need,
> If prosperous be the ray,
> That paints with gold the flowery mead,
> Which blossoms o'er our way.

A popular secular song-text, combined with a new parlor-song style of melody by a major American music publisher of both secular and Catholic sacred music, became part of the mainstream American Catholic repertory for over a century (fig. 5.2).

The Growth of American Catholic Song

The name of William Cumming Peters figured prominently in the music discussed in chapter 4, and does so again in the present chapter. While many of Peters' publications of Latin masses and hymns were republications or adaptations of European compositions, there appear to have been few European sources Peters could directly draw upon for Catholic sacred songs in English. Thus new pieces with either text or music composed in America figure more prominently in this chapter. Nicholas Tawa, in his study of American parlor song, notes the difficulty in distinguishing sacred songs, hymns, and parlor songs. He shows that within Protestant churches parlor songs dealing with sacred subjects were employed in church services, and hymns were sung both in concert and in the parlor.[8] The same was clearly true within American Catholic communities.

FIGURE 5.1
"Holy God We Praise Thy Name" from *English and Latin Hymns* (1884)

No. 6 HOLY GOD, WE PRAISE THY NAME.

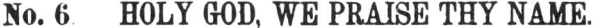

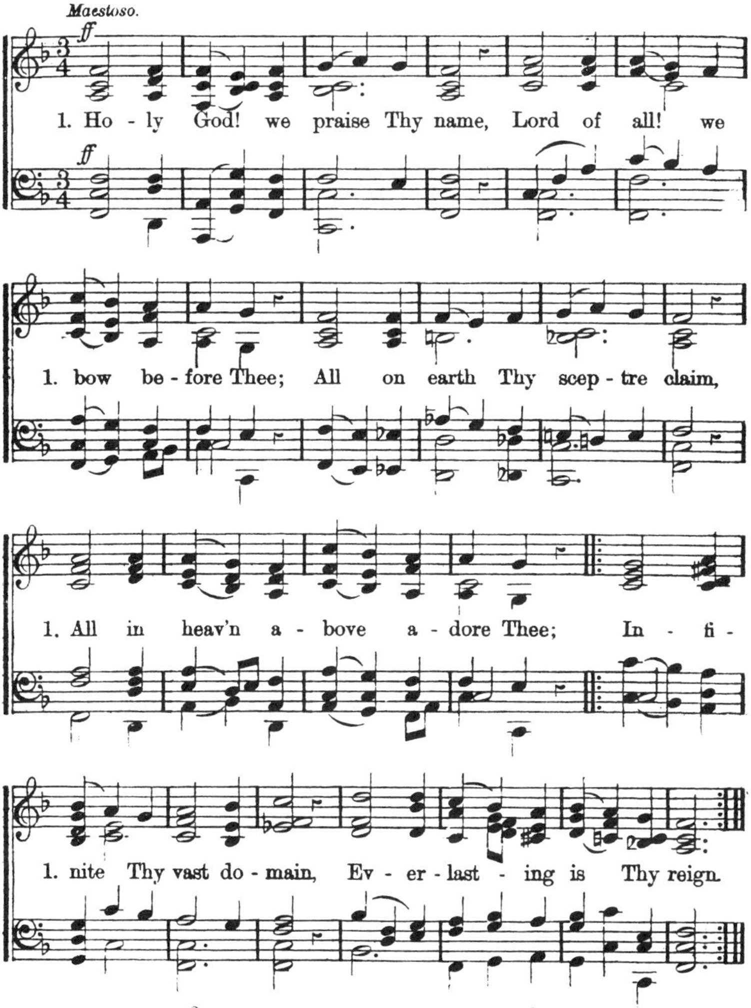

2.	3.
Hark! the loud celestial hymn,	Holy Father, Holy Son,
Angel choirs above are raising;	Holy Spirit, Three we name Thee.
Cherubim and Seraphim	While in Essence only One,
In unceasing chorus praising;	Undivided God, we claim Thee;
Fill the heav'ns with sweet accord:	And adoring bend the knee,
Holy, Holy, Holy Lord!	While we own the mystery.

8

FIGURE 5.2 "Mother Dear, O Pray for Me" from the *De La Salle Hymnal* (1913)

In 1838 George Willig of Philadelphia published two separate songs by W. C. Peters which illustrate the close relationship between parlor songs and hymns of the period. Peters' "The Babe Divine: Hymn for Epiphany" (fig. 5.3) was published in the same format as a parlor song and, except for the content of the lyrics, could easily be taken as a secular song of the late 1830s. The same is true of "Peters Evening Hymn" which bears no resemblance to anything in the Catholic vesper service; it is, however, not unlike T. V. Wiesenthal's "Fading, Still Fading," an American Catholic vesper hymn composed in the 1820s, which continued in popularity throughout the nineteenth century.

That a new category of Catholic music was emerging is clear, implicitly through the repertory, and explicitly through the comments contained in the prefaces to collections of Catholic music published in the 1840s. James Hoerner, in the preface to his 1843 collection, noted that

> the main objective of the work here presented to the public, is to furnish a manual of sacred music adapted to family use, devotional meetings, and the pious entertainment of youth on such occasions as first communion, confirmation, the opening and close of studies, catechism, &c.[9]

The Sacred Wreath, first published in 1844, was "designed not only for the church or chapel, but also for Sunday Schools and the domestic circles."[10] The surge of interest in providing Catholic music for American Catholics is at least partially explained by the preface to *The Catholic Harp*:

> As singing is considered of so much consequence at the present day, being taught and studied to a considerable extent, in the common schools of Boston and vicinity, Catholic children are in the habit of singing in these schools, hymns and songs used in Protestant worship, and when they go home, or are at play, they are singing them over, for want of a CHEAP *Catholic* Singing Book to practice and amuse themselves with in their leisure hours, and thus impart new vigor to the mind.[11]

The Catholic community felt it necessary to insulate themselves from the overwhelmingly Protestant culture in which they lived. But the dangers of Protestant music are not limited to children; they could enter the very worship of the church. W. C. Peters noted that "Owing to the absence of easy music, adapted to the capacity of small choirs, it frequently happens that Protestant music-books are used in our country churches; and to remedy this evil, the author has adapted melodies, carefully harmonized to Latin words, as used by the Church."[12]

FIGURE 5.3
W. C. Peters' "The Babe Divine: Hymn for Epiphany"
(transcription)

FIGURE 5.3
W. C. Peters' "The Babe Divine: Hymn for Epiphany" (cont.)

FIGURE 5.3
W. C. Peters' "The Babe Divine: Hymn for Epiphany" (cont.)

FIGURE 5.3
W. C. Peters' "The Babe Divine: Hymn for Epiphany" (cont.)

TRADITION OF VERNACULAR SONG 105

FIGURE 5.3
W. C. Peters' "The Babe Divine: Hymn for Epiphany" (cont.)

If Catholics were to develop their singing, and if music was to be marketed to the millions, it was necessary to provide some form of musical instruction. The phrase "music for the millions" harkens back to the title of an instructional book, *Singing for the Million*, published in England in 1841.[13] Joseph Mainzer, the author, was a German Catholic priest serving working-class Catholics in Prussia. His progressive views alarmed the government, and Mainzer fled both Prussia and the priesthood, arriving in Paris in 1834. There he set up singing schools for the workers; the classes were free and Mainzer earned his living through the sale of music textbooks. The same system was employed when Mainzer arrived in England in 1841.[14]

A contemporary account of a Mainzer singing class appeared in the London press of 1837:

> The room was crowded to overflowing.... The pupils sat without any distinction or classification, each holding a little well-thumbed book, containing M. Mainzer's simple and clear exposition of the elements of music and part-singing, and also a series of easy compositions, whence the exercises of the evening were to be selected.... When M. Mainzer appeared, he was greeted with a round of applause, and the business of the evening began. The pupils sung several of the little pieces I have mentioned-a few of these were of a sacred character, but most of them in the style of the livelier German *lieder*, with a spritely burden, and a solo part for two (never more than three) voices. I presume, from their style and easiness, that the class in question was not far advanced.... Nothing could be more admirable than M. Mainzer's manner with his pupils; it seemed to me the proper mixture of firmness and courtesy ... but, as a whole, the performances required but little indulgence. The singers attacked the forcible passages with a point and an energy I have never heard in England; and the mass of sound formed by so many voices was clear, but not crude.[15]

Although Mainzer himself never came to America, his system of music instruction did, in 1842, under the care of Madame Mecovino Malone. Malone came to the United States to sing in a season of opera to be presented in New York City by the Italian bass Giuseppe de Begnis. When the hopes for a New York opera season failed, de Begnis and Malone joined forces to begin a Mainzerian school in the city.[16] The local Irish-Catholic newspaper described the importance of the opportunity:

> The great advantages which this system possesses beyond all others are the almost incredible ease and quickness with which a just knowledge

of music and singing is attained; its enabling hundreds to be taught in one class, and thus placing its benefits within the reach of the humblest artisan, from the consequent smallness of expense. . . .

We are rejoiced to find that M. Mainzer has sent to our shores an agent in the person of Madame Mecovino Malone, for the diffusion of his system in this city and the vicinity. She intends opening classes in the middle of the present month, and we hope soon to see singing in unison under her tuition, hundreds of pupils of both sexes, and all classes, for she intends to place the means of acquiring this method within reach of the least opulent of our citizens.[17]

The next issue of the newspaper advertised a "Grand Concert" to be given by Malone and de Begnis, aimed at "all lovers of *Irish minstrelsy*, and more particularly of that people whose earliest associations are connected with the land of its origin, as well as all who generously sympathize in that country's misfortunes."[18] If it was not already clear that Malone was targeting an Irish audience, it was reported that the Mainzerian system was endorsed by one of the great contemporary Irish figures:

He who is justly titled the great Apostle of Temperance in Ireland, . . . Father Mathew sent a request to M. Mainzer . . . to be supplied with teachers of his system, to instruct the Teetotallers in singing. This proceeding of Father Mathew is a proof, how fully he estimates the solid benefits which would accrue to society from a more widely diffused musical education.[19]

It is difficult to determine with what, if any, success Malone and the Mainzerian school of singing met in New York City. But a writer for one New York newspaper characterized the system as "an outrage upon common sense and all established principles," and referred to Madame Malone as "the worst singer we have ever heard in public."[20]

Whatever the success of Malone's effort, it was the first attempt to introduce the immigrant to music instruction on a large scale. Catholic parishes had often opened individual singing schools, but they were usually on a small scale and reflected the pedagogical attitude of the musician who opened the school. In 1853 and 1854, however, two books designed to be used in Catholic singing schools appeared: W. C. Peters' *The Young Catholic's Vocal Class Book* and Anthony Werner's *The Catholic Singing Book*.[21] Perhaps reflecting the sudden growth of American Catholic parishes during the Irish famine years, these books provided standard models by which a parish could develop a singing school, and eventually a parish choir.

Anthony Werner, the author of *The Catholic Singing Book*, was a German immigrant and organist of Boston's Cathedral of the Holy Cross. In the introduction to his manual he notes that in "the original pieces contained in this work I have endeavored to give simple and progressive lessons, rather than difficult and classical music." The ninety-six-page work begins with simple exercises, followed by unison hymns with movement by seconds and occasional thirds. About halfway through the work, Werner introduces simple two-part hymns, and concludes with a setting of the ordinary of the mass for soprano, alto, and bass by F. H. Schmid. The inclusion of a bass part in the mass setting suggests that Werner did not intend his manual to be used by children alone. Advertisements for the work in the *Boston Pilot* referred to the manual as *The Young Beginner's Singing Book*, which was "designed principally for schools, but will answer for small choirs."[22] Werner's manual sold well. On February 24, 1855, the *Boston Pilot* noted that, just a few months after publication, the "little Catholic singing Book is meeting with a success unprecedented in the sale of Catholic music. The first edition of two thousand is nearly exhausted."[23]

The 1850s also witnessed the rise of concerts given by massed choirs of Catholic children. Beginning in 1855, the House of the Angel Guardian, a Catholic orphanage for boys in Boston, presented large-scale concerts to help support the institution. The orphanage regularly leased the new Boston Music Hall and filled it to capacity, normally charging twenty-five cents per person. A printed financial statement for the orphanage reported income of $3,720.14 from the concerts presented up to the end of 1857.[24] The explanation of the financial report, provided by the rector of the orphanage, the Reverend George F. Haskins, provides details concerning the idea behind the concerts:

> Three years ago, I proposed to have the boys instructed in music, both vocal and instrumental, in order that, by concerts and public exhibitions, they might, in some measure, contribute to their own support. The proposition was received with smiles of doubt or derision.... It is absurd, they said, to think of making singers, much less orchestral performers, of these uncouth, ill-bred, ignorant boys.... However, we did it.[25]

The same report also provides information concerning the financing of such a music program:

Many persons, naturally enough, greatly exaggerate our concert receipts. Seeing them attended night after night by a large number of persons, the conclusion is that the cash returns must be immense. The Music Hall, say they, is capable of containing three thousand persons. At each concert the music hall is filled. Therefore, at twenty-five cents a ticket, the receipts of each concert must be at least $750. Now here is the mistake in the onset. The largest number that can be seated in the Boston Music Hall is 2,463, including the seats on the stage. The Music Hall is said to be *filled* when every seat is occupied, and it *appears* to be filled when only two-thirds of them are occupied. Then there are to be considered the *expenses* of each concert, never less than $125, and frequently amounting to $200. Then, after deducting these expenses from the receipts, fifteen percent of the balance is paid to Mr. Werner, the teacher of the orchestra, and conductor of the concerts. The balance is credited to the House of the Angel Guardian, and small as it is, it is of infinite service.... The figures in the report show the exact amount received from all our concerts, both in the city and the country, up to January 1, 1858, viz, $3,720.14. From this we ought to deduct the cost of the musical instruments, $673.52, and the salary of the music professor, $600, and what have we left? Only $1,947.02, as the actual receipts for the benefit of the Institution.[26]

The young ladies of Catholic Boston were also involved in grand concerts. Michael J. Mooney presented a series of concerts in the early 1850s, given by larger and larger numbers of Catholic girls recruited from the Catholic Sunday schools of the city. For example, on St. Patrick's Day of 1850, Mooney presented a "Grand Union Concert" at the Melodeon, at which a choir of 500 Catholic girls performed the following program, typical of such a concert of the period.

Part I

Chorus: Invocation	G. Eck
Duett: Go, forget me	Moore
Hymn to St. Patrick	M. J. Mooney
Song: Angel's Whisper	S. Lover
Duett: Has sorrow thy young days shaded	Moore
Chorus: Mater Dei	St. Sulpice
Song: Silent O'Moyle	Moore
Doxology	Foulin

Part II

Hymn to St. Rose of Lima	W. Carr
Duett: The Harp that once thro' Tara's Halls	Moore
Chorus: Evening Hymn	M. J. Mooney
Duett: Piano Forte, four hands: The Legacy	Moore
Song: Be kind to thy loved ones at home	Woodbury
Chorus: Star of the Sea	Lambillotte
Song: Meeting of the Waters	Moore
Chorus: Hail Glorious Apostle	T. Comer

The concert was heralded in the press as a glowing success:

> In the evening, also, a Grand Juvenile Concert came off at the Melodeon where a very touching and delightful spectacle was presented to one of the greatest congregations the room ever held. There stood on the steps leading to the Organ about 500 children arrayed in white; and the mingling of their young sweet voices with the modulated thunder of the organ, gratified the audience of all demonstrations with one of those beautiful and solemn services which the Catholic Church loves to preside over. The Chaunts were admirably sung, under the leadership of Professor Mooney who was highly honored in the performance of his interesting pupils.[27]

The program combines Irish and Catholic selections in an interesting mix of sacred and secular. The traditional Irish songs of Thomas Moore are heavily represented, with three of Moore's songs on each half of the program. Both the first and second parts of the concert included four sacred pieces (presuming the "Invocation" by Eck was religious in nature). The attribution to St. Sulpice refers to a collection published in Paris in 1823, *Cantiques de Saint-Sulpice*, which was a popular source of melodies for Catholic hymnbook compilers; the Paris hymnal is cited as a major source in the introduction of both *The Sacred Wreath* (1844) and *Sacred Melodies* (1850).[28] French influence is also found in the inclusion of Louis Lambillotte's "Ave Maris Stella," sung in English as "Star of the Sea." The concert concluded with a song standard among Boston Irish of the period, "Hail Glorious Apostle," discussed in chapter 3. With nine stanzas composed by an Ursuline nun from the Charlestown convent, it was set to a "National air of good old Ireland" ("St. Patrick's Day") by Thomas Comer.[29]

The use of Irish traditional tunes as the basis of hymns appears to have had some currency during the 1840s. Kirk's *Catholic Harp* (1844) included a hymn to St. Patrick, "Hibernia's champion saint, all hail," set to the tune "The Harp that Once through Tara's Halls"; Kirk uses the same tune for the text "Bright Mother of Our Maker, Hail." Throughout the 1840s, Catholic hymnals include the hymn "See the Paraclete descending," to the melody Sir John Stevenson arranged with Thomas Moore's "Hark, the Vesper hymn is stealing."[30]

The use of traditional Irish tunes in church was not without some controversy. An exchange of letters in the *New York Freeman's Journal* of 1846 concerning the practice became somewhat heated. "Sigma," pen name of one opposed to the use of Irish tunes, dared the proponents of the use of "secular airs" in church to

> furnish us with something like an argument in favor of having the "Last Rose of Summer," or "Molly Ashtore," sung after the elevation at Mass instead of "O! Salutaris Hostia." I care not for the plea set up that the words were the beautiful composition of the pastor, who knew what to do in the matter. The *air* is what affects the feelings of the congregation, and not the *words*, for they are scarcely ever heard.[31]

"Sigma" saw the issue as a denominational one; the inclusion of secular tunes in worship was a Protestant device:

> The only instances that I know of such tunes being sung in church, were at the Baptist churches in Philadelphia, where I have heard "I see them on their winding way," sung in full choir at night. For such folks such an air was quite as appropriate as the weathercocks on the tops of their conventicles, but for the Catholic service, surely such are not in keeping with its practice.[32]

A response to "Sigma" from "A Reader" was printed in the *Freeman's Journal* a few weeks later:

> It appears that, to the refined ear of "Sigma," these beautiful conceptions of "modern" genius and piety, when adapted to the harmony of numbers, and breathed in the melody of sound, bring back remembrances quite *foreign* to *desired* thought, and irresistibly transports him to the *fatherland*, where he imagines he listens again to the inspiring music of a *good old Irish jig*, and fancies, perhaps, that he once more mingles in the mazes of the merry dance. In vain, it seems, do his prayerful aspirations strive to rise on the flippant wing of *such* music.[33]

"A Reader" closes his letter suggesting that the "agent of disease sometimes proves the agent of cure" and provides the following example which he clearly believes will convince "Sigma" of the value of new poetic compositions wed to traditional Irish airs, in this case, "The Harp that Once through Tara's Halls."

> A Vesper Hymn
>
> The wearied Dove now trembling flies,
>   And seeks the tranquil home,
> For clouds and tempests veil the skies,
>   And she is sad and lone:
> So plumes her wing my wearied soul,
>   So mounts the Spirit-Dove,
> And strives to gain her happy goal,
>   Where dwells her God, her Love!
>
> Then come, my dear, thy grace impart,
>   Come, guide my spirit home,
> For wearied is this trembling heart,
>   No more it seeks to roam:
> No joy like thine my spirit knows,
>   Then smile, dear Lord, on me,
> And grant my wearied soul repose
>   With Angels and with Thee![34]

While no response from "Sigma" has been discovered, one doubts that the above example convinced him of the value of the practice. The text is clearly of the same nature as contemporary parlor songs, and Thomas Moore's adaptation of the Irish air was as popular among the general American population as among Irish-Americans. These are the precise traits to which "Sigma" was objecting in Catholic church music.

But traditional Irish tunes were not the only airs borrowed for use in the American Catholic church; French tunes often found their way into the repertory. The above-mentioned *Cantiques de Saint-Sulpice* included many French folk tunes. Perhaps because they were not previously known to the immigrants, and thus lacked extramusical associations, the French airs often became quite popular without arousing opposition. The most popular and durable of the French tunes among American Catholics was the tune associated with the text "Hail heavenly Queen, Hail foamy ocean's star," a free translation of "Ave Maris Stella." The text and air were first printed together in a sheet-music edition published by John Cole in 1826.[35]

The translation and choice of tune is credited to the Revd. M. F. W. The arrangement is by P. Kelly, most likely Patrick Kelly, who for many years was professor of music at St. Mary's College (now St. Mary's Seminary and University) in Baltimore. The popularity of the combined translation and French air is attested to by the fact that it was included in almost every collection of Catholic music issued before the Civil War, and many after the war, even into the twentieth century (fig. 5.4).[36]

The practice of combining newly composed lyrics with existing tunes was not limited to the use of traditional or folk tunes. Well-known tunes used in the Catholic church were often given new lyrics so that they might be employed in different liturgical settings. Avison's "Sound the loud Timbrel," for example, was provided with the following Christmas lyrics by James Gibbons:

> Hail Bethlehem city! hail humble abode!
> That sheltered a Virgin, a Savior, a God:
> What hand would transcribe on the pages of story,
> As heaven threw open its portals of light,
> Revealing to shepherds bright legions of glory,
> Chaunting Hosannas in the stillness of night.

In the final verse Gibbons unites traditional Catholic images of the Virgin with images common to many secular songs of the time—images of a mother's care and life's troubled ocean.

> Hail Virgin of Virgins! by an angel addressed,
> With "hail full of grace" above all women blessed,
> Hail Virgin! all nations with filial devotion,
> Still call thee Mother; Oh list to our prayer!
> Obtain for us mercy on life's troubled ocean,
> Oh, take us sweet Mother to thy holy care.[37]

The practice of employing older tunes with new lyrics provides us with some indication of the more popular melodies employed by American Catholics during the antebellum years; authors would presumably choose tunes that were widely known. The preface to *The Sacred Wreath* (1844) suggests a number of "admired and generally known melodies [which] may be applied to various hymns of similar metres and character," and includes among these "See the Paraclete descending" (melody: Thomas Moore's "Hark! The Vesper Hymn") and "My God, My Life, My Love" (by Bishop David).[38] Other common airs employed include Benjamin Cross's "Like the

FIGURE 5.4
"Hail Heavenly Queen" as it appears in Garbett (1840)
Courtesy The Music Division, New York Public Library for the Performing Arts, Astor, Lenox, and Tilden Foundations.

FIGURE 5.4
"Hail Heavenly Queen" as it appears in Garbett (1840) (cont.)

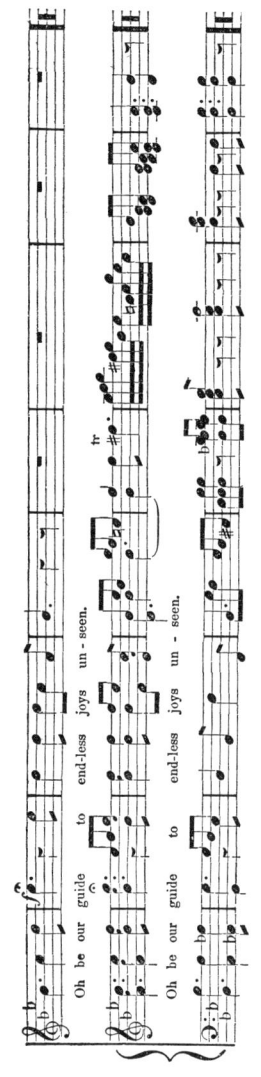

2
Hail! full of grace! with Gabriel we repeat,
Thee, Queen of heaven, from him we learn to greet;
Then give us peace, which heaven alone can give,
And dead thro' Eve, thro' Mary let us live.
Chorus. Hail! &c.

3
Oh break our chains! 'Thy guilty slaves release;
Oh give us light! and let our blindness cease:
Let every ill that preys upon our hearts,
Fly at thy voice, which every good imparts.
Chorus. Hail! &c.

4
Thy children save—oh gracious mother hear!
From brimful eyes, oh deign to wipe the tear!
Our anxious prayers to God thy Son present,
Whose life and blood for sinful man were spent.
Chorus. Hail! &c.

5
Oh Virgin meek! alone of all mankind,
In whom not God can stain or blemish find;
From Satan's chains our captive souls set free,
And be our lives from sin exempt by thee.
Chorus. Hail! &c.

6
Our lives unstained in purity preserve,
And ne'er permit our ways from truth to swerve;
That when our time has roll'd its rapid round,
We may with Christ in heavenly bliss be crown'd.
Chorus. Hail! &c.

Eternal praise to God the Father be!
Eternal praise to Christ's dread majesty!
Eternal praise the Holy Ghost attend!
To God triune be glory without end.
Chorus. Hail! &c.

children of Sion" and "O Power Divine," ascribed to "J. M. of P. T." None of these are surprising selections, for they had been current since the 1820s or earlier.

Newly Composed Songs

It should not be supposed, however, that newly composed songs were uncommon. The work of both Protestant and Catholic American composers came into the Catholic antebellum repertory. The songs are found in collections and in sheet-music editions, as in earlier years. A new vehicle for the dissemination of Catholic music was added to the more familiar methods; beginning around 1840, Catholic periodicals and newspapers began to publish music regularly or intermittently for American Catholics. *The Catholic Expositor* from New York and *The U. S. Catholic Magazine* from Baltimore are two of the more important of such publications.

The Catholic Expositor was the creation of Charles Constantine Pise, one of the best-known Catholic priests of the mid-nineteenth century. Pise, noted as an author, orator, and first Catholic to serve as chaplain to the United States Senate, had penned the lyrics "Like the Children of Sion," loosely based on Psalm 137. The enduring popularity of the hymn, first published in 1826 with music by Philadelphia's Benjamin Cross, may be due to the fact that it well describes the Irish immigrants' experience:

> Like the children of Sion on Babylon's shore,
> When Jerus'lem their country smiled round them no more;
> Their harps were all lonely and wet with their tears,
> And their bosoms were harrow'd with sorrow and fears.
>
> So in this dark shade of this valley of life,
> I recline me and think of my country above,
> Had I wings like the dove I should fly from this strife
> And repose in the arms of contentment and love.
>
> O when to thy beautiful visions I turn
> For thee like the love stricken turtle I mourn:
> O! when from the storms of this world shall I flee,
> And who would restore me Jerus'lem to thee.

In the 1840s, Pise was more interested in translating the Latin breviary hymns. The first issue of the second, and last, volume of the *Expositor* contained the first of a series of choral settings of Pise's translations, composed by Charles M. King, a noted New York City musician who directed music in a number of the city's Catholic parishes. The series of six hymns included two with traditional texts: "Spirit, Creator of Mankind" and "Jesus the Savior of Mankind," the latter with music by W. A. King, brother of Charles, and the noted organist of New York's Grace Episcopal Church. It should be noted that in Catholic circles the term *hymn* was employed for any type of musical setting of a hymn-text; the term did not refer to a particular musical form (e.g., four-part chorale).

The second hymn of the series, "Hymn for a Martyr," demonstrates the musical idiom King employed in these settings (see fig. 5.5). The text, which begins "Oh God! the portion, the reward," is set for one voice and organ or piano. The accompaniment begins with an Alberti bass pattern in the first two phrases, suddenly switching to a repeated chord pattern for the second half of the stanza. The harmonic structure changes rapidly as well: the first phrase begins and ends in G major, while the second phrase shifts abruptly to G minor and cadences on B-flat major. The third and fourth phrases are in G minor, while the next two phrases return to the major mode. A final "coda" remains in G major, although the iii and vi chords are emphasized. The harmonic structure and the thick texture of the accompaniment contribute a sense of drama to the short twenty measures, not unlike Italian operatic writing.

The four hymns by Pise and Charles King were published in 1844 as part 1 of a collection entitled *The Sacred Lyre: New Hymns*.[39] No later parts of the collection have been located. The setting of "Spirit, Creator of Mankind" was published in 1842, and dedicated to David Harrison, organist of St. Patrick's Cathedral in New York.[40] By reprinting the hymns in sheet-music form, the publishers made them available to a wider audience, including American Episcopalians who, under the influence of the Oxford movement, were becoming more interested in the hymns of the Roman Breviary, especially in English translation.

The *U.S. Catholic Magazine*, which attempted to become the first national Catholic periodical, began publishing music in 1846. The musical selections were of a greater variety than those of the *Expositor*, including both sacred and secular pieces from a number of different composers. One of the earliest selections published was a new musical setting of a familiar text in honor of St. Patrick, "Grateful notes to heav'n ascending." The composer was Henry Dielman, professor of music at Mount St. Mary's College in Maryland. Dielman holds the distinction of having received the

FIGURE 5.5
C.C. Pise and Charles M. King, "Hymn for a Martyr" (transcription)

FIGURE 5.5
C.C. Pise and Charles M. King, "Hymn for a Martyr" (cont.)

first (honorary) doctorate in music awarded in the United States: Georgetown University bestowed the honor upon him in 1849.[41] Dielman contributed several sacred pieces to the *U.S. Catholic Magazine* which were not published elsewhere. His "Hymn to the Blessed Virgin Mary," arranged for solo voice, SATB chorus, and piano, organ, or harp, reveals Dielman's admiration of Italian operatic style, although in a simpler style and clearer texture than Charles King's "Hymn for a Martyr" (fig. 5.6).

David R. Harrison, the organist of St. Patrick's Cathedral in New York, wrote a number of pieces for the *U.S. Catholic Magazine*, including a setting of the then-familiar hymn "Spirit, Creator of Mankind" (see fig. 5.7). This translation of the "Veni Creator Spiritus" was very possibly the text most often sung within American Catholicism, simply because it was employed for so many different occasions: before a sermon was preached, before catechism classes, to open and close religious meetings, and, of course, at Pentecost. Precisely because it was sung in so many contexts, it was a popular text with composers.

Harrison's setting of "Spirit, Creator" is scored for four-part chorus (treble, alto, tenor, bass) and organ, and set in D-flat major. The organ part doubles the choral writing in all but four of the twenty-four measures of the stanza. Harrison opens the piece with chorale-like four-part diatonic writing in the first two phrases. But at the third phrase of text, "And sweetly let thy grace invade," he introduces a "sweeter" chromatic harmony, before a return to chorale-like writing in the fourth, and last, phrase of text. The half cadence which concludes the fourth phrase allows Harrison to add a coda, repeating the second half of the verse. The fifth phrase begins as a solo with independent organ accompaniment, is repeated as a duet, harmonized in thirds and sixths, and returns to four-part chorale-like writing for the final phrase. Harrison combined a traditional style of church music composition with phrases of Italianate writing which he employed to color the text.

Although these compositions clearly borrow from traditional Irish and French tunes, as well as Italian operatic styles, the 1840s and 1850s are remarkable for the number of native-composed songs for American Catholics. A number of factors seem to have contributed to the phenomenon. In the early years of the nineteenth century, American Catholics, in common with most Americans, followed the lead of England and English taste. But English Catholicism does not appear to have produced much Catholic devotional music in a popular vein, perhaps due to the Oxford movement, with its emphasis on ancient Catholic hymns and plainchant. Furthermore, as the American Catholic church became more and more an Irish-American church, there was certainly less interest in following the lead of England in political or cultural affairs. As we will see in chapter 6, many Catholic parishes in the northeastern states hosted "Repeal Organizations" in the 1840s, that is, political organizations devoted to the repeal of the Act of Union of Great Britain and Ireland.

In addition, the nature of Irish Catholicism differed significantly from

FIGURE 5.6
Henry Dielman, "Hymn to the Blessed Virgin Mary"
Courtesy General Research Division, The New York Public Library, Astor, Lenox, and Tilden Foundations.

FIGURE 5.6
Henry Dielman, "Hymn to the Blessed Virgin Mary" (cont.)
Courtesy The Music Division, New York Public Library for the Performing Arts.

2. Thine own sinless heart was broken,
   Sorrow's sword had pierced its core;
   Holy Mother! by that token,
   Now thy pity I implore.
      (*Chorus.*) Holy Mother, &c.

3. Queen of Heaven! guard and guide me,
   Save my soul from dark despair,
   In thy tender bosom hide me,
   Take me, Mother, to thy care.
      (*Chorus.*) Holy Mother, &c.

FIGURE 5.7
David Harrison, "Spirit Creator of Mankind."
Courtesy General Research Division, The New York Public Library, Astor, Lenox, and Tilden Foundations.

Chase from our minds th' infernal foe,
And peace, the fruit of love, bestow;
And lest our feet should step astray,
Protect and guide us in the way.

Immortal honour, endless fame
Attend th' Almighty Father's name:
To the Son equal praises be,
And holy Paraclete, to thee.

the Catholicism of the English. The Irish often viewed their religion and nationality as two aspects of the same identity. Catholicism in Ireland, especially in contrast to the English Catholicism that emerged from the Oxford movement, had much in common with folk religions, including the retention of Celtic superstitions. It is not surprising that the differing nature of English and Irish Catholicism called for different types and genres of musical expression.

In 1851 an attempt was made to introduce the new English Catholic hymnody into the United States, with the publication of the American edition of *Lyra Catholica*.[42] Even before publication was announced, a writer for the *New York Freeman's Journal* expressed hope that a publisher would be found:

> By the way, will not he or someone else give us an American edition of the *Lyra Catholica*, which contains such beautiful translations of the Breviary Hymns? If these and other recent hymns composed by Fathers Newman, Faber, &c., were within reach we might hope never again to see the chirruping twitter of Mrs. Sigourney and Mrs. Hemans' rhymes figuring among Catholic hymns.[43]

The *Boston Pilot* reviewed the new work shortly after it went on sale:

> A splendid Catholic literature with all its branches is growing up in our midst and casting its refreshing shades upon our walks.
> The "Lyra Catholica" is proof of this. . . . All [the hymns] breathe a truly Catholic spirit and are full of unction.[44]

In spite of the writer's enthusiasm for the collection, the edition published by Dunigan and Brother of New York did not sell well. Most of the hymn texts were the work of men such as Newman, Faber, and Brydges who had converted to Catholicism after their association with the Oxford movement. Many of the hymns contained in the *Lyra Catholica* would eventually become part of the American Catholic repertory, but as late as 1856 the *Freeman's Journal* bemoaned the neglect of the hymnal:

> One of the least successful publications of this house [Dunigan & Bro.] is really one of the most meritorious. It is the *Lyra Catholica*, published in 1851. . . . The American Catholic public . . . [have] permitted a large part of the first American edition of this little volume to have remained for five years on the shelves of the publisher. What is the reason of it? Is it

mere inattention to the important subject of Catholic hymnody? Is it an innate and irreclaimable love of un-English and unmetrical doggerel?[45]

American Catholicism placed less stress on the liturgical revival that characterized the British Catholic church under Newman's influence. American Catholic parishes actively sought to become the social, educational, and even political centers of the community. Sodalities and similar pious organizations promoted the use of vernacular hymns and sacred songs among their membership. Sodality manuals regularly carried the lyrics to such songs so that they could be sung both at meetings and at home.

Music and the Schools

As the number of American Catholics increased, so did the number of Catholic schools. Catholic education originally was centered in boarding schools and colleges, although parochial grammar schools were founded as early as the end of the eighteenth century. By mid-century those responsible for the schools had learned the importance of music; Mother Rose White, second superior of the Sisters of Charity, noted that "the indispensable thing in this country, even for the poor . . . is music. No piano, no school!"[46] The popularity of music studies in the schools also helped sustain the institutions financially; instruction in instrumental music required an additional fee above the normal tuition. The fee was often quite high. At St. Stephen's School in New York City (a day school) tuition was three dollars per quarter (which included vocal music); instrumental music brought an additional charge of three dollars.[47] At Villanova College, room and board cost 125 dollars per year; music instruction cost an additional 40 dollars.[48]

The development of Catholic school music was speeded by two factors: the use of Protestant hymnody within the public school system,[49] and the desire to use music to teach Catholic beliefs, values, and identity. Catholic Sunday schools also employed music for the same reasons. In one of the many battles between the Catholic church and public schools in the antebellum years, Bishop Fitzpatrick wrote the following to the Boston School Committee:

> The chaunting of the Lord's Prayer, of psalms, of hymns, addressed to God, performed by many persons in unison, being neither a scholastic exercise, nor a recreation, can only be regarded as an act of public worship. Indeed it is professedly intended as such in the regulations which

govern our public schools. It would seem that the principles which guide Protestants and Catholics in relation to communion in public worship are widely different. . . . The Catholic cannot act in this manner. . . . His church expressly forbids him to do so.[50]

The early publications for Catholic children often contained a repertory similar to that in the collections intended for adults. But they also contained new texts, often to familiar melodies, that were more didactic in tone than other Catholic hymnody. For example, *The Sacred Wreath* (1844) included the following hymn:

> "It is holy and wholesome thought to pray for the dead, that they may be loosed from their sins."
> Air.-O Power Divine
>
> Pray for the Dead! at noon and eve
> Lift up to God thy young request,
> Implore his goodness to relieve
> The suffering souls and grant them rest.
>
> Pray for the Dead! though faithful they,
> Yet while the penalties remain,
> Must suffering purge the debt away,
> And penance cleanse the sinful stain.[51]

The hymn continues for three more verses, explaining the belief in purgatory and extolling the practice of praying for the dead, both characteristically Catholic. Jeremiah Cummings, pastor of St. Stephen's Church in New York City, wrote a number of Catholic children's songs which were set to music by Signor Domenico Speranza and published in 1860 as *Songs for Catholic Schools*.[52] A new edition, issued in 1862, attests to the popularity of the first. The following is fairly typical of Cummings's doctrinal formulations set to music:

> Great God, whatever through thy Church,
> Thou teachest to be true,
> I firmly do believe it all,
> And shall confess it too.[53]

It was not long, however, before children's songs became blatantly propagandistic, as well as doggerel. *Catholic Hymns and Canticles* (1863) included the song "I am a Little Catholic" (fig. 5.8) which proclaims both an identity and, in verse 5, a paternalistic image of parish life.[54]

Although the school songs were usually religious in nature, they often expressed the Catholic view of national and societal matters. Jeremiah Cummings included a song for the United States in his collection which reflects his position on a national debate (fig. 5.9).[55]

As the country drew closer to civil war, the Catholic position on slavery was somewhat unclear. Three factors contributed to the lack of clarity. First, the vast majority of Catholic immigrants lived in free states and had no direct experience of slavery; second, the abolitionist leaders were vocally anti-Catholic and anti-Irish in their rhetoric; third, the Irish immigrant

FIGURE 5.8
"I Am a Little Catholic," from *Catholic Hymns and Canticles* (transcription)

FIGURE 5.9
Jeremiah Cummings & Dominico Speranza, "God of Mercy"
(transcription)

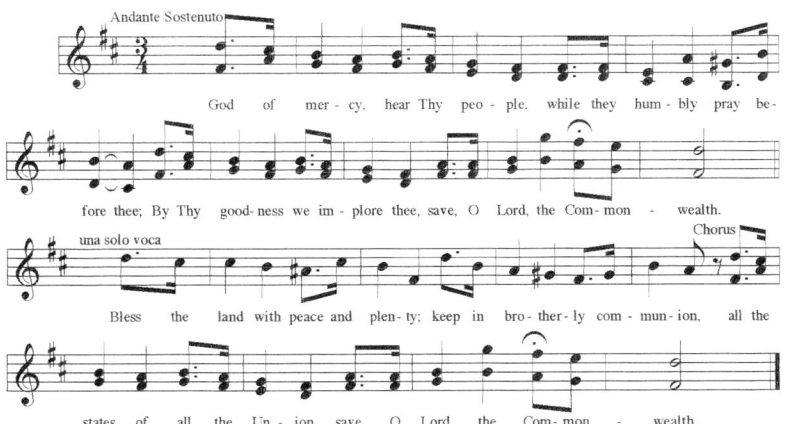

and the free African-American were in economic competition for the same jobs. Although generally opposed to slavery in principle, Catholics were unwilling to sacrifice the Union for abolition. Cummings's text expresses the fundamental position: "All the states of all the Union, save, O Lord, the Commonwealth."

Collections of Catholic Song

The single largest source of devotional music in the vernacular was contained in the various collections published between 1840 and the Civil War. While several of these have been mentioned in various contexts already, it would be helpful to give brief descriptions of some of the more important works that fall into the category.

Manual of Catholic Melodies or a Compilation of Hymns, Anthems, Psalms, &c., with appropriate airs, and devotional exercises for the Ordinary occasions of Catholic Piety & Worship. By Rev. James Hoerner. Baltimore: Printed and Published by John Murphy, 146 Market Street, 1843.

Hoerner's work, at 448 pages, was by far the largest Catholic hymnal assembled before 1860. In addition to a sixteen-page "Short Introduction to the Art of Singing," 58 Latin hymns, and 162 in English, the compiler provides the prayers of the mass, as well as other devotional exercises. It is clearly a devotional manual rather than a choir book. There are no musical settings of the ordinary of the mass, although the hymns and psalms for Sunday vespers are provided in settings by Jacob Walter, Richard Garbett, and George Loder. Hymns are generally printed without accompaniment; there is, however, an appendix containing only the vocal harmonies to selected hymns and songs contained in the main body of the work.

Both the *U.S. Catholic Magazine* [2 (1843): 512] and the *New York Freeman's Journal* [4 (1843): 113] reviewed the manual with high praise. Philadelphia's *Catholic Herald* recommended the work, "although we miss from its pages some of our favorite airs, and meet others arranged or retouched not altogether to our taste."[56] Indeed, a large number of the selections are listed as "melody arranged by J. H."

The size of the work may have been an obstacle to the manual's success, for a version "abridged for the use of schools, &c." was issued a year later, under the title *Catholic Melodies*. Even the abridged version, however, at 264 pages, was large for the time.

The Catholic Harp, containing the morning and evening service of the Catholic Church, embracing a choice collection of Masses, Litanies, Psalms, Sacred Hymns, Anthems, Versicles and Motetts. Selected from the compositions of the first masters. Compiled by Philip A. Kirk. Boston: Philip A. Kirk, 1844.

Philip Kirk was a Boston musician and printer. An 1839 advertisement noted that he was "ready to make arrangements with Musical Societies, Publishers and others, for PRINTING MUSIC in book, sheet, or any other form that may be required."[57] The same year he was also listed as the conductor of the St. Mary's Singing Society.

Shortly before his death, Kirk issued *The Catholic Harp*, an eighty-page book in its first edition and priced at $37\frac{1}{2}$ cents per copy.[58] The work begins with a nine-page section on "The Elements of Vocal Music," and contains four settings of the mass, the psalms for Sunday vespers, twenty-eight hymns in English, and seventeen in Latin. The work appears to be an inexpensive alternative to Garbett's 1840 hymnal which sold for $2.25; only three of the forty-five hymns in Kirk are not included in Garbett.[59]

A second edition of Kirk's compilation was issued by D. Reilly of Boston in 1845.[60] The work is described as "published by the late Philip A. Kirk," and was expanded to 112 pages by the addition of DeMonti's "Favorite Mass in Three Voices." The DeMonti mass includes only the vocal parts, not the accompaniment, which appeared in Garbett. Later editions, without changes, were published by D. J. Sadlier of New York and Montreal in 1848, 1852, and 1853, attesting to the popularity of Kirk's work.

Sacred Melodies, Containing a Selection of the Most Appropriate Airs, Arranged and Designed as a Companion to the Catholic Sunday School Hymn Book, Manual of the Sodality, Sacred Wreath, etc. Philadelphia: Published by Henry McGrath, No. 1 South Eighth St., 1850.

The title of the ninety-six-page book explains the purpose of the publication. Throughout the 1840s, various Catholic manuals had been published with hymn texts, but without melodies. The preface to the work noted that Catholics "had an abundance of beautiful devotional words, but no airs." The edition, priced at 18 ¾ cents, was designed to remedy that lack. In advertisements, the publisher offered the work bound together with the (text-only) *Sunday School Hymn Book* (1850) for 25 cents. An alphabetical index at the end of the volume provided page numbers for both books.

Sacred Melodies contains text and melody-line, without any harmony or accompaniment. Two litanies, four Latin hymns, and forty-six hymns in English are provided, although a few popular hymns such as "Spirit, Creator of Mankind" and "My God, My Life, My Love" are set to more than one melody. As noted earlier, many of the airs are taken from the French collection, *Cantiques de Saint-Sulpice*, although familiar tunes from Benjamin Carr and Bishop David are also included (without attribution).

The Chapel Choir Book. A Collection of Catholic Music, Consisting of Masses, Anthems, Chants, and Hymns, to which is prefixed a Short Treatise in the Art of Singing. Designed for Public Worship, and Sunday and Singing Schools. Edited by Geo. W. Lloyd. Boston: Published by Patrick Donahoe, 1850.

An advertisement in the *Boston Pilot* (owned by the publisher of the *Chapel Choir Book*) stated that the "object of the Editor and Publisher of the Chapel Choir Book has been to furnish a choice and correct collection of sacred music suitable for parish churches, singing schools and private devotion."[61] The first edition of 128 pages sold for 50 cents, and contained twenty-two hymns in English, including many familiar titles; unlike in most publications of the day, however, almost all of these hymns are set to new melodies, often by the editor of the hymnal. The one exception is "Jerusalem, My Happy Home." A second edition issued circa 1855 added sixteen pages to the original; the new appendix contained more traditional selections including "See the Paraclete Descending," to Stevenson's arrangement, and Dumont's "Missa Regia."

Rohr's Collection of Favorite Catholic Music for Church, School, and Home. Containing the greatest number of Hymns, Psalms, Antiphons, Masses, &c., &c., ever published. Particularly adapted to the wants of small Choirs, Sodalities, and Sunday Schools. Compiled with the assistance of several distinguished Clergymen. By Philip Rohr, Leader of St. Augustine's Choir, Philadelphia. Boston: Published by Patrick Donahoe, 1856.

Rohr's collection, which sold for 25 cents, is advertised as the fourth edition of the work.[62] The title is an exaggeration; at 126 pages, and containing two masses and a hundred hymns, psalms, and antiphons, *Favorite Catholic Music* is considerably smaller than Hoerner's manual. The hymns and songs contained in the work, however, are indeed favorites; almost every title can be found in an earlier Catholic collection.[63]

The Bristow School

In the present chapter, as in the last, we have encountered the names of many performers and composers who worked to some degree with the Catholic immigrant community in antebellum America. Some are names of men whose musical contributions have been largely forgotten, names such as Philip Rohr, James Hoerner, and George W. Lloyd. Others, however, are more familiar to us today because of their musical contributions in the mainstream of the mid-nineteenth-century United States, a roster which includes William Cumming Peters, William Bristow, George Loder, and the brothers Charles and William King. Carlo Bassini, Thomas Comer, Giuseppe DeBegnis and Samuel Lover are names prominent in both the musical history of the Catholic immigrants and at least remembered in the wider realms of the American musical past.

The exceptionally striking aspect of this list of names is that they have been linked in a context having nothing to do with the Catholic immigrant in America. Grace Yerbury, in her study *Song in America,* places all of these musicians within the same "school" of mid-nineteenth-century musicians in America, which she entitles the "Bristow School," in honor of its leading exponent, George F. Bristow.[64]

Yerbury suggests that there are four basic "schools" of mid-century song composition: in addition to the Bristow school, she points to the schools of Oliver Shaw, John Hill Hewitt, and Herrman Saroni. While there are a few musicians from the last three schools whose talents contribute to our story, notably Hewitt and T. V. Wiesenthal of the Hewitt school, and Henry Dielman of the Shaw school, the music of Catholic ritual, both canonical and popular, was to a great extent composed and performed and even published by musicians of the Bristow school. Moreover, Yerbury views the musicians of this ilk as descendants of Benjamin Carr, who had an important impact upon the music of American Catholicism from 1800 to 1830.[65]

Yerbury sees the characteristic quality of the Bristow school of song as a "harmonic density" strongly influenced by the composers of Italian opera, whose works began to attract attention and admiration in America in the 1820s.[66] Yet the new harmonic density is used within the framework of the sentimental ballad, as popular at mid-century in America as in 1800. Although Yerbury is speaking of secular song compositions, the characteristics that she spells out are descriptive of the hymns and sacred songs composed by the Kings, William Cumming Peters, and the others mentioned above. Yerbury notes extensive use of secondary dominants and diminished chords; Charles King's "Hymn for a Martyr," discussed above (fig. 5.5), is a good example of both chromaticism and the freer use of modulation, another practice of musicians of the Bristow school.

It is, perhaps, not surprising that the Catholic immigrant community had a taste for music influenced by Italian opera. Many of the touring opera companies in America featured Italian or Spanish singers, who were very often of the Catholic faith. The churches were not shy in requesting the services of such performers; in 1834, for example, the visiting Italian Opera Company provided the music for the dedication of St. Joseph's Church, the third Catholic parish in New York City.[67]

It also appears significant, however, that the composers of the Bristow school who figure in the musical history of Catholic immigrants were musicians mainly associated with New York City, Philadelphia, and Baltimore, cities in which Italian opera had its greatest popularity. But in the city of Boston, where the musical elite preferred the orchestral music of Germany, we find a somewhat different repertory of Catholic music than elsewhere. Garbett's collection of music for Boston in 1840 was quite similar to those found in other Catholic churches. By 1850, George W. Lloyd's collection retained familiar lyrics, but composed entirely new musical settings. By 1860, the influence of the German immigrant Anthony Werner was felt throughout the Boston diocese; his collections supplied mass settings by Buehler, Feltz, Schmid, and Wallenreiter, names unfamiliar to most antebellum Catholic musicians.[68] Even while the leadership of American Catholicism attempted to shelter its membership from the larger

American culture, societal influences—even regional influences—appear to have had a significant impact upon the musical life of the Catholic parishes.

Summary

We turn once again to six aspects of musical life delineated in chapter 2: performers, choice of music, economics, ritual, sources, and significance.

If the promotional phrase "Music for the Millions" is not an entirely accurate picture of the music of Catholicism, it does express a fundamental trend in the mid-nineteenth-century Catholic parish. There were deliberate attempts to extend the performance of sacred song into as many venues as possible. Collections of music were compiled to contain selections "extremely well adapted for introduction into families, schools, and (may we add?) congregations in the United States . . . a want long felt and often expressed."[69] Interest in music performed by large numbers of singers increased, as for example Mooney's choir of 500 in Boston. A popular collection of Catholic music noted that "when hundreds of voices are united, as in Sunday Schools and Sodalities, the effect is truly religious and most pleasing."[70] The publication of "simple" melodies, designed to complement rather than replace the more difficult choral music of composers from Mozart to DeMonti, fostered two goals: the expansion of devotional singing among Catholic immigrants and an alternative to the incursion of a Protestant repertory in a music-hungry country.

Because vernacular song was often sung outside the official solemn rituals of Catholicism, the choice of music was less constrained by rubrical considerations, and guided more by aesthetic preferences. The hymns and songs which became popular were those that people enjoyed hearing and performing. Tunes that became popular were often fitted with new lyrics to serve in other contexts. Members of the clergy—men as prominent as Charles C. Pise and Archbishop John Hughes—provided new hymn-texts. But unknown authors could also disseminate their newest creations through letters to Catholic and Irish newspapers. Both Catholic and Protestant musicians published sacred music for the immigrant community but, as we have seen, there appears to have been a strong preference for those musicians characterized as members of the "Bristow school" of song composition.

The most common word used in advertisements for these new collections of Catholic music is "cheap." The expensive collections of the 1830s and early 1840s, often costing well over two dollars per copy, were supplanted by inexpensive manuals which could be purchased by larger numbers of the faithful. Garbett's 1840 collection was published at the price of $2.25; Rohr's 1857 collection was priced at $2.00 per dozen. Boston is once again an exception; both of Anthony Werner's collections (1857 and 1862) were priced at over two dollars.

Vernacular sacred song was programmed for benefit concerts as well, concerts which often served to pay for construction of churches, purchase of organs, and support of choir directors. These concerts were also commonly used to serve the charitable work of the church, including the support of charity schools and orphanages. Schools charging tuition often supplemented their income through the demand for music lessons. In short, both music education and performances were important sources of income for many financially strapped institutions.

There is no doubt that vernacular sacred song was on occasion used within solemn celebrations of Catholicism. The exact extent of the usage is difficult to determine; the number of instructions condemning the practice indicates it must have been fairly common. Philadelphia's *Catholic Herald* refers to the use of vernacular song within solemn worship as having "hitherto widely prevailed."[71] But even these instructions specifically refer to solemn celebrations of mass and vespers, implying a tacit acceptance of their use within the so-called "low" mass, the most common ritual within an ordinary parish. The *Herald* urged the proper use of vernacular song, so that "the rite of the Church will be disfigured by no anomalies, and the power of hymns in the vernacular language, on children and the community at large may still be felt."[72] With the growth of popular organizations connected to the parish, the nonliturgical opportunities for the use of vernacular sacred song increased; as the Catholic church in America became more Romanized—and consequently stricter in regard to rubrical matters—the vernacular sacred song of Catholics found a home in nonliturgical settings.

The music for Catholic vernacular song emerged from many sources, including Irish and French traditional melodies, clergy, professional musicians (both Catholic and Protestant), and anonymous individuals. There was far more music available than any given community could use, a significant change from thirty years earlier, allowing a given parish a far greater degree of musical choice than had been previously known among American Catholics. The dependence on British Catholicism and its music grows weaker between 1840 and 1860, a fact made evident by the popularity of home-grown compositions and the unpopularity of the American edition of *Lyra Catholica*, the most important British Catholic musical publication of the mid-nineteenth century. The British hymns of Faber and Newman would, however, grow in popularity in the years following the Civil War.

The growth of vernacular hymnody, which was often composed in a style similar to that of secular song popular at the time, coincides with the growth of interest in performances of the "masterpieces" of Catholic music. As early as 1842 the *Catholic Herald* published an article that appears to reflect a growing split in the musical styles preferred by Catholics at worship:

> For what and for whom is it that we have music in our choirs at all? Is it to furnish a rich musical treat to persons of cultivated minds? ... if ecclesiastical music be only intended for persons of refined taste, and if the efforts of composers and of the leaders of the orchestra are to be directed to the refinements which education teaches the few to understand, rather than to the simpler cadences which can be relished by all—in such a case we say, Heaven help the unlearned! Heaven help those who are innocent of concerts and unskilled in opera.[73]

The Irish immigrant parish would employ the works of the Viennese composers for special occasions, but they often appear to do so not from a love of the music itself but from a desire to impress the non-Catholic world.[74] The vernacular sacred music which developed between 1830 and 1860 became an important part of the musical life of the immigrant parish, surviving the opposition of both the Gregorian and Caecilian reforms later in the century; indeed, some of these songs survived even the acculturation of the immigrants themselves.

As the nineteenth century unfolded, music took a more and more important place in the mainstream of American life. The rise of public-school music education reflected a growth in the educative and formative role that music was expected to fill.[75] Within the Catholic immigrant community it is clear that music was valued as well. But the nature of the values which music instilled differed in the eyes of Protestant and Catholic. Within public schools music was thought to instill discipline, democracy, and Christian ethics. Within the immigrant community, music "raises the soul to heaven, inspires sublimer feelings, and helps human infirmity to support itself longer in contemplation."[76] In short, each group found music capable of instilling the values that it held dear.

The immigrant also understood music to serve a social function, and music was often employed to maintain a sense of national identity.

Although we have examined only liturgical and religious music and song, the musical life of the immigrant parish was clearly not limited to those genres. In chapter 6 we look at the popular rituals of the mid-nineteenth-century Catholic parish, including the retention and revival of Irish culture, as well as the music of social and political parish organizations.

CHAPTER SIX

𝔐usic of 𝔓opular ℜitual: 𝔖ong and 𝔓arish 𝔒rganizations

The preceding chapters have documented aspects of the significant musical culture that existed within American Catholic parishes of the 1840s and 1850s, parishes that had become the center of Catholic immigrant life. But it would be a mistake to assume that the practice of music within the parish was limited to music of a religious nature. As the parish was more and more consciously organized to serve as the central institution of immigrant life, new parish organizations were formed to meet the needs of the community; yet the organizations were often only tangentially connected to explicitly religious ends. Because the life of these groups was often of short duration, and they often swiftly evolved in both function and purpose, information concerning them is sketchy. The use of music by immigrant parish organizations is frequently mentioned in newspaper accounts, yet rarely with much detail. But the nature of the various organizations appears to have been similar from parish to parish, thereby allowing us to gain an overview of the use of secular music within the Catholic parish.

Two types of organizations arose in the Catholic parishes of the early 1840s: the temperance society and the repeal organization. The temperance, or total abstinence, society originated within New England Protestantism, with the goal of ending the use of alcoholic beverages; the temperance movement was accepted into Catholic circles, but with significant changes, to be discussed. Repeal organizations, on the other hand, were Irish-American political societies, formed to support Ireland in the fight to repeal the Act of Union of Great Britain and Ireland (1800). Although the two organizations appear to be quite different in nature and orientation, both served similar functions within parish life.

Temperance Songs

There is evidence that sporadic attempts at introducing a Catholic temperance movement in America existed before 1840. The formation of the Catholic Total Abstinence Society of Pennsylvania in 1840, however, marks the first appearance of a large-scale temperance movement among Irish Catholic immigrants. The Catholic Total Abstinence Society, although sharing similarities with Protestant temperance organizations, was inspired by and modeled after the movement begun by Capuchin Father Theobald Mathew in Ireland in 1838.[1] News of the spectacular success of Mathew's societies in Ireland soon reached American shores, and elicited praise from Catholic and Protestant alike.

Rev. Charles Constantine Pise of the diocese of New York visited Mathew in 1842 and on his return to America published the following description of the "apostle of temperance":

> He can scarcely walk the streets of Cork, he is so followed and saluted by rich as well as poor. In his person are combined with curious felicity the blandest and most elegant manners with a high-toned and gentlemanly reserve. He is equally courteous to all, addresses all in terms of affection, and shows peculiar interest for the lowest of the people. He seems ever engaged in works of benevolence and charity. The alleviation of the hardships of the laboring classes engrosses his attention. He is now exerting his influence to abolish night work among the bakers.[2]

Father Mathew's Temperance Crusade was marked by several characteristics which distinguished it from American Protestant temperance movements; these characteristics were not always retained in the American Catholic counterpart. First, although clearly a religious movement, Mathew's crusade was not denominational. Mathew moved freely among Catholics, Anglicans, and Presbyterians. The ecumenical character of his work, however, aroused suspicion among the Catholic bishops of the United States, who tended to view American society as a denominational battleground.[3] Secondly, Mathew also saw the temperance movement as one aspect of a larger social-reform movement, and he himself was active in promoting numerous social reforms, as is evident from Pise's description of Mathew. Within the American context, the Catholic temperance movement was closely linked to efforts to change the American stereotype of the Irish immigrant as a lazy and ignorant drunkard. Finally, all descriptions of Mathew and his style of preaching stress the quiet and rational nature of the movement. The contrast with the emotive style of Methodist temperance preaching in America seems to have been generally retained in the Catholic Total Abstinence Movement in America.

Father Mathew encouraged the formation of "temperance bands" in the branches of the movement in Ireland. The use of music within the crusade appears to differ sharply from the use of music in American Protestant temperance movements. The large repertory of temperance songs in America is often didactic or even propagandistic in style. Couched in a popular medium, Protestant temperance songs attempt to portray the evils of alcohol and the abuses which stem from its use, often in highly emotional displays. But within the Catholic temperance movement, both in Ireland and America, musical activity is used primarily as a diversion from drinking; song lyrics rarely tell a story relating the dangers of alcohol. It is musical activity which is important in the Catholic temperance movements rather than the specific music employed.

The Catholic parish in Fall River, Massachusetts, for example, opened a singing school in connection with the temperance movement. In a letter to the *New York Freeman's Journal*, a parishioner noted that "many are they who visit this school, who, were it not in existence, would, according to the order of the day, be seduced by those who haunt our taverns and groceries." The writer also went on to note that "the Temperance movement has done much here."[4]

Particularly on holidays that were associated with drinking, the Pennsylvania Catholic Total Abstinence Society planned elaborate temperance celebrations, before the anti-Irish riots of 1844 made such public demonstrations dangerous to public safety. Thus, in 1843, the society held a "GRAND CONCERT and ORATION in the *Saloon of the Chinese Museum*" with proceeds applied to the city's Catholic orphanages.[5] Independence Day of 1843 was celebrated with a "GRAND PROCESSION, ORATION and CONCERT" at the same site and for the benefit of the same charities.[6]

The formation of temperance bands, so popular in Ireland, does not appear to have been as widespread in America. Accounts of Catholic temperance activities often are unclear as to whether the society possessed its own band, or simply hired a band, for its events. For example, at the closing of the Provincial Council of Baltimore in 1843, the procession of bishops was escorted by the St. Patrick's Temperance Society with "a large complete band of music to itself."[7] In Philadelphia, St. Augustine's church sponsored a temperance band that performed at Catholic parishes in the mid-1840s.[8] At Hartford's Holy Trinity Church, the "entire parish renounced alcohol" in 1842, and sponsored a "fine brass band" during the mid-1840s.[9] But a letter to the editor of the *Boston Pilot* in 1846 seems to indicate that Catholic temperance bands were not common in Boston:

> An Irish Band. *Mr. Editor*:-Permit me, through the columns of your valuable paper, to solicit the attention of young men not otherwise engaged, to the above-named object in this city. There is a large number of young men, good performers on various instruments, who have been members of bands in Boston and elsewhere, to whom I think this suggestion will be useful. . . . it would prove a useful medium for the cause of Total Abstinence, to say nothing of cultivating the taste for music so natural in the Irish people.[10]

It is unclear whether the effort to form an Irish band in Boston was successful, but a "Hibernian Band" is mentioned in the Boston Irish press of the early 1850s.[11] In New York, the St. Patrick's Total Abstinence Beneficial Society hired Dodworth's Band for its third annual boat ride and picnic. The advertisement includes the caution "N. B. Private musicians will not be allowed to play on the boat or barges," suggesting earlier excursions were accompanied by music provided by members of the society.[12]

The nature of Catholic temperance songs was often guided by the purpose for which they were written, for example, the celebration of St. Patrick's Day without the use of intoxicating beverages. In the lyrics of the songs, themes of temperance are linked with the glories of Ireland. A song composed for the Albany Catholic Total Abstinence Association in 1841 saw temperance linked to the success of the Irish race:

> This day we sons of Erin sigh,
> Long life and health to Innisfail,
> Since clouds no more their shadows fling,
> To robe her in a mourning veil.
> She now shines forth an Em'rald bright,
> Gemming the seas with rays of light.
>
> Her noble sons were once enslaved;
> Their gen'rous hearts were crushed with shame,
> Until the Temp'rance banner waved,
> And poured cold water on the flame.

> And then an army gladly rose,
> To fight and conquer all its foes.[13]

One of the few Catholic temperance songs that directly dealt with the evils of alcohol appeared in the *Boston Pilot*. A new set of lyrics to William Dempster's "Lament of the Irish Emigrant" changed the subject of the song from an oppressed Irishman to a drunken one:

> I'm thinking on the night, Mary,
> The night of grief and shame,
> When with drunken ravings on my lips,
> To thee I homeward came:-
> O, the tear was in thy earnest eye,
> And thy bosom wildly heaved,
> Yet a smile of love was on thy cheek,
> Though thy heart was sorely grieved.
>
> O, my words were harsh to thee, Mary,
> For the wine-cup drove me wild,
> And I chid thee when thy eyes were sad,
> And cursed thee when they wailed,-
> God knows I lov'd thee even then,
> But the fire was in my brain,
> And the curse of drink was in my heart
> To make my love a bane.[14]

Such lyrics were, however, an exception. Many songs composed for total abstinence organizations had only vague references to temperance, often an image related to the purity of water, and are perhaps best classified as songs for temperance societies rather than temperance songs. James Gibbons composed the following lyrics, probably sung to a traditional tune such as "Sheela na guira" or "Paddy Whack," for the Pennsylvania Catholic Total Abstinence Society celebration of March 17, 1843:

SONG OF THE EXILE

> Hail, thrice happy day to the exile endearing
> As he wanders afar o'er life's troubled sea,
> And sacred's the tie that still binds him to Erin,
> While the pulse of his heart throbs for Cushlamachree.
> No hills are so green as my own native mountains,
> No valley so fertile, no flowers so fair;

> No nectar more pure than thy crystal-like fountains,
> Whose murmurs are fann'd by thine own balmy air.
>
> Behold our loved Erin in bold agitation,
> Combating with despots to sever her chains,
> Proclaiming aloud that she must be a nation,
> Free as the breezes that sweep o'er her plains.
> Nations have sunk 'neath the lash of oppression,
> Their glory departed all shrouded in gloom,
> Whilst Erin Mavourneen resisting aggression
> Thy spirit ne'er slumbered in slavery's tomb.
>
> Oh! Harp of my country, the pride of her sages,
> In vain would the tyrant thy numbers control.
> Thou'rt the gift of our fathers, the boast of past ages,
> Thy music still lives in each Irishman's soul.
> Then hail to thee, Erin! wherever I wander,
> My spirit still lingers around thy loved shore,
> Where nature appears in her own native grandeur,
> And thy sons are as brave as their fathers of yore.[15]

Repeal Songs

While the use of music within the Catholic total abstinence societies was rarely didactic or sensational, the music employed by repeal associations was often a tool of propaganda. Although the songs of Thomas Moore were still popular among the Irish immigrants—and in the country at large—there was a growing sense that Moore's message was too passive, even defeatist, in regard to the fate of Ireland. It was not uncommon for a contemporary poet to add an extra verse, changing the tone of the song. For example, the final verse of Moore's "Blame not the Bard" foresees little hope for the future of Ireland:

> But, though glory be gone, hope fades not away;
> Thy name, loved Erin! shall live in his songs;
> Not even in the hour when his heart is most gay,
> Will he lose the remembrance of thee and thy wrongs!
> The stranger shall hear thy lament on his plains;
> The sigh of thy harp shall be sent o'er the deep,
> Till thy masters themselves, as they rivet thy chains,
> Shall pause at the song of the captive, and weep!

In the 1840s, Thomas Mooney excused the tone of the song, for Moore had
been a living witness of his country's glory, and her fall. He saw her deprived of freedom, bleeding, prostrate, and destitute even of the hope to recover.... But Ireland's wounds are almost healed; her tears are dried up; her vigor and courage have returned.... At such a moment, I may be pardoned by the patriotic for adding an appropriate stanza to this beautiful song. It is the concluding one,—in italics.[16]

> *But arise, dearest Erin! the home of the brave!*
> *The birthplace of heroes, and sages of light!*
> *Send your voice of complaint and resolve o'er the wave,*
> *And the nations shall join in your cause and your fight!*
> *And the God that protected his children before,*
> *Whom the tyrant of Egypt oppressed in his might,*
> *Shall watch o'er the struggle around your green shore,*
> *And bless the brave arms of your sons in the fight!*[17]

The supporters of Irish nationalism in the 1840s were aware that their cause was a difficult one, and would never be achieved without assistance from outside of Ireland. In the revolt of 1798, the Irish looked to the revolutionary government of France for assistance; in the 1840s they looked to their countrymen in America. The leader of the movement to repeal the Act of Union of Great Britain and Ireland was Daniel O'Connell, elected to the British Parliament in 1828. By 1840, when the Tories had regained control of British government, O'Connell despaired of government-led social reform in Ireland and began a popular movement for repeal, the first step toward Irish self-government. Associated with O'Connell's repeal movement, but somewhat less patient and more radical, was the Young Ireland movement, whose views were expressed in a Dublin newspaper, *The Nation*. Both of the organizations were active in America's immigrant community, and both of them employed song for disseminating their message. Many repeal songs were simply new lyrics for traditional Irish tunes. There were, however, at least a few newly composed songs, both text and music. The *New York Freeman's Journal* reported the beginning of a series of new repeal songs of American origin:

> We are gratified to learn that a new and splendid series of Repeal Songs—the words by J. AUGUSTUS SHEA, the music, for voice and piano forte, by CHARLES M. KING—will shortly be published in rapid succession, to be continued, we understand, *until Repeal is achieved*. The subject of these Songs will be taken from the principal circumstances recently at-

tending the great struggle. It is much to be regretted that hitherto some of the finest effusions of Patriot and Poet, on this inspiring subject, have been sadly distorted by the inappropriate, and often incongruous *Melodies* adapted to them, but we may now hope for something worthy of the "Harp of Erin" and the glorious *Theme*, from the pens of such competent gentlemen as the above named.[18]

The article goes on to note that the first of the songs would be based on "The Trial," would include a picture of the "Liberator," that is, Daniel O'Connell, and would be issued in two days. "Every friend to the cause, and especially all of either sex (the better half more especially) who can play, or sing, should encourage this spirited and interesting undertaking."[19] It is unclear why the *Freeman's Journal* felt women "especially" should support the endeavor.

American interest in the repeal of the Act of Union is demonstrated by the prominence the cause was given in Irish-American societies other than repeal organizations. For example, the St. Patrick's Day dinner of the Washington, D. C., Benevolent Society in 1844 featured toasts and songs in support of repeal. The fourth toast of the evening was to "Repeal: By right, or might, now or never." At least three repeal songs were included on the program: a Mr. McConnell sang "The Land of O'Connell and Repeal," Mr. J. Reilly sang "Arise, arise, Hibernia's Sons, arise," and George Washington Parke Custis, a descendant of the first American president, composed "An Ode to Young Ireland" to the air "Believe me if all those endearing young charms":

> Oh, where is the star that shall guide the opprest—
> Where refuge the poor Exile find?
> 'Tis the young Eagle Empire, "enthroned in the West,"
> The beacon of Hope to mankind;
> 'Tis the Star of our Washington, honored and bright,
> Undimmed in its luster by time,
> That sheds on fair Freedom its glorious light,
> In every country and clime.
>
> Arouse thee, oh Ireland! while long thou hast slept
> Oppression has stalked through thy land;
> No tears for thy sorrows, too long hast thou wept,
> Thy day of Redemption's at hand.
> The shadowy forms of thy Heroes repair
> To gatherings on mountain and height;

> The cries of thy Martyrs are heard in the air,
> Young Ireland arise in thy might.[20]

The third and fourth stanzas of the ode promise that "Columbia will ever be first in thy cause" and urge the Irish to "strike for the Rights of Mankind," indicating to the listener the importance of American support for repeal, while placing the issue of repeal within the broader context of inalienable rights.

Charles Soran's "Arise, arise, Hibernia's Sons, arise" was probably sung to the tune "The Battle of the Nile." The melody was a popular patriotic air in both England and the United States; in Britain the first line of text was "Arise, arise, Britannia's Sons, arise," while in the United States it was "Columbia's Sons" who were addressed.

> Arise, arise, Hibernia's Sons, arise,
> And strike for your altars, for your freedom, for your homes!
> The cries, the cries of Bondsmen rend your skies,
> Then resolve ye for Repeal or for your tombs.
> Too long has Britannia ruled your noble Nation,
> Arise, and no longer submit to degradation;
> With O'Connell as your chief,
> Up! and make the battle brief;
> Lift your banner from the ground,
> Every Paddy rally round,
> And Freedom, Erin's Freedom, o'er the Nations shall resound
>
> CHORUS
>
> Repeal, Repeal, Repeal, your chorus be, boys!
> Shout till John Bull shall acknowledge the decree,
> Till Peel shall feel he must give you Repeal,
> And Erin take her place among the Free![21]

Figure 6.1 provides another example of a repeal song, written by an Irishman in America to a preexisting tune. Thomas Mooney traveled throughout the United States, first to raise support for repeal of the Act of Union and, later, to promote the revival of Irish culture among the immigrants in America. His annotation before the song notes that he wrote the lyrics "on the Mississippi, while on my Western Repeal Mission, in 1841–2," and that the song was first published in the *Dublin Pilot*. The arrangement in figure 6.1 was published in Boston, in 1845, as part of a large collection of lectures and songs. The third verse of "Come, Raise a

FIGURE 6.1
"Come Raise a Cheer for Erin," from Thomas Mooney's *History of Ireland* (transcription)

COME, RAISE A CHEER FOR ERIN!
Words by T. Mooney
Written on the Mississippi while on my Western Repeal Mission in 1841-2, and published in the Dublin Pilot, in one of a series of letters, addressed by me to that paper, under the title of "American Correspondence."   T.M.

Cheer for Erin!" clearly states the goal of repeal: the restoration of self-rule by an Irish parliament:

> Then rouse your heart, dear Erin,
> And sound your voice from shore to shore!

SONG AND PARISH ORGANIZATIONS 147

> Demand your rights, brave Erin,
> And your parliament they'll restore;
> And lift on high your streaming
> Green banner, as in days gone by.
> The nations aid you, Erin!
> And Heaven smiles a cheer from high![22]

The organ of the Young Ireland movement, the *Dublin Nation*, regularly printed poems and lyrics that dealt with political situations in Ireland. They were collected into book form and first published in Ireland. In 1844 Patrick Donahoe, publisher of the *Boston Pilot*, issued the first American edition.[23] The *Boston Pilot* announced the publication with the following description of the collection:

> We are glad that these far-famed and noble national lyrics are now before the American people. It will give them, better than any amount of cold logic, an idea of the great and universal spirit of the Irish people, and may we not hope that the wild pathos, the fiery energy, and all-absorbing love of liberty, which so strongly marks these ballads, will win many a warm heart to our cause.
>
> O'Connell has bestowed strong praise upon these thrilling songs, and Alderman Butt, an opponent of Repeal, confessed their power and influence.... It will be the best "Repeal speaker" in the country.[24]

The *New York Freeman's Journal* noted that the American edition is "the only one which contains a table of contents, with *the airs to which the songs are to be sung*, an all important feature."[25]

Many of the songs were widely available, because individual selections often appeared in both Irish-American and Catholic newspapers. Donahoe's own newspaper printed "The Saxon Massacre," described as "noble and truthful":

> The sword of the Saxon with slaughter is red—
> But the blood on his blade in no battle was shed;
> For—heavens! the babe, and the maid, and the mother,
> Have shared the same fate with the sire and the brother!
> It is not the blush by the morning sun spread
> That tints the horizon so luridly red—
> It is not the heath on the mountain side high,
> Whose blaze brings the glare on the far flushing sky—
> 'Tis the flame of the village illumines the air,
> Where the shriek of the maiden, in maddened despair,

> Pleads to the heart of the monster in vain,
> Who are dyed with the blood of her kindred slain![26]

Other songs were less lurid, but no weaker in the resolve finally to take control of Ireland:

> Air-Mrs. Casey
>
> Too long our Irish hearts we schooled
> In patient hope to bide;
> By dreams of English justice fooled
> And English tongues that lied.
> That hour of weak delusion's past,
> The empty-dream has flown;
> Our hope and strength, we find at last,
> Is in OURSELVES ALONE.[27]

The repeal movement met with a rather sudden end. The leaders of the Young Ireland movement, impatient with O'Connell's small measure of success, attempted an armed rebellion in 1848, which was quickly put down. The imprisonment or exile of the Young Ireland leaders ended the repeal movement. Moreover, the concern with repeal was overshadowed by the agricultural news which began coming out of Ireland in 1845: the potato blight and the beginning of the great famine.

The Great Famine

The immigrants were well aware of the importance of the potato to Ireland. Among the toasts at the Philadelphia Hibernian Society St. Patrick's Day dinner in 1843 was one to "*The Potatoe*. The root of health, strength and increase."[28] The effects of the great famine would be felt within the American Irish community as well. Repeal associations were replaced with relief organizations. Concerts and benefits were held to raise money to buy food for the Irish people.

The *Catholic Herald* printed the following description of a sermon given in a Catholic church with the goal of raising funds for the starving and sick of Ireland:

> The hearers were principally Irish, some of them but recently from the scene described: the theme awfully distressing: the speaker one of the most moving, most eloquent we have ever heard. . . . he produced a portrait of her [Ireland's] present condition, the most frightful and

heartrending, the mind of man can entertain. . . . The effect on the audience was such, as I never have, nor ever again expect to witness. "These famished beings, (exclaimed he,) are your friends, your relatives, amongst them the very mother, who bore you near her heart." There was a general burst of tears all over the Church; for many of them, it was but too true; many of the little children looking up to their parents and seeing them so intensely agitated, wept aloud. . . . I actually saw persons take their crosses from their necks and rings from their fingers, and throw them in the box, not having the money they wished to contribute. One person told me he could not resist throwing in the very house-rent, he had collected with pain, and was to be paid that very day."[29]

The bitterness and mistrust toward England, already strongly expressed in repeal songs, would increase; the increase led some immigrants to a rejection of English culture and a renewed interest in the culture of Ireland. But certainly the most long-lasting effect of the famine would be the sheer numbers of Irish who came to America to escape hunger, disease, and poverty.

Irish-Americans were not alone in their concern for famine victims. Although strain, at times even violence, had marked the relationship between the Irish in America and the so-called Nativists, news of the severity of the famine and the suffering it was causing brought forth a charitable response from Americans of all national backgrounds. Protestants were often prominent in famine relief organizations. For example, Boston held a "Grand Entertainment for the Relief of Ireland" on March 20, 1847, at the Melodeon. The "committee of arrangements" included the publisher J. T. Buckingham, the piano-builder J. Chickering, and the music publisher Oliver Ditson, along with men of Irish surnames.[30] A collection at Grace Church (Protestant Episcopal) in New York City raised two thousand dollars for famine relief, and the *New York Herald* estimated that over one hundred and fifty thousand dollars had been raised in America by March of 1847. Three ships sailed from Boston loaded with 51,577 bushels of corn, 2,100 bushels of rye, and 500 bushels of corn meal.[31] In five years the place of the potato in Irish life had radically changed: a toast at a Boston St. Patrick's Day dinner in 1848 wished that Ireland "may declare her independence by substituting the culture of grain for that 'root of all evil,' the potatoe!"[32]

George Loder, a British-born Protestant influential in Catholic church music in New York City, composed a song in response to the famine, "The Dying Emigrant's Prayer," dedicated to the Irish Relief Committee (fig. 6.2).[33] Loder's setting of a text by Henry Plunkett Grattan is a typical sentimental ballad composed in the style of the Bristow school discussed in chapter 5. In his secular songs such as "The Dying Emigrant's Prayer," however, Loder employed a greater degree of chromaticism and dissonance than is found in his sacred compositions. The extent to which Loder's song was employed by the Irish immigrant community is unknown, but the composition does demonstrate the concern of the non–Irish American for the plight of Ireland during the famine.

Traditional Irish Song

Historians of mid-nineteenth-century music in America recognize the "Irish song" as a category of music popular throughout much of the country. The popularity of the songs of Thomas Moore and Sir John Stevenson has already been noted. During much of the 1840s Samuel Lover, whom Charles Hamm calls the most popular Irish writer of song after Moore, was presenting an entertainment called "Irish Evenings" throughout the United States.[34] Lover's performances were not without controversy within the Irish-American community. His 1846 performances in New York City were warmly received by the local Irish press:

> Mr. Lover's Evenings were a source of unalloyed pleasure to the crowded audiences attending each representation in our city. His numerous narratives and pathetic recitals kept the audience from the commencement to the close either in roars of laughter or overcome with tears. His songs elicited unbounded applause—compositions that for their music or poetry are the admiration of the world.[35]

Lover's later performances in Washington, D.C., were less well received by at least one Irish-American:

> [Lover's] pictures of Irish life and manners, which are principally copied from the coarsest and vulgar originals, covered over it is true with a very small amount of drapery, may amuse a mixed mass of persons, already but too well inclined to sport with the feelings and foibles of his countrymen. . . . Mr. Lover is, I am sure, a very clever man, and an accomplished scholar, but lacks, I think, a reasonable share of that national pride that belongs to men of his acquirements in his native land. . . . Whatever may be Mr. Lover's talents, or his love of fatherland, the line of life he has adopted for a living is not very well calculated to enhance the former in the estimation, at least of his countrymen.[36]

FIGURE 6.2

Loder & Grattan, "The Dying Emigrant's Prayer" (first verse) (transcription)

FIGURE 6.2

FIGURE 6.2
Loder & Grattan, "The Dying Emigrant's Prayer" (cont.)

The critic appears to have been concerned with the way Ireland and its people were viewed both by the Irish immigrant and American society in general, and found Lover's presentations reinforcements of undesirable characterizations of the Irish. A writer to the *Boston Pilot* complained that the music of Ireland had been suppressed by "Doctors" and "Professors"

of music, both in England and America: "[Ireland] is viewed only through the ridiculous prism afforded by such stories as . . . [Lover's] Handy Andy, to be laughed at or pitied."[37] Just as the choice of music in the churches was calculated to impress the non-Catholic world, so some immigrants hoped that Irish entertainments would promote the image of the Irishman before a society hostile to the Irish.

The Irish and Catholic press in America printed numerous articles extolling the history of Irish music. The motivation behind the articles may well have been an urgent concern among some immigrants to preserve the Irish culture. A letter to the editor of the *New York Freeman's Journal* expressed this concern in the following fashion:

> Often I have been struck with wonder and regret, at the apathy which prevails on a subject, so indissolubly linked with the dearest associations of our native land; and long have I hoped that some public-spirited individual would adopt measures for the revival of those beautiful airs, which appeal with such touching fidelity to every feeling of the human heart. This is no isolated question; but a subject of deep and abiding interest to every individual who boasts an Irish name; to the antiquarian and the man of letters, a source of delight and pride; to the politician, a powerful means of moulding the minds of his fellow men;—and to the humble poor one of the "greenest spots in memory's waste."[38]

The *Boston Pilot* noticed the letter, and agreeing wholeheartedly with the sentiments, reprinted the final paragraph. The editor of the *Boston Pilot* introduced the excerpts with comments such as these:

> Aye, our divine melodies have been shamefully neglected, when millions of the accomplished children of Irish parents cannot play a single strain of their father's land. We cannot wonder that anti-Irish feelings spring from such un-Irish education—that the American of to-day feels not for the Irishman—that parents feel the dreadful bitterness of filial contempt.[39]

The remarks seem to indicate the children of Irish immigrants were, at least to some extent, becoming assimilated into American society; the rejection of Irish identity concerned at least some Irish leaders in America. But the interest in repeal, concern over the famine, and the phenomenal increase in Irish immigration all contributed to both the growth of Irish-American identity and a revival of interest in Irish culture.

Thomas Mooney, mentioned above in connection with the repeal movement, toured the United States giving "Lectures on Ireland." The "lectures" were actually a mix of history, oratory, and music designed to increase American sympathy for the Irish cause. The following advertisement for a Mooney lecture appeared in the *Boston Pilot* and is typical of the program for one of Mooney's presentations:

Fourth Lecture on Ireland

With Concert of Irish Music, on Monday Evening, Oct. 23 Mr. Mooney will deliver his fourth lecture on Irish History, Poetry and Music, at the Marlboro Chapel, on next Monday Evening, Oct. 23rd, at seven o'clock.

Principle topics—The Revolution of 1782—the Revolution of 1798—the Life and Times of Robert Emmet and the Revolt of 1803, and the trial and last speech of the Martyred Patriot. Mr. Mooney will recite the authentic speech of Robert Emmet in nearly the manner it was delivered on the trial.

After the lecture a MELODIANA of Irish Music will be introduced in which MRS. FRANKLIN will sing the following melodies.

She is far from the Land	Moore
Oh! breathe not his name	Moore
The Exile of Erin	Campbell[40]
The meeting of the Waters	Moore

The celebrated Irish trio, "Peace to the souls of the heroes!" will be sung by three young gentlemen amateurs.

The following melodies written specially for these Lectures will be introduced.

Repeal is o'er the Billows	T. Mooney
We'll knock up the union says Steele to Peel	T. Mooney
The gathering of Leinster	O'Callaghan of the Dub. Nation
The Discovery of America	T. Mooney

MR. TOWNLEY will preside at the Pianoforte.

Time, Seven o'clock precisely
Admittance 25 cents. Children with their parents, half price.[41]

In a review of the evening, the *Pilot* noted that the "singing by Mrs. Franklin electrified the audience.... She has a voice that seems fitted alone for the plaintive songs of the Irish people."[42] The songs of the first half of the concert are well known even today; the songs of the second half are rare. Figure 6.3 gives the melody and first verse of O'Callaghan's "The Gathering of Leinster" as printed in Mooney's *History of Ireland*.[43]

Mooney's book, which includes both his lecture series and a printed edition of the music performed at the concerts, was first published by Patrick Donahoe (owner of the *Boston Pilot*) in 1845. The printed work was far more extensive than Mooney's live performances, running over one thousand pages. A chapter was devoted to the history of Irish music, and each chapter of the book ended with appropriate songs and tunes of Ireland. An advertisement for the first edition described the music included as:

> One Hundred and Fifty Irish Melodies
> (Poetry and music combined) arranged for Pianoforte, Violin, Flute, or Clarionet, and presented as specimens of our ancient and modern composition, embracing every measure, whether of love, sorrow, joy, merriment, war or patriotism, well calculated to soothe the heart in Exile, or to animate it in bondage.[44]

FIGURE 6.3
"The Gathering of Leinster," from T. Mooney's *History of Ireland* (transcription)

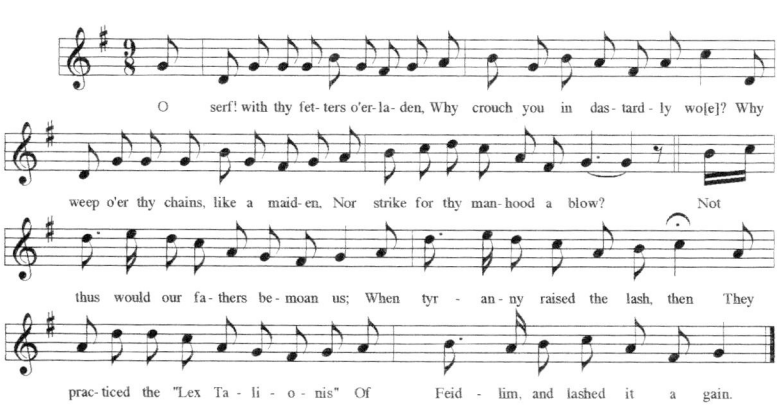

Editor's note: The irregular number of beats in measures four and five are in Mooney's original.

The publication of Mooney's work was accompanied by a concert and lecture in Boston at the Odeon. The *Boston Pilot* reported that although the hall could hold "several thousand persons. . . . several thousands went away unable to enter."[45] Among those reported in attendance were the Catholic bishop of Boston, John Fitzpatrick, and the noted journalist and Catholic convert Orestes Brownson.

Although the concert and book proved popular in Boston, Philadelphia's Catholic newspaper found Mooney's work wanting.

> The only merit Mr. Mooney could fairly claim is for an extensive compilation, made up of *verbum-berbo* extracts from Irish historians and poets. Even in this he has not made a happy or judicious arrangement. . . . Mr. Mooney's songs in juxtaposition with Moore's charming melodies—who can tolerate them? Some indeed of our historian's verses are passable when not in rude contrast with the "Irish Melodies," but many of them would be pronounced barbarous by the ballad singers of Dublin.[46]

Although the *Catholic Herald* was a staid and generally conservative paper—the anti-Catholic riots of 1844 in Philadelphia did not merit front-page coverage—the paper's review of Mooney's book is generally quite accurate. Mooney's song compositions do not seem to have made an impact upon the Irish in America. Yet the publication was popular, being issued in a number of editions between 1845 and 1857. And the book made notated versions of traditional Irish tunes readily available to the immigrant musician.

In 1839 and 1840 the Irish singer and songwriter P. F. White toured in the United States, armed with letters of recommendation from the great Thomas Moore himself, playing in such cities as Boston, Providence, and New York. White's concerts were less politically motivated than Mooney's, and included short lectures on music history, especially that of Ireland. White's song repertory was a mix of Thomas Moore ballads and his own compositions, some with piano accompaniment and others in which White accompanied himself on guitar. Among White's compositions are the songs "This Heart is Thine," "Oh! Yes I Remember," and "Come, Come Away."

White was received with great acclaim. The *Boston Pilot* described his oratorical style. "He rolled out sentence after sentence in stately rhetorical grandeur, illustrating his arguments relative to Irish music with unbounded power, and encircled them in beauty of imagery, felicity of illusion, and impressive magnificence of thought and language."[47] The *Courier* of Providence, Rhode Island, noted that "his reception here has been flattering; and the best conducted newspapers in N. York, Boston, Lowell, and other cities, have accorded the highest praise to his performances."[48] In Boston, White appeared as guest soloist with the Gregorian Society, the chorus associated with the Catholic cathedral. His reception in Boston was so favorable that a dinner was held in his honor, arranged by leading members of Boston's Irish community, including Patrick Donahoe, publisher of the *Boston Pilot*.[49]

The Irish Keen in America

A Mr. McMichael toured the United States with success, presenting evenings of Irish minstrelsy. *The New York Freeman's Journal* assured its readers that "unlike too many performers of the same class, Mr. McMichael does not caricature his countrymen," and noted his success in concerts in Boston and Saratoga.[50] An advertisement for McMichael's New York concert appeared in the same paper and listed the songs to be performed:[51]

The Deserter's Meditation	Let Erin Remember the days of old
As down on Bannas Banks	The Roving Blade
Silent oh! Moyle	The Exile
When I was younger	The Irish Mother's Lament
Molly Brallaghan	The Old Man's Lament
Terence's Farewell	The Irish Sailor

Of particular interest in Mr. McMichael's repertory is the song "The Irish Mother's Lament." The *Boston Pilot* described McMichael's performance:

> As we entered, he was reading from his manuscript in a clear, firm, well-managed voice, some historic illustrations and introductions to the ancient Caoine, or Keen, for the dead. After repeating a very romantic legend, of three brothers drowned in a lake, on whose shore their frenzied widow-mother mourns their loss, he at once proceeded with the lament. His blanched and reverent hair, and highly expressive features were but the indexes to a voice of surprisingly sorrowful power. There has never been heard so truly pathetic a voice, in this city.[52]

The song described appears to be John Barton's "The Irish Mother's Lament," which is subtitled "Song introducing the Irish Cry for the Dead."[53] It is reproduced in figure 6.4.

FIGURE 6.4

John Barton's "The Irish Mother's Lament" (first verse) (transcription)

160 HOW SHALL WE SING?

FIGURE 6.4
John Barton's "The Irish Mother's Lament" (first verse cont.)

It has been suggested that keening is the oldest form of Irish music to have survived into modern times.[54] While an extensive investigation of the nature of keening is beyond the scope of this work, a few remarks on the practice in Ireland will aid in the understanding of the practice in America. Travelers to Ireland were often struck by the strange nature of keening. Mr. and Mrs. S. C. Hall visited Ireland shortly before the great famine, and described an Irish wake:

> The body, decently laid out on a table or bed, is covered with white linen.... The women of the household range themselves at either side, and the keen at once commences. They rise with one accord, and moving their bodies with a slow motion to and fro, their arms apart, they continue to keep up a heart-rending cry. This cry is interrupted for a while to give the *ban caointhe* (the leading keener) an opportunity of commencing. At the close of every stanza of the dirge, the cry is repeated, to fill up, as it were, the pause, and then dropped; the women then again proceed with the dirge, and so on to the close.[55]

The *ban caointhe*, or leader of the keen, was always a woman, either a close relative of the deceased or a keening specialist. Each round of keening consisted of three parts. The first is sometimes referred to as the "salutation," the murmuring of the name of the deceased over and over in a low voice. Others have suggested that the keener is actually running quickly through the text that will be used in the following section. The second part is the verse, in which the keener sings of the goodness of the deceased or the impact of the loss. For example, the following lines were printed in a Boston publication of 1856, described as a (prose) translation of an actual keen:

> My sunshine you were. I loved you better than the sun itself; and when I see the sun going down in the west, I think of my boy and of my black night of sorrow. Like the rising sun, he had a red glow on his cheek. He was as bright as the sun at midday; but a dark storm came on, and my sunshine was lost to me forever. My sunshine will never again come back. No! my boy cannot return. Cold and silent is his bed.[56]

The final section of the keen was the cry in which all present joined in, often employing sounds such as "Och-ochone."[57]

The sound of the keen must have been a powerful memory for many Irish-Americans, for it was not only sung at the time of death; as the emigrant was leaving for America, those left behind would keen the departure. The night before departure from Ireland, the family and friends of the emigrants would gather for what was termed an "American wake." An unsympathetic English visitor to Ireland in 1852 happened upon a family leaving their native town for America:

> We were startled—to say the truth, our blood ran cold—at the loud cry of a young girl who ran across the road.
> ... A man, his wife, and three young children were going to America.... All eyes were fixed on the neighbors who were going away for ever.... The last embraces were terrible to see.... When we saw the wringing of hands and heard the wailings, we became aware, for the first time perhaps, of the full dignity of that civilization which induces control over the expression of emotions. All the while ... this lamentation was giving a headache to all who looked on.... and the shrill united cry, when the car moved on, rings in our ears, and long will ring when we hear of emigration.[58]

Although sympathetic to many Irish customs, the hierarchy of the Catholic church in America frowned upon the continuance of the Irish wake in America.[59] Because of a lack of church buildings in Ireland, as well as from centuries of persecution, many Catholic rituals in Ireland had been centered in the home rather than the church, most notably funerals and weddings. While the hierarchy would eventually be successful in promoting a parish-centered faith, it is clear that traditional practices continued in the Irish immigrant community before the Civil War. George Templeton Strong happened upon a construction accident in New York City which had killed two Irish workers. In his diary, Strong describes his first experience of keening:

> Yesterday morning I was spectator of a strange, weird, painful scene.... Seeing a crowd on the corner, I stopped and made my way to a front place. The earth had caved in a few minutes before and crushed the breath out of a pair of ill-starred Celtic laborers.... Around them were a few men who had got them out, I suppose, and fifteen or twenty Irish women, wives, kinfolk or friends, who had got down there in some inexplicable way. The men were listless and inert enough, but not so the women. I suppose they were "keening"; all together were raising a wild, unearthly cry, half shriek and half song, wailing as a score of daylight Banshees, clapping their hands and gesticulating passionately.... It was an uncanny sound to hear, quite new to me.... Our Celtic fellow citizens are almost as remote from us in temperament and constitution as the Chinese.[60]

New York's *The Musical World* printed an article on "The Irish Keen" which included a transcription of keening originally published in the Halls' previously cited work on Ireland (fig. 6.5).[61] This transcription and the descriptions of a keen given above afford us some basis for evaluating John Barton's composition.

The sheet music edition of *The Irish Mother's Lament* notes that it is printed "as sung by Mrs. Seguin," a noted operatic soprano of the day. The fact that keens were the exclusive domain of Irish women suggests that Mr. McMichael conceived of "The Irish Mother's Lament" as a ballad rather than a keen. The piece lacks the traditional first section, the salutation, and the second section is more of a narrative than a keen text should be. And of course, a keen is neither sung in English nor accompanied by a piano.

The subtitle of the composition, "Song introducing the Irish Cry for the Dead," suggests that the keen is only a part of the whole song and, indeed, that appears to be the case. The third part of the keen, the wail, is artistically recreated at the end of each verse. The syllables "O Hone" and "Philla lilla leu" that Barton employed are very similar to the texts used in the last part of a keen.[62] The shape of the melody is similar enough to the Hall transcription to suggest Barton based the "O Hone" section on actual knowledge of keening.

Before a non-Irish-American audience, Barton's song could be passed over as a novelty. But the fact that the song was included in the repertory of both Seguin and McMichael, singers popular within the immigrant community, suggests that "The Irish Mother's Lament" represented something more within the Irish immigrant community. Even in recent times, Irish women have been reticent to keen outside of the proper context, believing that doing so would bring ill fortune upon them or their families.[63] Thus, it is hard to imagine a mid-nineteenth-century Irishman requesting to hear a keen for entertainment purposes. But in recreating a part of the keen within the artistic framework of another culture, the practice of keening loses some of its ritual "power"; keening becomes "safe," a reminiscence of the old country and its beliefs rather than an efficacious ritual act.

The survival of keening as an active tradition also depended upon the retention of the Irish language. In the mid-1850s, over 20 percent of the people of Ireland spoke Gaelic. But the retention of the Irish language was strongest in the western parts of Ireland, the very counties from which most of the emigrants to America departed. John Ridge has estimated that close to one-third of Irish-born New Yorkers would have spoken Irish in

FIGURE 6.5
Hall's Notation of Keening (transcription)

the years immediately before the Civil War. But Ridge has also noted the fact that Irish was a *spoken* language; the lack of Irish literacy doomed the survival of the language within a literate culture. Neither the Irish language nor the art of keening was fostered by the Catholic parish; neither practice would long survive in the new world.[64]

Irish Instrumental Music

Traditional Irish instrumental music was in a steady decline even in Ireland during the early nineteenth century. While the harp was still considered the national symbol of Eire, the great Irish harp tradition was fast waning. The *New York Freeman's Journal* noted a concert to be given in New York City by a certain Mr. Wall. As was not uncommon among Irish harp players, Mr. Wall was blind. The paper noted that he was "one of the few living representatives of the Irish Harper."[65] Thomas Mooney, always the champion of Ireland, was forced to acknowledge, in a roundabout fashion, that the Irish harp tradition had been lost or, at the very least, supplanted. "The harp of Erin is still vital, and, as it were, doubled in power by its transposition into the piano box, where, though struck by machinery instead of fingers, it preserves its original figure, and is governed by the original *laws* framed by the bards of that forgotten land."[66]

The tradition of Irish fiddling undoubtedly existed, but the fiddle was primarily used for accompaniment of dancing; the instrument was rarely employed in concerts, and is rarely mentioned in articles about Irish music. Casual references to the playing of the fiddle in relation to dancing aboard the ship bound for America or saloons have already been cited. The fiddle tradition does not seem to have been considered a part of the treasures of Irish civilization, and thus was neither included in concerts of Irish music nor referred to in the various articles which praised the music of Ireland.

There are few references to the *uillean* (or Union) pipes, the Irish form of bagpipes, and those references are often derogatory. But there appears to have been something of a revival of interest, or at least respectability, in the uilleann pipes in Boston of the mid-1850s. Regular advertisements began to appear in the *Boston Pilot* for a manufacturer of pipes:

IRISH BAG PIPES

Edward White, manufacturer of the union IRISH and SCOTCH BAG PIPES, Dallas Place (Ruggles St.) Roxbury, would most respectfully return thanks to his friends and customers for their former patronage and is hoping a continuance of same. By prompt attention and facilities which he now has, he can furnish the purchaser with an article superior to anything of the kind to be found in this country. . . . He also holds himself prepared to be present at all parties that his services are required to play upon the Union Pipes.[67]

Later that same year, the *Boston Pilot* noticed a concert by an Irish piper, Mr. C. Ferguson, and related that "he is said to be one of the best performers on the Union Pipes now living. Those who wish to hear the soft, plaintive melodies of the old land will not lose the present opportunity of hearing one of Ireland's most gifted sons."[68]

Music for St. Patrick's Day

Although not exclusively the preserve of the Catholic parish, St. Patrick's Day was celebrated with music in American parishes as early as the eighteenth century. The controversial Abbé de la Poterie, the first resident Catholic priest in Boston, announced in 1789 that "On the 17th of March, next, there will be sung at 11 o'clock A.M. a high mass in musick to honor St. Patrick, apostle of Ireland. All persons, particularly the Catholics, are desired to attend and join to our prayers for the propagation of the faith."⁶⁹

Mention has already been made of Catholic St. Patrick's Day celebrations in connection with temperance songs and devotional hymns. In the celebrations of the saint's feast day, many of the basic issues of the Irish Catholic immigrant are joined: the oppression of Ireland, the immigrant experience, and Catholic identity. The following song—attacking the taxation of the Irish to support the Church of Ireland—was sung "by a select choir, accompanied by a band" at the celebration of the Boston Charitable Irish Society on March 17, 1837:

> Air: "Paddy's Land"
>
> Poor Ireland! how long shall thy hardly earn'd treasures
> Be wrung from thy hand, that a priesthood may gorge,
> Who, year after year, are abroad on their pleasures,
> Or swelling the train of a William or George!
> 'Tis not so with thy sons on this side of the Ocean;
> Here we open our hands from the grateful emotion
> We feel to our priests, for their zeal and devotion,
> In removing our sins and the fetters they forge.⁷⁰

That the author of the lyrics was the Reverend Mr. Pierpont, a Catholic priest of Boston, suggests that the church was not opposed to using the celebrations to foster the image and importance of the Catholic church for the Irish immigrant.

Many of the new lyrics for traditional Irish tunes were composed to be sung during the series of formal toasts that followed St. Patrick's Day banquets. Between each formal toast appropriate music was scheduled, either instrumental or vocal. The first toast was inevitably to the day itself, accompanied with the air "St. Patrick's Day." The second toast was always to Ireland, accompanied by "Erin Go Bragh." A toast to the president of the United States was always made early in the proceedings, usually accompanied with "The President's March." "Yankee Doodle," "The Star Spangled Banner," and "Hail Columbia" were often heard with toasts to American figures; "Remember the Glories of Brian the Brave" and "The Meeting of the Waters" were popular tunes to accompany toasts related to Ireland. The following lyrics were written to the tune "The Meeting of the Waters" for the Young Men's Carroll Club celebration in New York, 1841, by Charles James Cannon:⁷¹

> O! well may his bosom with rapture expand,
>   Who boasts the Columbia his own native land:
> When freedom no longer by tyrant oppressed,
>   Has found for her sons an asylum of rest.
>
> But he whose cold breast no emotion inspires,
>   When insult is cast on the land of his sires:
> Who listens unmoved to the tale of her whoes [*sic*],
>   Deserves not the blessings that freedom bestows.
>
> O! Erin, our childhood was lulled with thy songs,
>   Our boyhood had burned at the tale of thy wrongs:
> And whilst we exult in our country's true fame,
>   Our best recollections are linked to thy name.
>
> Then drain we the wine cup, O Erin! to thee,
>   Not as thou now art, but as thou shalt be:
> And when the lost rights of thy nation's restored,
>   Thy perch thou shalt make where the Eagle has soared.[72]

The immigrants sang not only about their hopes for Ireland; they sang of their gratitude to America as well. Thomas Power penned the following lyrics to the air "Gramachree":

> There rose a light in western sky
>   One hundred years ago;
> It beamed from Pity's melting eye
>   To calm the sufferer's woe:
> The exile from his native shore
>   Beheld the gentle light,
> And dear the hope its promise bore
>   Upon the wanderer's sight.[73]

Parades celebrating St. Patrick's Day were held in cities such as New York and Philadelphia as far back as the eighteenth century. Originally organized by Americans of Scotch-Irish heritage, the parades saw Catholic influence and participation increase; by mid-century New York's parade was coordinated by a committee made up of representatives from all the major Irish Catholic organizations.[74] The parade, of course, employed a great number of bands to supply music, which included "the soul-stirring national airs of Old Ireland."[75] The 1856 parade in New York City included the Washington Brass Band, Stewart's Band, Whitworth's Band, Rohner's

Band, Robertson's Band, and Monahan's Band, as well as many more unnamed instrumental groups.[76] The names of the various bands suggest that many were non-Irish organizations. Manahan's Band, however, was noted for wearing the uniform of the Irish Volunteers, "a green frock coat and gold lace facings."[77] An advertisement indicates Manahan's Band was a professional organization, adaptable to the nature of the event: "Manahan's Brass Band. Civic and Military parades attended. Manahan's Quadrille Band attends balls, excursions, and private parties, supplying any number of musicians. Apply to Thomas Manahan, 270 Bowery, New York."[78]

Catholic parishes occasionally sponsored bands, either as temperance organizations, as noted above, or simply as a parish activity. In the 1850s both St. Mary's Church and St. Patrick's Church in Boston supported bands. Irish immigrants were also involved in professional bands. The noted American composer John Hill Hewitt recalled that the band at West Point was directed by an Irishman, Richard Willis: "To Captain Willis I am indebted for my musical education, for he was a good theorist as well as performer."[79] Perhaps the most famous Irish-American musician of the time was Patrick S. Gilmore, noted leader of the Boston Brass Band, the Boston Brigade Band, and, later, a band under his own name. Gilmore's active participation in parish musical affairs appears to have been limited. He did, however, conduct five soloists, a chorus of thirty, and an orchestra of twenty-one in Haydn's Mass No. 4 at Boston's Church of the Immaculate Conception on Easter Sunday, 1873.[80]

Summary

Because this chapter deals with many different sorts of music and musical activity, it is more difficult to provide simple answers to the questions used to summarize the previous chapters. Nevertheless, certain tendencies become apparent within each of the areas covered by the questions laid out in chapter 2.

First, it appears that performances of most of the music detailed in the present chapter were executed by a specialist of some sort. The practice of keening, requiring a knowledge of traditional form and practice, is an obvious example. But traditional Irish song was largely becoming the province of professional entertainers, who combined their performances with lectures on Irish music, culture, and history. The scant information available on Irish instrumental music is limited to the few teachers and manufacturers of uillean pipes. Much of the music for St. Patrick's Day celebrations was provided by hired—and often non-Irish—musicians.

The two exceptions to the specialization of musical performance are repeal and temperance songs. While repeal songs were often sung by professional musicians during rallies to gain support for the Irish cause, the songs were also published and distributed for use at home. As noted above, music associated with Catholic temperance societies was designed to be performed by the membership at large; musical activity was stressed, rather than any particular repertory of music.

Second, the choice of the music employed was governed by both traditional guidelines and public preferences. Keening, although frowned upon by church authority, remained a necessary element of death rituals for many of the immigrants. Irish song and instrumental music was a repertory including both the traditional airs, as adapted by Moore, and new compositions by composers such as Lover. The choice of repertory was guided largely by the performer, who presumably blended his own preferences with those of the paying public. The repertory of repeal songs was largely chosen by leaders of the political movement, whether the songs were adaptations of Moore's ballads, as in Thomas Mooney's works, or new texts wedded to new music, as in the Shea-King collaboration. Finally, the Catholic temperance movement can scarcely be said to have had a repertory. There were no collections of temperance songs as found in the Protestant movement. The stress on musical activity rather than repertory meant that temperance music within the Catholic movement consisted of whatever music a temperance organization performed.

The third concern is the financial aspect of musical performance. Musical organizations within temperance societies performed to raise money for the support of charitable organizations, particularly orphanages. Repeal songs financed activities that were more political in nature. The major goal of repeal organizations in America was to encourage support, both moral and financial, for the independence movement in Ireland. Thus, when food became a higher priority for Ireland than independence, the repeal organizations were supplanted by relief organizations. In both cases, musical activity was one means employed to raise the necessary funds.

The concerts of Irish song performed by artists such as Lover, McMichael, and White were business ventures, designed to raise money for the performer and promoter. For many of the immigrants, coming from the rural west of Ireland, Irish concerts were the immigrants' first experience of being consumers of music. The hiring of bands for St.

Patrick's Day was yet another aspect of the commercial development of music within the Irish-American community. Perhaps only the keen, when performed within the rites for the dead, retained a noncommercial status.[81]

On one level, the ritual contexts of each of the types of music discussed appear quite different. Temperance music was performed within a meeting of a moral "support-group." Repeal songs were sung as part of political rallies. Keening was an expression of grief within traditional death rituals. Irish song was more and more performed within the emerging rituals of the concert hall. The celebration of St. Patrick's Day was a complex mix of civic, national, and religious ritual. Yet all the diverse ritual contexts served similar purposes, providing a sense of community identity and stability within a community experiencing rapid change. The most enduring of all these rituals, the celebration of St. Patrick's Day, was in a sense the combination of all the others. The celebrations of the day uplifted the community just as the temperance movement did and expressed support for Ireland as the repeal organization did. The celebrations reminded the immigrants of what they had left behind, as did the keening heard at their departure from Eire; the traditional Irish songs were sung now, not in the homeland, but in ritualized concerts which recreated that home, if only for an evening, and displayed the "glories of Irish culture" to America.

The sources of texts and tunes is the fifth area of concern and is, perhaps, the clearest connection between the diverse musical activities surveyed in the present chapter. In much of the music employed, there is a conscious use of traditional tunes, particularly the tunes as transmitted through Thomas Moore and Sir John Stevenson. When new tunes were composed, such as by Lover or Mooney, the tunes are clearly modeled on traditional techniques. The lament by John Barton demonstrates the combination of Irish phrases into a popular style of song writing. The relative ease with which Irish traditional material could be received into Anglo-American song was largely due to Thomas Moore's recension of the material; Moore had, in effect, already Anglicized Irish music to an extent the Irish themselves would realize only in later years.

Although traditional texts—that is, Thomas Moore texts—remained current, the immigrant community frequently altered or entirely recomposed texts to suit the new surroundings. Many texts were written for use at a particular occasion and then forgotten; some few gained a lasting place in the repertory of Irish-American secular song. For example, dozens of texts written to the tune "St. Patrick's Day" can be located; only a few, such as "Hail Glorious Apostle," endured more than a short time in active use.

Finally, running through most of the music discussed in the present chapter is the tension between love of Ireland and devotion to America. The Irish immigrants felt themselves exiles, forced from their native land; yet they prized the ideals of the new country they had entered. As they had demanded their rights in Ireland, but lost them there, so too would the immigrants demand their rights in America, even in the face of the hostility of the so-called nativists. The music of temperance stresses Irish responsibility to exercise the rights of freedom; repeal songs show the Irish fighting for their rights in Ireland, and implicitly, in America as well.

The music employed in the celebration of St. Patrick's Day suggests not so much a melting pot as an eclectic mix. Erin was toasted to the sounds of "Gramachree"; the United States Constitution toasted to "Yankee Doodle." No societies or choirs were founded specifically to preserve the musical culture of Ireland, as they were among German and later Eastern European immigrants. The Irish immigrants employed the music at hand, both traditional, borrowed, and newly composed, to suit the needs and goals of the growing Irish-*American* community.

CHAPTER SEVEN

"We Hung Our Harps on the Willows"

> On the willows there
> We hung up our harps....
> How shall we sing ... in a foreign land?
> (Psalm 137)

In an 1844 article in the *New York Freeman's Journal*, an Irish immigrant to America wrote, "We hung our harps on the willows, and mourn ever the departed glories of our native land."[1] But the harp had already ceased to be the heart of Irish music, and remained only the symbol of Eire: a people brought low by famine, and a culture and economy destroyed by colonial rule. A Donegal woman recalled the famine she had survived thirty years before:

> It didn't matter who was related to you, your friend was whoever would give you a bite to put in your mouth. Sport and pastimes disappeared. Poetry, music, and dancing stopped. They lost and forgot them all, and when the times improved in other respects, these things never returned as they had been.... The famine killed everything.[2]

A new musical life would grow up in Ireland from the vestiges of the old, just as an Irish-American musical life would develop in the United States. But the two paths had parted, and would go on in different directions.

Recent ethnomusicological studies of immigrant populations have stressed the necessity of investigating three dimensions of the immigrant musical experience. Adelaida Reyes Schramm refers to the divisions as pre-departure features, departure-related features, and resettlement features.[3]

The first has been the traditional focus of ethnomusicological studies, while the third has lately become a subject of investigation. It is the second division, the departure-related features, that Schramm suggests is overlooked.

The predeparture features of Irish musical life have been studied elsewhere, and have been only peripherally noted here.[4] It is necessary, however, to point out that the musical life of prefamine Ireland was already in a period of rapid change. The transcriptions of traditional Irish song recorded by Edward Bunting in the last years of the eighteenth century marked the transition of Irish song from an oral to a written form of transmission. Bunting's transcriptions became a primary source for the work of Moore and Stevenson. And we have already seen that the Thomas Moore–John Stevenson edition of traditional Irish tunes was an Anglicized recension of the songs. In the nineteenth century, Ireland was hearing English and American songs, and the songs were becoming a part of Irish musical life.

An American visitor to Ireland just before the great famine provides a fine example of the eclectic repertory heard in mid-nineteenth-century Ireland. Mr. DuSolle, editor of the *Philadelphia Times*, spoke with his driver in Ireland:

> We coaxed him to give us an Irish song, and for an hour he delighted us with old ballads, in a language that was, discourse, all Lyrine or Coptic to us, but that was enlarged to the wildest melodies that ever entered the music-chambers of a human heart.... Imagine our surprise, when he suddenly stopped and sang, in a touching style that would have done credit to a drawing room, "Woodman, spare that tree."[5]

Henry Russell's song—from a poem by George P. Morris—had been popularized in both the United States and England through Russell's tours. But Russell brought more than his own compositions across the Atlantic. Mr. DuSolle went on to note that

> as for the "Ethiopian melodies" they are as common here as at home. Russell has been singing them all over England, (claiming the music as his own—'Heaven save the mark!') the theatres in Dublin, Cork, etc. furnish them nightly, and we heard two urchins whistle one in the streets of Ballyvourney.[6]

Chapters 3 through 6 of the present work have been concerned with resettlement-related features. But just as British and American songs had been heard in Ireland before the great famine, Irish music had made its presence felt in England and America as well. The popularity of Moore's songs in the United States, together with the earlier transmission of Irish folk tunes into America through the Scotch-Irish immigrants, meant that the Irish immigrant did not enter into an entirely foreign musical culture. Charles Hamm has succinctly noted that "the Irish came early and often to America."[7] But the continuous exchange of musical repertory back and forth across the Atlantic makes the tracing of musical influences difficult; it is entirely possible that an Irishman first learned a traditional Irish tune in Boston or New York and an American minstrel-show tune in Cork or Limerick.

Deciphering the impact on American musical development of the great Irish migration of the mid-nineteenth century is also a difficult, perhaps impossible, task. For example, Peter Van der Merwe has noted that musical features considered characteristically African appear in Celtic music as well, citing the falling melodic line of an Irish keen as an example.[8] Furthermore, the close contact between African- and Irish-Americans in the pre–Civil War years suggests that musical features may have been exchanged between the two groups in spite of racial barriers. Charles Dickens's description of a dance hall in New York's Five Points slum, quoted in chapter 1, suggests one point of contact between Irish-Americans and African-Americans. Van der Merwe quotes an 1876 description of "these negro singers . . . [who] can mimic the Irish accent to a degree of perfection which an American, Englishman or German could not hope to acquire."[9] While the two races rarely lived together harmoniously, elements of their traditional musics may well have.

Departure-related features of the Irish immigrant musical experience have been noted whenever available. Perhaps the most striking contrast is between the keening at the "American wake" the night before departure from the emigrant's home, and reports of fiddling and dancing on board the ship to America. But unlike many immigrants, the Irish rarely encountered other cultures on the trip across the Atlantic. Although the majority of the Irish traveled first to Liverpool, in England, to embark on the Atlantic crossing, mid-nineteenth-century passenger lists show that vessels crossing from Liverpool to New York with Irish immigrants carried almost exclusively Irish passengers.

But perhaps the most important departure-related feature, according to Schramm, is the nature of the migration: is the migration voluntary or involuntary?[10] The sense of loss is tempered for the voluntary migrant by the possibility of return; the sense of loss is compounded for the involuntary migrant by the lack of that possibility. In the case of the early- and mid-nineteenth-century Irish emigration, the question is not simply answered.

The Irish were both attracted to the freedom and economic possibilities in America and repulsed by the repression and poverty of Ireland. But the Irish who fled the great famine are more properly called refugees than emigrants. Although some emigrants did return to Ireland, even after 1850, the famine seems to have acted as a symbol of the hopeless future of life in the old country. In the years after the Civil War a distinctive Irish-American musical culture developed; but the ideas and attitudes which formed this culture are evident even in the antebellum United States.

There are many possible ways in which the music-making of the mid-nineteenth-century Irish immigrant can be viewed. One could look to the issue of music literacy and publishing, for example. The earliest Catholic hymnbooks produced in America were text-only collections, such as Challoner's *Garden of the Soul* or Cheverus's *Roman Catholic Manual*, suggesting that tunes were usually transmitted orally. The early notated-music collections of Catholic church music, such as Aitken's, Carr's, and Walter's, were directed toward musicians. As non-Catholic musicians were hired to direct music in Catholic churches, the collections served as a means of transmitting the Catholic repertory to musicians largely ignorant of it. But a third stage begins in the 1840s, with inexpensive notated hymnals, directed at the general Catholic public, hymnals such as Hoerner's, Kirk's and Rohr's. These publications, as well as the growing amount of sheet music published for Catholics, enabled the literate amateur to recreate hymns and songs in the home or school, without a professional musician.

As the arrival of immigrants was transforming American Catholicism into an urban church, the music of the immigrants, both sacred and secular, was being transformed as well. Advances in printing encouraged the production of "cheap" editions of music; the urban setting led to a greater exposure to styles and types of music. In rural Kentucky, however, less influenced by the arrival of the immigrants, the repertory remained remarkably stable. Elliott's 1855 collection of church music could easily be mistaken for a Catholic music book of the 1830s: many of its selections were contained in Aitken's 1787 collection. In urban New York, Boston, or Philadelphia, on the other hand, the repertory changed and grew quickly after 1840.

But the history of music is not simply about changes in repertory or technology. John Blacking has noted that musical changes occur because *individuals* make creative decisions about music and the process of music-making within their own social context.[11] Individuals are not isolated from one another; they learn from teachers and peers, and are influenced by events and developments around them. Two examples, one from Boston, the other from Philadelphia, may help illustrate the connections linking some of the individuals previously mentioned.

In Boston, as elsewhere in America, the musical compositions of the Englishman Samuel Webbe were an important part of the Catholic church-music repertory. Webbe, trained by Carl Barbandt, was most likely his daughter Cecilia's music teacher; Cecilia married D. L. Brown and came to Boston, where she was organist at the Catholic cathedral throughout the 1830s, as noted earlier. Mrs. Browne, described by her choir members as having a "tyrannical mode of proceeding," undoubtedly was a significant force in the musical education of one Walter Madigan, a member of the Cathedral choir throughout the 1830s. Madigan, in turn, became a significant figure in Catholic Boston of the 1850s as conductor of the choir of St. Mary's church, the largest Catholic parish in Boston. Madigan used one of the few surviving copies of Fenwick's hymnal of 1833, a hymnal that contained a number of compositions and chant arrangements by Samuel Webbe and one by Cecilia Brown, even though it had been superseded by Richard Garbett's 1840 collection.[12] Thus the London embassy-chapel tradition of music was passed on in Boston until broken by Anthony Werner's influence as cathedral organist, publisher of musical instruction books, compiler of music collections, and composer.

In Philadelphia, an individual such as William Augustine Newland was linked to many important aspects of American music, aspects which reach back to the eighteenth century and look forward to the twentieth. Newland was trained by Leopold Meignen and Benjamin Cross; Newland in turn would teach Cross's grandson. His friendship with Charles Zeuner brought him into contact with American Protestant music; as professor of music at Villanova and St. Charles Seminary, Newland had a virtual monopoly on music in Philadelphia's Catholic men's colleges. He helped William Henry Fry with the musical preparation for the premiere of Fry's opera *Leonora*, and was prompter at the first performance. Among the members of his choir at Philadelphia's Holy Trinity church was Francis Drexel, founder of the famed banking company. Drexel and his sons collected a vast musical library, unsuccessfully offering to purchase items from Newland; the Drexel collection was given to New York's Lenox Library, eventually forming the basis of what is now the New York Public Library's Music Research Division.[13]

From the documentation of the immigrant musical life within the Catholic parish contained in the preceding chapters, a number of attitudes toward music emerge, attitudes which would help shape the Irish-American community's future musical preferences: first, the way in which the immigrant community regarded the European fine art musical tradition; second, the broad musical preferences of the community; and third, the adaptation of the immigrant musical life as the community moved from a largely rural colonial environment to an urban capitalist economy.

Fine Art and the Immigrant

The mid-nineteenth-century United States experienced the beginnings of modern music education, the movement Charles Seeger has called the "urban, make-America-musical intellectualism."[14] But the stress on the intellectual nature of the movement is perhaps misplaced; as I endeavored to show in chapter 2, the advocacy of the European fine-art tradition of music, especially by a man such as John S. Dwight, might be styled as much a religious movement as an intellectual one. Irving Lowens has referred to Dwight as "virtually the Transcendental pope of music."[15] Influenced by Transcendentalist philosophy and Unitarian theology, he considered the works of the great masters a sort of divine revelation, "the language of *natural religion*" according to Dwight.[16]

> This is the love of God, as it is also, from the first, the inbreathing of God, who is love; to whom the soul seeks its way.... Music is its natural language, the chief rite of its worship ... for music cannot cease to be harmony, cannot cease to symbolize the sacred relationship of each to all.[17]

Dwight, as editor of *Dwight's Journal of Music*, the leading American music journal from 1852 until it ceased publication in 1881, had an enormous influence on the development of the musical "establishment" in the United States. Dwight's celebrated battle with William Henry Fry made Dwight's position clear: only the highest forms of musical art should be cultivated in America, and the greatest manifestations of musical genius were German, with Beethoven the highest of all.[18]

Dwight was certainly not alone in the nineteenth-century sacralization of art, a movement which contributed to the construction of music halls as "temples," and the development of the elaborate concert "rituals" prevalent even today. But the movement was not shared by the Irish immigrant to America. As demonstrated in chapters 3 and 4, Catholic choirs, frequently made up largely of Irish parishioners, performed the liturgical works of Haydn, Mozart, and Beethoven, perhaps most often within worship, but occasionally in concert as well. But while Protestant visitors to a

Catholic church, such as George Templeton Strong, may have appreciated a Mozart mass *as* worship, the Catholic community heard the composition as music *for* worship.

The distinction does not mean to imply that Catholic immigrants had no aesthetic appreciation of the works of Haydn and Mozart they often heard in their churches, but that the ritual context for which the masses were written was still a living tradition for the immigrant. The Latin texts were neither foreign nor exotic, even if the listener knew no Latin. The minimal exposure to the "great composers" of Western music did not suggest to the immigrant that musical creations are autonomous, but rather that even art music was inherently functional. Music was used *for* some practical purpose, whether worship or dancing, story-telling or lamentation. The purely aesthetic contemplation of music was as foreign to the Irish immigrant in America as it was to the Irish peasant in the west of Ireland.

The difference in attitude between the growing musical establishment and the Irish immigrant is significant because the musical establishment tended more and more toward the "enthronement" of Western art music, with the effect of distancing compositions of this kind from people who conceived of music in a much more practical way. Thus Mozart and Beethoven became "high-brow." Irish-American musicians and entertainers, however, who came to dominate the popular stage, became famous as performers of "low-brow" music in the post–Civil War era.

Italian versus German

As earlier chapters have shown, the small repertory of music brought from Ireland was not sufficient to meet the needs of the immigrant community. New music, composed from within and without the immigrant community, was accepted into the repertory. The most striking aspect of the new repertory, ranging from orchestral masses to popular songs, is the Italianate character of much of the music. Some compositions were from Italian composers such as Mercadante; others were adaptations of Donizetti or Bellini arias; still other compositions were of American origin, but display influences derived from nineteenth-century Italian opera, as in the songs of the so-called Bristow school.

The popularity of the works of Donizetti, Bellini, and Rossini was, of course, widespread across America. Performances of Italian opera were given by touring European companies; arias and duets from the operas appeared with English lyrics (either translations or entirely new verses) in sheet-music form for use in the home. Yet the Irish appear to have had a particular affinity for nineteenth-century Italian music. An early article in the Irish-American press attempted to "prove that our [Irish] music is only inferior to the Italian, in affecting eloquence, touching expression, and euphonious harmony."[19] At times extraordinary claims were made for the influence of Irish music: an 1847 article held that "the fragmental remains of Ireland have supplied England, Scotland, aye, and Italy, with a great part of their present stock of music."[20] The validity of the claims is unimportant; both statements reflect a level of esteem for Italian music.

The affinity between Irish musicians and Italian music is also highlighted by the two most successful non-Italian composers of "Italianate" opera: Michael William Balfe and William Vincent Wallace. Both men were Irish by birth, although the former received much of his training in Italy, while the latter was Dublin-trained. Nevertheless, two Irishmen were the best and most popular imitators of the operatic school of Donizetti and Bellini.

Extra-musical forces may also have helped sway Irish-Americans toward Italian rather than German musical preferences. By mid-century the most prominent German composers were often Protestants, while the Italian composers were considered coreligionists. The *Boston Pilot*, as quoted earlier, held that "there are no musicians like the children of the Catholic faith."[21] As American Catholics increasingly looked to Rome for guidance, the same newspaper extolled the papacy as the true benefactor of music.[22] Rossini's *Stabat Mater*, performed in whole or part during numerous Catholic concerts, was held to be "the gem of Catholic music."[23] Italian singers touring America were often persuaded to donate their services for the Sunday mass or for a benefit concert for a Catholic charity; these performances exposed the Irish immigrants to a caliber of singer they might not have otherwise heard.[24]

But while Italianate music continued to hold sway over the immigrant community, German orchestral music was becoming the preference of the musical establishment. John Dwight acknowledged his "strong preference of German to Italian music," focusing on the music of Mozart, Beethoven, and Mendelssohn. Dwight also admitted that "should some meteoric Wagner or other musical comet strike both the Verdi and Bellini operas out of existence, we could contemplate without more dismay than when we part with the peculiar beauties of one tract of country on a journey."[25] In contrast to Italian opera, the work of the German masters was sacralized by musicians such as Dwight which, as Lawrence Levine has noted, "rendered it inviolate, exclusive, and eternal."[26] Indeed, Italian opera eventually underwent a similar process, but as early as 1858 *Dwight's Journal* would look with relief "upon the decent, well-dressed audience ... upon the general aspect of refinement which so distinguishes an opera from a common theatre audience."[27] Yet the journal also reminded its readers that "to be a popular Italian *prima donna* or *tenore* it is not thought at all indispensable to be in any deep sense a musician."[28]

Dwight was not alone in the campaign for the "best musical taste." A writer for New York's *Evening Post* held that

> the history of music in this country shows that by a few only, patiently and in silence, has the tender spark, wafted here from the parent fire in Germany, been nursed; only by degrees has it grown under their care to a steady flame. Recently, however, the happy issue of their labors has become apparent.... Their disciples are increasing, and a taste for the best music is gradually increasing.[29]

The *New York Musical Review* and *Dwight's Journal* held hope that the powers of music might even save the "forsaken boys and girls, with strong Irish accent, who ... sleep in carts and coal boxes" of New York's worst slum:

> Thus does the music to which they listen become to them, like Noah's dove, a harbinger of better things.... Who does not see that music is thus exerting a powerful influence for the redemption of this district of vice and crime? ... If, therefore, instead of a chapel holding three or four hundred persons, the House of Industry, or some similar institution, were provided with one accommodating one thousand or fifteen hundred, what a powerful auxiliary free concerts might become, in connection with the other agencies employed, for the redemption of the Five-Points![30]

To the chagrin of the reformers, the Irish immigrant—unlike the German—preferred what was characterized as "illiterate music":

> There is such a thing as illiterate music; rude, low, vulgar, it is made up of cant phrases, disconnected melodies, usually, not necessarily erroneous harmony; it has a kind of "hum-drum" rhythm, all of which are offensive to good taste and refined musical sensibilities. It is generally found among the ignorant and the rude; always among the low and vulgar.[31]

At least one correspondent for *Dwight's Journal* found the Catholics of Maryland—economically better established than most Catholics in America—an obstacle in the development of a proper musical culture:

> I do not think our city would have been so slow in acquiring a taste for High Art, if it were not for the influence of the Catholic schools in this part of the State. With more wealth than is usual with Catholic communities, with everything calculated to bring them in connection with the highest music, so much of which has been composed for the Church, *our* Catholics . . . have an obstinate fondness for Russell's "thrilling flights," (witness "Maniac," "Newfoundland Dog," &c,) or Dempster's "soul-and-eye-filling pathos" (See "Blind Boy," "Irish Emigrant's Lament," &c.)...[32]

The writer goes on to note that the state of affairs has improved somewhat in recent times. At the Georgetown Convent school, for example, "Opera (Italian) music is kept on hand, and considered a sort of angel's food. It is safer not to ask for any German music, lest you should get it."

Robert Toll, in his study of the minstrel show, notes the hostile attitude of the early minstrels toward the Irish. He shows that in the 1840s the Irishman was portrayed as a stupid, violent drunkard who represented a real danger to the country. But in the 1850s, as Irishmen such as Dan Bryant, Matt Campbell, and George Christy became prominent figures on the minstrel stage, minstrelsy's view of the Irishman was softened.[33] In the process of urbanization, many Irish musicians evolved from itinerant rural entertainers to stage personalities. When Edward Harrigan removed his blackface in the 1870s, he created a new opportunity for the Irish performer, and a new image of the Irish immigrant.

The Irish immigrant community did not follow the lead of the musical establishment; rather, the immigrants held fast to the types of musical expression which they had previously enjoyed and they created new ones. The German orchestral tradition remained foreign to them, and the reform of Catholic church music at the end of the nineteenth century resulted in less familiarity with the works of Haydn and Mozart, whose liturgical works had commonly been heard in Catholic parishes. But while the concert hall became the temple of a sacralized art for the musical elite, the Irish immigrants' church remained their temple, and theater their entertainment. In the years following the Civil War, few Irish were involved in the performance of "classical" music, yet the popular musical theater would be filled with "Irish" performers performing "Irish" music.

Adapting to a Not-So-Foreign Land

Lawrence Levine has noted that the trend toward the sacralization of the fine art of music was accompanied by a rejection of what had been standard concert programming: the mixture of various styles and genres of music, the interpolation of a folk song into an Italian opera, Mozart and Moore intermingled.[34] But the repertory the Irish immigrant encountered in the Catholic parish was an eclectic one, preserving elements of a folk tradition, incorporating elements of European art music, and creating a variety of new compositions to meet the needs of the community.

The religious toleration which the Irish encountered in the United States had allowed an institutionalized church to develop. Where Ireland had few Catholic churches relative to the population, parishes were founded in the United States wherever the immigrants settled. In contrast to the silence of Irish worship services, the American church could call upon a variety of Catholic musical traditions for services. The liturgical works of Haydn and Mozart, Gregorian chant, folk tunes, and contemporary compositions from American, Italian, and even Spanish composers form the diverse repertory to which the immigrant worshiper was exposed.

The growth of devotional practices, Sunday schools, and sodalities provided occasions for the use of English-language songs within the parish. Often the songs were composed in easily accessible styles, popularly employed for secular compositions as well as sacred. Although some Irish musical elements were retained, the "popular songs of ritual" generally maintained a stylistic similarity with contemporaneous American song. But American song had already been influenced by, among other things, Irish song, particularly the ballads of Thomas Moore.

The "music of popular ritual" surrounding the parish aided the survival of particular Irish melodies and musical features, but it also facilitated the immigrants' exposure to American compositions. Lawrence McCullough has suggested that it was precisely the fusion of American and Irish musical traditions which led to many of the popular musical forms of the post–Civil War period, particularly Irish "stage" music.[35] The final years of the nineteenth century witnessed the birth of a truly Irish-American repertory of song, identified by American Irish as symbolic of their heritage, but vastly different from the traditional music of Ireland, which began to be revived about the same time.

Musically, the Irish immigrants did not find themselves in such a foreign land. The Irish community preserved aspects of an earlier culture but swiftly adapted themselves to become producers and consumers of an American product. McCullough has noted that Irish musicians in mid-nineteenth-century America swiftly moved into the growing entertainment industry in America, and by the last decades of the century Irish-American performers—identified as Irish—reached their greatest fame.[36] In the twentieth century, Irish-American musicians did not disappear but became so identified with the mainstream of American music that their "foreign" identity was lost. For example, Nicholas Tawa, in his study of ethnic music in America after the Civil War, does not consider the Irish community as part of "ethnic America."[37] Irish traditional music endured in America, as McCullough has documented, but as a specialized tradition even within the Irish-American community. And for many Americans of Irish heritage, the ancestral land is celebrated in songs such as "My Wild Irish Rose" and "McNamara's Band," as foreign to traditional Irish music as any American composition.

History has not treated the music of the Irish immigrant community well. Histories of American Catholic music speak of the mid-nineteenth century as a period of "general decline in church music . . . hastened by the large number of English and Irish immigrants."[38] But the present study has shown that the Catholic parish was a rich center of musical life for the Irish immigrant in America. Judgment of the musical repertories employed by the immigrants has been clouded by the reform of Catholic church music in the early years of the present century, a reform that rejected orchestral masses and contemporary musical styles in favor of a restored plainchant. The extensive employment of music considered "illiterate" by the musical establishment also injured the reputation of Irish-American musical life. But the immigrants themselves appear to have been content with the music encountered through the parish, participating in its creation, adding to the repertory, and employing the music in a myriad of circumstances.

The harps may have been hung on the willows, but only to allow free hands to play the piano and organ, the guitar and horn. And while a part of the immigrant mourned the native land, another part of the immigrant embraced the possibilities that America provided. The culture the Irishman knew was gone. The farmer had moved to the city, the oppressed became a capitalist, the harpist became a pianist. The immigrant retained some traditions, adapted others, and accepted entirely new ideas. The Irish in America would have a profound effect on the development of popular music in America, as performers and consumers of American culture. And the musical traditions that developed made the immigrants feel less and less that they were singing in a foreign land.

Appendix

AMERICAN CATHOLIC MUSIC COLLECTIONS TO 1860

Sigla

US Bp	Boston Public Library—Music Department
US Cn	Newberry Library, Chicago
US NYp	New York City Public Library, Lincoln Center
US NYts	Union Theological Seminary Library, New York City
US PROu	Brown University Libraries, Providence
US Ps	Pittsburgh Theological Seminary
US Wc	Library of Congress, Washington, D.C.
US Wcu	Catholic University Library, Washington, D.C.
US WOa	American Antiquarian Society, Worcester
US Wgu	Georgetown University, Washington, D.C.
EAI	Early American Imprints, 1638–1820 (Readex Corp. Microprint edition)

The following list provides the location of copies of the works cited which the author has viewed; it does not intend to be a comprehensive list of extant copies.

1774

The Garden of the Soul, or Manual of Spiritual Exercises and Instructions for Christians Who (Living in the World) Aspire to Devotion. London printed, Philadelphia reprinted: Joseph Crukshank, 1774.
Text only.   US Wgu

1787

A Compilation of Litanies, Vesper Hymns and Anthems as They Are Sung in the Catholic Church Adapted to Voice or Organ by John Aitken. Philadelphia: John Aitken, 1787.
Re-issued in facsimile edition. Philadelphia: Musical Americana, 1956.
                                                                                        EAI, US NYp, WOa

1791

A Compilation of Litanies, Vesper Hymns & Anthems As They Are Sung in the Catholic Church. Philadelphia: Printed and Sold by John Aitken, 1791.
                  EAI, US NYp, WOa

1798

Cantique Français à l'usage du Catéchisme de l'Eglise de Saint-Patrice de Baltimore. Baltimore: Jean Hayes, pour le compte de Jacques Rice et Comp., 1798.
Text only.   US Ps, Wc, WOa

1800

Anthems, Hymns, &c. Usually Sung at the Catholick Church in Boston. Boston: Printed by Manning & Loring, 1800.
Text only.   EAI, US Wgu

1803

Roman Catholic Manual, or Collection of Prayers, Anthems, Hymns, etc. Boston: Printed by Manning & Loring, No. 2 Cornhill. December, 1803. 287 pp.
Text only.   EAI, US Wgu

1804

Hymns of the Roman Catholic Church: As Now Sung in the Different Churches Throughout the United States, on Days of Worship and Devotion. Baltimore: By John B. Dizabeau, 1804.
Only known copy (at Loyola College, Baltimore) was destroyed by fire in 1956.

1805

Masses, Vespers, Litanies, Hymns, Psalms, Anthems and Motetts. Composed, selected and arranged for the use of the Catholic Churches in the United States of America and respectfully dedicated by permission to the Right Reverend John Carroll, D.D., Bishop of Baltimore by Benjamin Carr. Sold by J. Carr, Baltimore; G. Blake, Philadelphia; J. Hewitt, New York; & F. Mallet, Boston, 1805.
                 EAI, US NYp, Ps, WOa

1807

Hymns for the Use of the Catholic Church of the United States of America. A new edition, with additions and improvements. Baltimore: John West Butler, 1807.
Text only   EAI, US NYts, Wgu, WOa

1808

A New Edition with an Appendix of Masses, Vespers, Litanies, Hymns, Psalms, Anthems & Motetts, Composed, Selected and Arranged for the use of the Catholic Churches in the United States of America Respectfully Dedicated by permission to the Right Rev. John Carroll by Benjamin Carr. Sold by J. Carr, Baltimore; G. Blake, Philadelphia; J. Hewitt, New York; & F. Mallet, Boston [before 1808].

US NYp

1809

Catéchisme, ou Abrégé de la Doctrine Chrétienne. Suivi de la Prière du Matin et du Soir, des Prières pour la Ste. Messe. Pour la Confession et la Communion; et de Quelques Cantiques Spirituels. Baltimore: Imprimé, pour Bernard Dornin, 1809.

Pages 222–76 contain the texts of numerous Cantiques spirituels. EAI

1811

Recueil de Cantiques à l'usage de la Congrégation établie parmi les élèves du College de Ste. Marie Sous le Nom de Société de la Ste. Familie. Baltimore: G. Dobbin & Murphy, 1811.

US Wgu

Roman Catholic Manual, or a Collection of Prayers, Anthems, Hymns, &c. With approbation of the Rt. Rev. Bishop. Boston: J. T. Buckingham, 1811. 184 pp.

EAI, US Wgu

1814

A Compilation of Litanies, Vespers, Chants, Hymns, and Anthems As Used in the Catholic Churches of Philadelphia and throughout the United States. A New Edition, Carefully revised and corrected from the former editions. Philadelphia: published and sold by Charles Taws, at his music store No.61, South Third Street, 1814. 87 pp.

A revision of Aitken's 1791 collection. US Wc, WOa

The Roman Catholic Prayer-Book, or Devout Christian's Vade Mecum; being a summary of select and necessary devotions, hymns, etc. Third Baltimore edition. Baltimore: Printed by William Werner, 1814.

US WOa

1815

Collection of Sacred Hymns, for the Use of the Catholic Churches, in Kentucky. Bardstown: Bard and Edrington, 1815.

US NYts, WOa

1816

Collection of Sacred Music, Chants, Anthems, Hymns. Philadelphia: B. Carr, 1816.
US NYp

A Short Abridgment of Catholic Doctrine, newly revised for the use of the Catholic Church, in the United States of America. To which is prefixed a short daily exercise. . . . Georgetown, D.C.: Printed by Wm. Duffy, 1816.
US WOa

1817

The Pious guide to prayer and devotion. Containing various practices of piety, calculated to answer the demands of the devout members of the Roman Catholic Church. The fourth edition, revised and augmented. . . . Georgetown, D.C.: Printed by William Duffy . . . , 1817.
Text only
US WOa

1820

Marianisches Blumen-Gärtlein, oder vollständiges Gebet-Buch, Zu der schmerzhaften Mutter Gottes Maria, das ist: Auserlesenes Marianisches Gebet-Buch, in sich begreifend; Morgen- Abend- Mess- Beicht- und Communion-Gebete. Libanon, [PA]. Gedruckt bey Joseph Hartman, 1820.
US WOa

1823

Cheverus, Bishop John. *Roman Catholic Manual, or a collection of prayers, anthems, hymns, &c. With approbation of the Rt. Rev. Bishop.* Boston: Ezra Lincoln, 1823.
Text only.
US Wgu

1825

Ancient and Modern Music selected for the use of the Catholic Church, containing litanies, masses, vespers, anthems, hymns, and choruses for the seasons, festivals or other occasions. Arranged for the pianoforte or organ by Jacob Walter. Baltimore: George Willig, Jr. [c.1825].
US NYp

1830

A Collection of Psalms, Hymns, Anthems, etc. (With the Evening Office.) For the Use of the Catholic Church Throughout the United States Permissu Superiorum. Washington, J. F. Haliday, 1830.
Text only.
US NYts, Wcu, Wgu

1832

A Collection of Psalms, Hymns, Anthems, etc.(With the Evening Office.) For the Use of the Catholic Church Throughout the United States Permissu Superiorum. Second edition. Washington, Thompson & Homans, 1832.
Text only.
    US Wgu

1833

The Catholic Church Service Book. Comprising a choice collection of Gregorian and other Masses, of Sacred Hymns, Anthems, Versicles and Mottets, both for the morning and evening service; taken out of the public liturgy of the Catholic Church. The whole Composed, Selected and Arranged by the first Masters, with a Separate Accompaniment for the Organ or Pianoforte. Part I. Boston: Published at the request of the present bishop of Boston for the use of his diocese, 1833 [Preface].
    US Bp

1834

Ancient and Modern Music selected for the use of the Catholic Church, containing litanies, masses, vespers, anthems, hymns, and choruses for the seasons, festivals or other occasions. Arranged for the pianoforte or organ by Jacob Walter. Baltimore: John Cole, 1834.
Same contents as 1825 edition.
    No copy located.

1835

Vesper Book, containing chants for Vespers; hymns and motetts, for morning and evening service; with a separate accompaniment for the organ or pianoforte, respectfully inscribed to the Rev. James Cummiskey & Rev. C.C. Pise, D.D., pastors of St. Joseph's church, New York, by the American publisher. Philadelphia: Eugene Cummiskey, n.d. [1835].
    US NYts

1836

Twelve Easy Masses. Philadelphia: Eugene Cummiskey, 1836.
This is the second installment of a projected four-part series which began with the *Vesper Book*: for contents, see *Catholic Herald* 4 (1836): 180.
    No copy located.

1840

The Morning and Evening Service of the Catholic Church, Comprising a Choice Collection of Gregorian and other Masses; Litanies, Psalms, Sacred Hymns.

Anthems, Versicles and Motetts . . . Compiled and Respectfully Dedicated to Rt. Rev. Dr. Fenwick by R Garbett, Professor of Music.* Boston: Oliver Ditson, 1840.

US NYp

1842

The Morning and Evening Service of the Catholic Church, Comprising a Choice Collection of Gregorian and other Masses; Litanies, Psalms, Sacred Hymns. Anthems, Versicles and Motetts . . . Compiled and Respectfully Dedicated to Rt. Rev. Dr. Fenwick by R. Garbett, Professor of Music. Boston: Kidder and Wright, 1842.

US Bp

1843

Manual of Catholic Melodies, Or, A Compilation of Hymns, Anthems, Psalms, etc. With Appropriate Airs and Devotional Exercises, For the Ordinary Occasions of Catholic Piety and Worship. By Rev. James Hoerner. Baltimore: John Murphy [c.1843].

US NYts, Ps, Wc

1844

A Collection of Psalms, Hymns, Anthems, etc., to which is added the Rosary of the Blessed Virgin, etc. Selected from an approved Catholic work. New York: Robert Coddington, 1844.
Text only.

US NYts

The Child's Prayer and Hymn Book, for the use of Catholic Sunday Schools throughout the United States. Baltimore: John Murphy [c.1844].
Text only.

US Wc

The Sacred Wreath; or, A Collection of Hymns and Prayers for the Use of the Youthful Members of the Sodality of the Blessed Virgin Mary, In the United States of America. Philadelphia: Eugene Cummiskey, 1844.
Text only.

US Wcu, Wgu

The Catholic Harp, containing the morning and evening service of the Catholic Church, embracing a choice collection of Masses, Litanies, Psalms, Sacred Hymns, Anthems, Versicles and Motetts selected from the compositions of the first masters. Boston: Philip A. Kirk, 1844.

US NYts (unlocated)

Catholic Melodies, or a compilation of Hymns, Anthems Psalms, &c., with appropriate airs and devotional exercises for the ordinary occasions of Catho-

lic Piety and worship; abridged for the use of schools, &c. by James Hoerner. (Baltimore: John Murphy [1844?]).
No copy located.

1845

The Catholic Harp, containing the morning and evening service of the Catholic Church, embracing a choice collection of Masses, Litanies, Psalms, Sacred Hymns, Anthems, Versicles and Motetts selected from the compositions of the first masters. Boston: D. Reilly, No. 32 Endicott Street. A. B. Kidder, Stereotyper and Printer, 7, Cornhill. 1845.
Enlarged from 1844 edition.
US Wc

1847

The Catholic Choralist: to be issued regularly every two months; to contain a choice collection of Catholic Music, viz. . . . Philadelphia: W. J. Ashe, 1847. First issue is reviewed in *Brownson's Quarterly Review*, n.s. 1(3):411. July 1847.
No copy located.

1848

Peter's Catholic Harmonist, a collection of sacred music appropriate for morning and evening service. Consisting of motetts, masses, hymns, chants, etc. suitable to the principal festivals throughout the year. Composed, selected and arranged for the use of small choirs with a Separate Accompaniment for the Organ and Piano=Forte. By W. C. Peters. Louisville, W.C. Peters & Co., 1848.
No copy located.

1850

The Chapel Choir Book. A Collection of Catholic Music, Consisting of Masses, Anthems, Chants, and Hymns, to which is prefixed a Short Treatise in the Art of Singing. Designed for Public Worship, and Sunday and Singing Schools. Edited by Geo. W. Lloyd. Boston: Published by Patrick Donahoe, 1850.
US NYp

A Catholic Sunday School Hymn Book. Consisting of Hymns contained in the Manual of the Sodality, and a selection of other Hymns Adapted to Children. Philadelphia: Henry McGrath, No. 1 South Eighth St., 1850.
Text only.
US NYts

Sacred Melodies, Containing a Selection of the Most Appropriate Airs, Arranged and Designed as a Companion to the Catholic Sunday School Hymn Book, Manual of the Sodality, Sacred Wreath, etc. Philadelphia: Henry McGrath, No.1 South Eighth St., 1850.
US NYts, Wc

A Catholic Hymn Book. Boston: Joseph A. Copes, 88 Endicott St., 1850.
No copy located.

W. A. Newland's *Collection of Sacred Music.* Philadelphia: Published and for sale by W. A. Newland, 1850.
US Wc

1851

The Catholic Hymn Book: A collection of hymns, anthems, etc., for holydays of obligation and devotion, throughout the year. Selected from approved sources and adapted to general use. New York: E. Dunigan and Bro., 1851.
US NYts

Peter's Catholic Harmonist, a collection of sacred music appropriate for morning and evening service. Consisting of motetts, masses, hymns, chants, etc. suitable to the principal festivals throughout the year. Composed, selected and arranged for the use of small choirs with a Separate Accompaniment for the Organ and Piano=Forte. By W. C. Peters. Baltimore, John Murphy and Co., No. 178 Market Street, 1851.
US Wc

The Chapel Choir Book, a collection of Catholic music, edited by George F. Lloyd. 2nd edition Boston: Patrick Donahoe, 1851.
US Ps, Wc

Rohr, Philip. *Favorite Catholic Melodies.* Boston: Patrick Donahoe, 1851.
No copy located.

The Little Catholic Hymn Book; containing a collection of Hymns, Anthems, etc., For Schools and Private Use. Selected from Approved Sources. New York: Edward Dunigan and Bro., 151 Fulton-Street, 1851.
Text only.
US NYts, Wc

Lyra Catholica: containing all the hymns of the Roman Breviary and Missal, With Others From Various Sources, with a selection of hymns, anthems and sacred poetry. New York: Dunigan and Bro., 1851.
Text only.
US NYts, Wcu

The Catholic Choralist: Containing A Selection of Hymn-Tunes and Litanies. Adapted to Latin and English Words. New York: E. Dunigan and Brother, 151 Fulton St., 1851.
US NYts

Youth's Catholic Hymn Book, Compiled from the Lyra Catholica. Boston: J. A. Copes, 1851.
No copy located.

1852

The Catholic Harp, containing the morning and evening service of the Catholic Church, embracing a choice collection of Masses, Litanies, Psalms, Sacred Hymns, Anthems, Versicles and Motetts selected from the compositions of the first masters. New York: D. J. Sadlier & Co., 164 William Street; Boston: 128 Federal Street; Montreal, C. E.: Cor. Notre Dame and St. Francis Xavier Streets, 1852.
Same as 1845 edition. US Wc

The Golden Manual: Being a Guide to Catholic Devotion, Public and Private, Compiled From Approved Sources With the Approbation of the Most Rev. John Hughes, Archbishop of New York. New York: D. J. Sadlier & Co., 1852
Text only. US Wcu

1853

Collection of Sacred Hymns for the Use of the children of the Catholic Church; compiled chiefly from a little work published by Father David in 1815, to which are added selections from other approved sources intended principally for the use of schools and academies &c. Louisville: Webb & Levering, 1853.
US NYts

The Young Catholic's Vocal Class Book, Designed for the Use of Churches, Schools and Associations. Cincinnati: W. C. Peters & Sons [c.1853].
US Wc

1854

The Catholic Singing Book, containing the elements of music, progressive lessons and exercises for singing schools, a Mass by F. F. Schmid, the Vespers and other Pieces for the Use of Choirs. By A. Werner, Organist of the Cathedral in Boston. Boston: Donahoe, 1854.
US Cn

The Hymn-book, containing a collection of the most popular Catholic hymns, arranged for the use of Sunday schools and Catholics throughout the United States. 250th thousand, enl. and rev. With the approbation of the Rt. Rev. Bishop of Philadelphia. Philadelphia: P. F. Cunningham [c.1854].
Text only. US NYts

1855

Manual of the Sodality of the Blessed Virgin Mary. Third Revised Edition. Baltimore, Murphy, 1855.
Text only. US NYts

The Catholic Melodist, a collection of masses, vespers, anthems and sacred hymns chiefly from the manuscripts of the late Right Rev. John B. David, coadjutor bishop of Bardstown, designed primarily for the use of country congregations, small choirs and schools. Compiled and arranged by Rev. James Elliott with the approbation of the Right Rev. Bishop of Louisville. Louisville: Webb & Levering, 1855.

US PROu

The Chapel Choir Book. A Collection of Catholic Music, Consisting of Masses, Anthems, Chants, and Hymns, to which is prefixed a Short Treatise in the Art of Singing. Designed for Public Worship, and Sunday and Singing Schools. Edited by Geo. W. Lloyd. [Expanded edition] Boston: Published by Patrick Donahoe, 1855.

US Bp

1856

Hundert fromme Lieder. Sechs Sammlung. Erste amerikanische Stereotypausgabe. New York: Matthaus Reichert, 1856.

No copy located.

Walter, Jacob. *Ancient and Modern Music selected for the use of the Catholic Church, containing litanies, masses, vespers, anthems, hymns, and choruses for the seasons, festivals or other occasions. Arranged for the pianoforte or organ.* Baltimore: George Willig, Jr., 1856 [original printing, 1825].

US NYp

Rohr's Collection of Favorite Catholic Music for Church, School, and Home. Containing the greatest number of Hymns, Psalms, Antiphons, Masses, &c., &c., ever published. Particularly adapted to the wants of small Choirs, Sodalities, and Sunday Schools. Compiled with the assistance of several distinguished Clergymen. By Philip Rohr, Leader of St. Augustine's Choir, Philadelphia. Fourth edition. Boston: Published by Patrick Donahoe, 1856.

No copy located.

1857

The Memorare, a collection of Catholic Music containing six masses, a short requiem mass, vespers and a variety of miscellaneous pieces, suitable for Morning and Evening Service, and for Family or Private Devotion. With Accompaniment for Organ or Piano-forte. By Anthony Werner, Organist and Director of the Choir of the Cathedral of the Holy Cross, Boston. Boston: Oliver Ditson, 1857; New York: S. T. Gordon; Philadelphia: Beck and Lawton; Cincinnati: Truax & Baldwin.

US Cn

Roman Vesperal: containing the complete Vespers for the whole year with Gregorian chants in modern notation. Baltimore: J. Murphy and Co., 1857.
US NYp, Ps

Manual of the Sodality of the Blessed Virgin Mary. Fourth Revised Edition. Baltimore: Murphy & Co.; Pittsburgh, George Quigley, 1857.
US NYts

1858

Hellebusch, B. H. F. *Katholisches Gesang- und Gebetbuch eine Auswahl der vorzüglichsten Choräle und Kirchenlieder, für zwei Stimmen gesetzt, mit der gewöhnlichen Andachtsübungen von B. H. F. Hellebusch.* New York, Cincinnati, Chicago: Benziger Brothers, 1858.
No copy located.

Catholic Soldiers and sailor's prayer book; or, Complete manual of spiritual devotions. To which are added choice selections of psalms, hymns, . . . compiled by a priest returned from the Crimea. Richardson & Son, 1858.
No copy located.

1859

Cummings, Rev. Dr. [Jeremiah Williams]. *Songs for Catholic Schools.* Published by St. Stephen's Sunday School. New York: P. O'Shea, 1859.
US NYts

Wuerth, Aloys *Katholisches Gesangbuch.* Detroit: Verlag von Aloys Wuerth, 1859.
US Wc

1860

A Manual of Roman Chant, compiled from the most authentic Roman sources, for the use of Ecclesiastical Seminaries, Religious Communities and Churches. By a priest of the Congregation of the Most Holy Redeemer. Baltimore, 1860.
No copy located.

The Little Vesper Book, being a supplement to the Manual of Roman Chant by a priest of the Congregation of the Most Holy Redeemer. Baltimore: Kelly, Hedian and Piet, 1860.
US Bp, Wc

Songs for Catholic Schools and Aids to Memory for the Cathechism. By Rev. Dr. Cummings, Pastor of St. Stephen's Church, New York; with original music, by Domenica Speranza. New York: P. O'Shea, 1860.
US NYp

Catholic Hymns. Albany, New York: Munsell and Rowland, 1860.

US NYts

Peters' Mass in G, for Soprano and Bass Voices. With Spirit, Creator of Mankind, Panis Angelicus, O Salutaris Hostia, Asperges Me, Domine. Also the Cantica Vespera, . . . Harmonized to the Gregorian Tones. To which is added the German Te Deum Grosser Gott! or, God of Might! The whole selected and arranged by W. C. Peters. Cincinnati, Published by A. C. Peters & Bro., No. 94 West Fourth Street, Opposite Post Office (successors to W. C. Peters & Sons). St. Louis Missouri, J. L. Peters & Bro., No. 49 North Fifth Street. 1860.

US Wc

The Catholic Vocalist, a New Collection of Sacred Music. . . . Philadelphia: Henry T. Rocholl, 1860.

No copy located.

Notes

Introduction

1. Andrew Reed and James Matheson, *A Narrative of the Visit to the American Churches by the Deputation from the Congregational Union of England and Wales* (New York: Harper & Brothers, 1835), 77–78.

1. The Irish Immigrant and the Catholic Parish

1. St. Mary's Seminary, Baltimore (founded in 1791), Mount St. Mary's College in Emmitsburg (1808), and Georgetown College in the District of Columbia (1787). Georgetown's student body included many Protestant students throughout this period.
2. U.S. Bureau of the Census, *Historical Statistics of the United States: Colonial Times to 1970* (Washington, D.C.: U.S. Government Printing Office, 1975), 106. Only in 1821 did the government record a larger immigrant group, that from Great Britain. Clerks were, however, inconsistent in recording the originating point. Many Irish traveled first to Liverpool before embarking for America, and were consequently listed as arriving from Great Britain.
3. James Hennesey, *American Catholics: A History of the Roman Catholic Community in the United States* (New York: Oxford University Press, 1981), 119; and Thomas T. McAvoy, "The Formation of the Catholic Minority in the United States, 1820–1860," *Review of Politics,* 10 (1948): 27.
4. Ray Allen Billington, *The Protestant Crusade, 1800–1860: A Study of the Origins of American Nativism* (Chicago: Quadrangle Books, 1964), 32ff.
5. Gerald Shaughnessy, *Has the Immigrant Kept the Faith? A Study of Immigration and Catholic Growth in the United States, 1790–1920* (New York: Macmillan, 1925), 78.
6. Dale T. Knobel, *Paddy and the Republic: Ethnicity and Nationality in Antebellum America* (Middletown: Wesleyan University Press, 1986), 33.

7. Francis J. Grund, *The Americans in Their Moral, Social, and Political Relations* (New York and London: Johnson Reprint Corporation, 1968 [1837]), 61.

8. Francis Lieber, *The Stranger in America: comprising sketches of the manners, society, and national peculiarities of the United States* (London: R. Bentley, 1835), 43–44.

9. "The Minstrel Boy in America," *Boston Pilot*, 4 (1841): 340.

10. Oscar Handlin, *Boston's Immigrants, 1790–1865: A Study in Acculturation* (Cambridge: Harvard University Press, 1941), 42.

11. Lucille O'Connell, "Kealing Hurley's Scrip Book: An Irish Immigrant in America, 1847–48," *Eire-Ireland*, 15 (1980): 108.

12. *Boston Pilot*, 12 (September 15, 1849): 6.

13. Handlin, *Boston's Immigrants,* 60.

14. Ibid., 140. A somewhat different perspective is found in Lynn H. Lees and John Modell, "The Irish Countryman Urbanized: A Comparative Perspective on the Famine Migration," *Journal of Urban History*, 3 (August 1977): 391–408, who view the Irish immigration as "part of a long-term process of rural to urban migration within a developing Atlantic economy" (p. 391).

15. Isabella Lucy Bird, *The Englishwoman in America* (Madison: University of Wisconsin Press, 1966 [1856]), 381.

16. Allan Nevins and Milton Halsey Thomas, *The Diary of George Templeton Strong: The Turbulent Fifties, 1850–1859* (New York: Macmillan, 1952), 56–57.

17. Jay P. Dolan, *The Immigrant Church: New York's Irish and German Catholics, 1815–1865* (Baltimore: Johns Hopkins University Press, 1975), and Robert Ernst, *Immigrant Life in New York City, 1825–1863* (New York: King's Crown Press, 1949), provide detailed descriptions of the Irish wards of New York City.

18. U.S. Bureau of the Census, *Historical Statistics of the United States: Colonial Times to 1970* (Washington, D.C.: U.S. Government Printing Office, 1975), 106.

19. Frederick Marryat, *A Diary in America with Remarks on Its Institutions* (London: Longman, Orne, Brown, Green & Longmans, 1839), 395.

20. Hasia R. Diner, *Erin's Daughters in America: Irish Immigrant Women in the Nineteenth Century* (Baltimore: Johns Hopkins University Press, 1983), 31. Diner points out that the German immigration to America, which occurred during roughly the same period as the Irish, was 41 percent female; among the Irish, women made up 52.9 percent.

21. William Sanger, *The History of Prostitution* (New York, 1859), quoted in Carol Groneman, "Working-Class Immigrant Women in Mid-Nineteenth-Century New York: The Irish Woman's Experience," *Journal of Urban History*, 4 (May 1978): 265.

22. Michael Curley, *Venerable John Neumann* (Washington, D.C.: Catholic University of America Press, 1952), 459.

23. If there were any doubt of Hughes's position on Catholicism in America, it would be dispelled by his letter to the American convert to Catholicism Orestes Brownson, ordering him to stop his apologetic arguments on the compatibility of the American and Catholic ways of life. See McAvoy, "The Formation of the Catholic Minority in the United States, 1820–1860," 30.

24. Sean Connolly, *Religion and Society in Nineteenth-Century Ireland* (Dundalk: Dundalgan Press, 1985): 47–48.

25. Emmet Larkin, "The Devotional Revolution in Ireland, 1850–1875," *American Historical Review*, 77 (1972): 627–31, 644, and David W. Miller, "Irish Catholicism and the Great Famine," *Journal of Social History*, 9 (1975): 81–98. Desmond J. Keenan's *The Catholic Church in Nineteenth-Century Ireland: A Sociological Survey* (Totowa, N. J.: Barnes and Noble, 1983) suggests that the famine was not a primary cause for this change as it was already taking place well before the 1840s. Sean Connolly's *Religion and Society in Nineteenth-Century Ireland* responds to Keenan's work, acknowledging that the "devotional revolution" indeed began before the famine, but was intensified and ultimately succeeded because of social conditions in post-famine Ireland.

26. *New York Freeman's Journal*, 9 (March 24, 1849): 5.

27. Charles Dickens, *American Notes* (London, 1842), quoted in Carol Groneman, "Working-Class Immigrant Women in Mid-Nineteenth-Century New York: The Irish Woman's Experience," *Journal of Urban History*, 4 (May 1978): 265. It is somewhat uncertain whether Dickens was describing an Irish dance hall or a black one. While the dance hall is in the heart of the Irish ghetto, he makes mention of "mulatto couples."

28. J. B. McMahon, Ptre, M. D., "To the Late Irish Immigrants of the City of Boston," *Boston Pilot*, 9 (July 4, 1846): 3.

29. The distinction between liturgical and extraliturgical worship is a canonical one. The liturgy includes the mass, the divine office (e.g., vespers), and the celebration of the sacraments. Extraliturgical worship refers to all other church-approved forms of devotion (e.g., stations of the cross, novenas, missions).

30. For example, it is clear that the liturgical singing of the Boston cathedral choir in the 1830s was dominated by men; at the same time the Baltimore cathedral choir was entirely female. Oddly enough, the Boston cathedral organist of the period was a female, Mrs. D. L. Brown, daughter of the English composer Samuel Webbe, while Baltimore's organist was male.

31. Handlin, *Boston's Immigrants, 1790–1865*, 132.

2. Music in the Press

1. In spite of the growing American belief in the "melting pot" image of America, Catholics began setting up parallel social institutions, most notably the parochial school system, which fostered a separateness from American

society. The Fourth Provincial Council (1840) spoke of a "separate system of education."

2. The 1816 charter of the Handel and Haydn Society stated that the organization existed "for the purpose of extending knowledge and improving the style of performance of Church music."

3. The *Boston Pilot* originated as a weekly newspaper entitled *The Jesuit*, a somewhat provocative title in the Protestant-dominated city of Boston. It was published by private individuals (during this period by Patrick Donahoe), and did not become the official diocesan newspaper until the early twentieth century. It currently is published as such by the Roman Catholic Archdiocese of Boston.

4. This controversy and the hymnal will be discussed at length in chapter 3.

5. See Hans Nathan, "The Tyrolese Family Rainer, and the Vogue of Singing Mountain-Troupes in Europe and America," *Musical Quarterly*, 32 (1946): 63–79. An item in the *Boston Pilot* of July 30, 1842, suggests that the Rainer Family volunteered their services: "The Catholic population of Boston are much indebted to them [the Rainer Family] for the generous manner in which they have at all times volunteered their services to aid in many charitable objects" (5:256).

6. Nathan, "Tyrolese Family Rainer," 65.

7. The citation given is usually for the issue before the concert, as this issue often gives the program of music to be performed. The *Boston Pilot* usually printed a short article describing the concert in the issue following the date of performance.

8. The Boston Gregorian Society was founded in 1836 by members of the various Catholic choirs of the Boston area for the improvement of Catholic church music. The society is discussed in Paul Eric Paige, "Musical Organizations in Boston: 1830–1850" (Ph.D. diss., Boston University, 1967). Paige found no evidence of the group's existence after the public rehearsal of January 20, 1839. As the table indicates, they were operative for some time after that date.

9. Other music journals existed in Boston at this time, but their nature was such that they would not be expected to report such events: *Proceedings of the Musical Convention* (1838–?) printed the texts of speeches given at the annual music conventions; *Musical Cabinet: a Monthly Collection of Vocal and Instrumental Music and Musical Literature,* and *The Seraph* (1842), contained printed music. *The Singer* (1840–1842) and *Juvenile Minstrel* (1840–1841) were both aimed at schools and youth groups.

10. *The Musical Magazine*, 1 (1839): 48.

11. *Boston Musical Gazette*, 1 (1839): 205.

12. *Musical Reporter,* 1 (1841): 138. The hymn was Bishop J. B. David's "My God, My Life, My Love." The *Musical Reporter*'s version of the hymn dif-

fers significantly from that printed in the hymnal *The Morning and Evening Services of the Catholic Church*. The title is changed from "Aspirations before Communion" (which is actually the name of a division of the Catholic hymnal in which this hymn appears first) to simply "Aspiration." The attribution to Bishop David (formerly Catholic bishop of Bardstown, Kentucky) is omitted, as are the second through fifth verses of the hymn, many of which have very "Catholic" themes (e.g. "My faith beholds thee, Lord, Concealed as human food . . ."). The designation for "short meter" (S.M.) is added. In the Catholic hymnal the hymn is arranged for three voices, except for the final four-bar phrase, which includes an optional fourth voice. This fourth voice is omitted in the *Musical Reporter*.

13. Louis C. Elson, *The History of American Music* (New York: Macmillan, 1904), 33.

14. Ibid., 56, 107.

15. H. Earle Johnson, "Early New England Periodicals Devoted to Music," *Musical Quarterly*, 26 (1940): 153–61.

16. Lois Ibsen al Faruqi, "What Makes 'Religious Music' Religious?" in *Sacred Sound: Music in Religious Thought and Practice*, ed. Joyce Irwin (Chico, Calif.: Scholars Press, 1984), 22.

17. Ibid., 29.

18. "Music in Boston," *Musical Magazine,* 1 (1839): 303. The concern for the use of the vernacular in worship parallels the popularity of Italian opera in English which was so favored at this time. See Charles Hamm, *Music in the New World* (New York: W. W. Norton, 1983), 197–200.

19. "Nature of Music," *Musical Reporter,* 1 (1841): 57–58.

20. "Protestant and Popish Music [from the New England Puritan]," *Boston Musical Gazette*, 2 (1848): 202. In fairness to the *Boston Musical Gazette* (1846–50), it should be noted that they also occasionally printed objective accounts of musical life in Boston Catholic churches.

21. *A Letter to a Friend in the Country, Concerning the Use of Instrumental Musick in the Worship of God: in Answer to Mr. Newte's Sermon Preach'd at Tiverton in Devon, on the Occasion of an Organ being Erected in that Parish-Church* (London, 1698), 16–17. Quoted in Gretchen Finney, "'Organical Musick' and Ecstasy," *Journal of the History of Ideas*, 8 (1947): 287–88.

22. The first account of St. Joseph's organ is found in Peter Kalm's *Travels into North America*, translated by John Reinhold Forster (Warrington: William Eyres, 1770). Justin Winser's *Memorial History of Boston* (Boston: J. Osgood, 1880) records that Francis Mallet performed on the organ at the dedication of Boston's original Holy Cross Church (later Cathedral).

23. *Musical Library*, 1 (1835): 1.

24. "Protestant and Popish Music," *Boston Musical Gazette*, 2 (1848): 202.

25. "Italian Opera," *New York Musical Review and Choral Advocate*, 5 (1854): 257.

26. Irving Lowens, "Writings about Music in the Periodicals of American Transcendentalism (1835–50)," *Journal of the American Musicological Society*, 10 (1957): 75.

27. A notable exception to this was the Boston Handel and Haydn Society. Selections from Haydn's *Mass in B-flat* were offered by that organization as early as 1829, and regularly performed up to 1837; Mozart's *Requiem* was first given in 1857.

28. "Haydn's Masses," *Journal of the Fine Arts*, n.s. #48, 1851. Some caution most be employed when dealing with references to Mozart's *Requiem*. At the time, a second requiem mass (K. Anh. 237) was attributed to Mozart, published by Novello as Mass Number 18. The first movement of the "Dies Irae" from this mass was published in the *Boston Musical Gazette*, February 1, 1850, in an English translation, "Day of Vengeance."

29. John S. Dwight, "Mozart's Twelfth Mass," *Saroni's Musical Times*, 2 (1851): 148–49. Mozart's Twelfth Mass refers to the mass numbered *twelve* in Novello's edition, a mass which is incorrectly attributed to Mozart. It was, however, probably the most popular of all the orchestral masses employed in America, both by Catholics and Protestants alike, and was often cited as Mozart's greatest choral composition.

30. "Musical Review," *Harbinger*, 3 (1846): 152.

31. Frederick H. Hedge, "Romanism and Its Worship," *Christian Examiner and Religious Miscellany*, 56 (1854): 235.

32. The term "primitive church" refers to the early centuries of Christianity before its establishment as a state religion under Constantine.

33. "Review: 'Hymns of the Primitive Church,'" *Christian Examiner*, 28 (1840): 2. The author of the review was, in fact, correct. This collection, put together by early supporters of the Oxford movement in England, contained many Catholic hymns which dated from the seventeenth and eighteenth centuries.

34. "Ancient Chant," *Musical Magazine*, 2 (1836): 79.

35. C. M. Cady, "Music in America," *American Musical Review and Choral Advocate*, 3 (1852): 132.

36. "Congregational Singing," *New York Musical Pioneer*, 3 (1858): 135.

37. Dr. Cummings, "Music in Worship," *Saroni's Musical Times*, 1 (1850): 429. This article appears to be reprinted from a British journal.

38. C. P. C., "The Concert and the Church," *Western Messenger*, 6 (1839): 339–41.

39. While the article does not give the title of the song, it is clear that it was *Evening Song to the Virgin at Sea*, with words by Mrs. Hemans and music by her sister, Mrs. Brown. The problem discussed in the *Western Messenger* does not appear to be an isolated one; when the song was sung by the Hutchinson Family, its title became *Vesper Song at Sea*, and the offending lines were changed: "Ave Sanctissima" became "Jesus, most holy one," and "Ora pro

nobis" became "Plead for us, Savior." *Vesper Song at Sea. As Sung by the Hutchinson Family.* (New York: Firth & Hall, 1843), copy at NYPL.

40. C. P. C., "Concert," 340.

41. Ibid., 341. A similar controversy and response were reported in the *Musical World,* 12 (1855): 50.

42. Rev. Henry Giles, "Music," *American Musical Review and Choral Advocate,* 3 (1852): 36.

43. John A. Albro, "Sacred Music," *Literary and Theological Review,* 3 (1836): 78.

44. "Address of Edward Hodges, Mus. Doc.," in *Proceedings of the American Musical Convention* (New York: Sexton and Miles, 1845), 43.

45. "Christmas in Philadelphia," *Harbinger,* 6 (1848): 69.

46. Ibid.

47. "Ceremonies and Superstitions of the Catholic Church in Rome," *Christian Examiner and Theological Review,* 2 (1825): 353–54.

48. T. J. Headley, "The Miserere at Rome," *Boston Musical Gazette,* 2 (1847): 141.

49. "Allegri's Miserere," *Musical World and Times,* 8 (1854): 113.

50. These hymnals are discussed in chapter 3.

51. "Ceremonies and Superstitions of the Catholic Church in Rome," *Christian Examiner and Theological Review*, 2 (1825): 354.

52. For a full treatment of Nativism, see Ray Allen Billington, *The Protestant Crusade, 1800–1860; A Study of the Origins of American Nativism* (Chicago: Quadrangle, 1964).

53. "The Artistic and Romantic View of the Church of the Middle Ages," *Christian Examiner and Religious Miscellany*, 46 (May, 1849): 31.

54. Dr. Cummings, "Music and Worship," *Saroni's Musical Times,* 1 (1850): 442. Protestant attendance at the Catholic Embassy Chapels in London in order to hear the music had been a popular practice since the late eighteenth century. Numerous articles indicate that the practice also began in urban areas of the United States. See, for example, the article cited in note 45 above, and the discussion of St. Peter's Church, New York City, in chapter 4.

55. Frederick H. Hedge, "Romanism and Its Worship," *The Christian Examiner and Religious Miscellany*, 56 (1854): 243.

56. Southey, "Effect of Music in the Conversion of Savages, from Southey's *History of Brazil*," *New York Musical Pioneer,* 3 (1858): 119. The newspaper misprinted the name, which should be "Nobrega," the one-time Jesuit provincial of Brazil. Robert Southey, *History of Brazil* (New York: Greenwood Press, 1969 [1822]), 1: 267.

57. Dr. Cummings, "Music and Worship," 442–43. This is an article reprinted from a British publication. There is, however, nothing in the text of the article itself that would make the reader believe it was not referring to America.

58. "Address of Rev. Raymond Seely," in *Proceedings of the American Musical Convention* (New York: Sexton and Miles, 1845), 57.

59. For example, "Different Kinds of Religion," *World of Music*, 2 (1844): 38.

3. Change and Adaptation in the 1830s, Boston

1. Patrick W. Carey, "American Catholic Romanticism, 1830–1888," *Catholic Historical Review*, 74 (1988): 590.

2. Ibid., 597.

3. The newspaper was founded in 1829 as *The Jesuit*. Its name was changed a number of times during the 1830s, and it was known at various times as the *United States Catholic Intelligencer*, *The Literary and Catholic Sentinel*, and finally *The Boston Pilot*, the name by which it exists today.

4. William Forbes Adams, *Ireland and Irish Emigration to the New World from 1815 to the Famine* (New York: Russell and Russell, 1932), 196ff.

5. *United States Catholic Intelligencer,* 3 (1832): 120; *The Jesuit, or Catholic Sentinel*, 4 (1833): 156.

6. *Boston Pilot*, 2 (1839): 190.

7. *The Catholic Church Service Book. Comprising a choice collection of Gregorian and other Masses, of Sacred Hymns, Anthems, Versicles, & Mottets, both for the morning and evening service; taken out of the public liturgy of the Catholic Church. The whole Composed, Selected, and Arranged by the first Masters; with a Separate Accompaniment for the Organ or Pianoforte. Part I.* (Boston: Published at the request of the present Bishop of Boston for the use of his Diocese [1833]).

8. Although not a great deal is known about Mrs. Brown, a few interesting facts have emerged. She was the daughter of the English composer Samuel Webbe, according to the *Boston Pilot*, 13 (February 23, 1850): 5. The *Journal of the Diocese of Boston*, preserved in the archives of the Boston archdiocese, contains a number of references to her. In November of 1832 the men of the cathedral choir resigned to protest Brown's "tyranical mode of proceeding," and because she "does not shew that respect to them in the Choir to which they think themselves entitled." The conflict was resolved and the men rejoined the choir. In November of 1839 Bishop Fenwick asked for Brown's resignation as "her extreme old age and increasing infirmities have long since incapacitated her from discharging her duty to the satisfaction of the community."

9. *The Jesuit*, 4 (1833): 11.

10. Accounts of Fenwick's piano playing come from an odd source, Rebecca Reed's *Six Months in a Convent*, a vicious anti-Catholic pamphlet which helped produce the riot that burned the Ursuline Convent in Charlestown. Rebecca Reed, a postulant for a few months at the Ursuline Convent, makes reference to Fenwick's playing of the piano on his visits to the nuns.

11. *The Jesuit*, 4 (1833): 21.
12. Ibid., 34.
13. Ibid., 84.
14. Ibid.
15. Ibid., 40, 184.
16. *Daily Evening Transcript,* November 23, 1833. In Paul Eric Paige, "Musical Organizations in Boston: 1830–1850," 110–11.
17. *The Jesuit,* 4 (1833): 190.
18. Ibid., 194.
19. *Illinois Catholic Historical Review,* 10 (October 1927): 161.
20. *Boston Pilot,* 2 (April 9, 1836): 3
21. Ibid., 2 (May 14, 1836): 3
22. Charles C. Perkins & John S. Dwight, *History of the Handel and Haydn Society* (New York: Da Capo Press, 1977 [1883]), 106.
23. *Boston Pilot*, 2 (January 26, 1836): 3
24. Ibid., 1 (1838): 271.
25. DeMonti's compositions are discussed further in chapter 4.
26. *Boston Pilot,* 2 (1839): 103. The program does not provide the names of many of the composers. Those in parentheses come from other concert programs given by the Society. Those with a question mark are composers who had published a piece with the given title.
27. Ibid., 2 (1839): 315.
28. Ibid., 1 (1838): 224.
29. Ibid.
30. Ibid., 2 (1839): 315.
31. Ibid., 2 (1838): 383.
32. Ibid., 1 (1838): 359.
33. Ibid., 2 (1838): 383.
34. For example, ibid., 2 (1839): 400.
35. Ibid., 199.
36. Ibid.
37. See figure 2.1 for a list of these concerts.
38. *Boston Pilot,* 20 (October 24, 1857): 6.
39. *Catholic Church Service Book*, [i].
40. The 1840 version merely adds the words "under the immediate" before the word "inspection."
41. Vernacular singing was at least tolerated, and often promoted, by the clergy in the United States. John Carroll, first Catholic bishop of the United States, held that congregational singing was not actually a part of the liturgy itself, and could therefore be in the vernacular. See *American Catholic Historical Researches* 14 (1897): 21.
42. *The Jesuit,* 4 (1833): 10.
43. *Catholic Church Service Book*, [i].

44. Ibid.
45. Today the site is part of Somerville, Massachusetts.
46. Billington, *The Protestant Crusade*, 71.
47. *Catholic Church Service Book*, [ii].
48. *Journal of the Diocese of Boston, Volume I*, p. 194. In the Archives of the Archdiocese of Boston.
49. Quoted in Rosemary Radford Ruether and Rosemary Skinner Keller, eds., *Women and Religion in America* (San Francisco: Harper and Row, 1981), 135.
50. *Catholic Church Service Book*, [iii].
51. "Ut omnia juxta ordinem fiant, et solemnes Ecclesiae ritus integri serventur, monemus Rectores Ecclesiarum ut sedulo invigilent ab abusus eliminandos qui in cantu ecclesiastico in his regionibus invaluerunt. Curent igitur ut sacrosancto Missae sacrificio et alliis divinis officiis musica, non vero musicae divina officia inserviant. Noverint juxta Ecclesiae ritum, carmina vernaculo idiomate, inter Missarum solemnia, vel Vesperas, decantare non licere." *Concilia Provinciale Baltimori, habita ab anno 1829 usque ad annum 1849: Decreta* (Baltimore: apud Joannem Murphy et socium, 1851).
52. The dates of Garbett's life were obtained from the biographical card catalog in the music division of the Boston Public Library, which in turn is based upon Boston city directories and newspaper obituaries.
53. *Illinois Catholic Historical Review,* 10 (October 1927): 165–66.
54. A incorrectly dated copy is in the Union Theological Seminary Library, New York City.
55. *Boston Pilot,* 4 (1841): 200.
56. Ibid., 5 (1842): 40.
57. *Journal of the Diocese of Boston, Volume III*, p. 55. In the Archives of the Archdiocese of Boston.
58. Quoted in Kevin G. Kenny, "Religion and the Rise of Mass Immigration," *New York Irish History*, 5 (1990–91): 29.
59. *Literary and Catholic Sentinel,* 1 (September 26, 1835): 2.
60. Ibid.
61. Ibid., 1 (March 14, 1835): 3.
62. Ibid.
63. Ibid., 1 (April 4, 1835): 1.
64. Ibid.
65. *The Jesuit,* 4 (1833): 83.
66. Ibid.
67. The practice is discussed further in chapter 5.
68. *Boston Pilot,* 1 (1839): 415.
69. *Boston Musical Gazette,* 1 (1839): 157.
70. See chapter 6 for a more detailed discussion of Irish musical practice in America, including P. F. White's concerts.

71. David J. Ferland, "Plenary, Provincial, and Synodal Legislation Concerning Liturgical Music in the United States as Causative and Resultant of the Enactments of the Third Plenary Council of Baltimore" (M.A. thesis, Catholic University of America, 1955), 17.

4. Canonical Music of Ritual: Art Music and the Immigrant

1. John Grady, "Roman Catholic Church, Music of the." In the *New Grove Dictionary of American Music* (New York: Macmillan, 1986): 4: 80.
2. The Roman legislation of the period can be found in Robert Hayburn, *Papal Legislation on Sacred Music, 95 A.D. to 1977 A.D.* (Collegeville, Minn.: Liturgical Press, 1979). David J. Ferland's thesis "Plenary, Provincial, and Synodal Legislation Concerning Liturgical Music in the United States as Causative and Resultant of the Enactments of the Third Plenary Council of Baltimore" (M.A. thesis, Catholic University of America, 1955) summarizes similar American legislation. A review of the legislation shows that it was singularly ineffective in changing the practice of music in the antebellum United States in all but the most general of matters.
3. *The Lyre,* 1 (1824): 5–6. The article contains a full stop-list of the organ.
4. Harold Earle Johnson, *First Performances in America to 1900* (Detroit: Published for the College Music Society by Information Coordinators, 1979), 286.
5. *Catholic Herald,* 2 (1834): 66.
6. Ibid., 9 (1841): 40. An orchestra of sixty-four musicians was led by L. Meignan, with Benjamin Carr Cross at the keyboard. The singers included Mr. and Mrs. Seguin. The Masonic nature of the work must have produced some embarrassment for the Catholic church. The issue of the *Catholic Herald* following the performance simply stated: "We have authority to state that the nature of the allegory of the Musical piece performed on Monday evening last, was not known to any of those immediately connected with St. John's Orphan Asylum" (9 [1841]: 41).
7. Vera Brodsky Lawrence, *Strong on Music* (New York: Oxford University Press, 1988), 9.
8. Ibid., 12–13.
9. Ibid., 127–28.
10. Ibid., 14.
11. *New York Freeman's Journal,* 1 (1841): 407.
12. Lawrence, *Strong on Music,* 155.
13. *New York Daily Tribune,* 2 (October 10, 1842): 2.
14. *Dwight's Journal of Music,* 21 (June 28, 1862): 100.
15. Ibid.
16. Ibid.
17. *New York Freeman's Journal,* 9 (March 3, 1849): 4.

18. *Boston Pilot*, 6 (1843): 53.
19. Johnson, *First Performances in America to 1900*, 185, 53, 272, 155.
20. *New York Freeman's Journal*, 2 (March 26, 1842): 309.
21. Ibid., 309 (emphasis added).
22. *Boston Pilot*, 9 (October 24, 1846): 6.
23. Lawrence, *Strong on Music*, 363.
24. *New-York Musical Review and Choral Advocate*, 6 (February 15, 1855): 61.
25. *Boston Pilot*, 5 (October 15, 1842): 345.
26. *Boston Musical Gazette*, 2 (March 1, 1847): 22.
27. There is some question as to whether the Handel and Haydn Society gave a complete performance or merely selections from the *Requiem*. The *Handel and Haydn Society List of Concerts, Seasons 1–75*, in the New York Public Library, classmark *MA, lists the 1857 performances as "selections," although Johnson, *First Performances in America to 1900*, implies a full version. One comment in Dwight's review of the Catholic choir's performance suggests an irregularity in the Handel and Haydn Society performance: he notes that the 'Lacrymosa' was "sung here, as it should be, as chorus and not quartet."
28. *Boston Pilot*, 20 (May 2, 1857): 4. The article also notes that "All the pieces to be performed are in the Latin language, and a translation of each piece into English is given with the programme. This is a great improvement."
29. *Dwight's Journal of Music*, 11 (1857): 45.
30. Ibid.
31. Ibid., 46.
32. *Saroni's Musical Times*, 2 (January 4, 1851): 148–49.
33. *Dwight's Journal of Music*, 2 (1852): 76.
34. *Musical World and New York Musical Times*, 11 (April 14, 1855): 170.
35. *Musical World and Times*, 8 (March 18, 1854): 123.
36. *New York Freeman's Journal*, 11 (July 6, 1850): 5.
37. *Musical World and Times*, 8 (March 18, 1854): 123.
38. *Dwight's Journal of Music*, 18 (March 16, 1861): 404.
39. A finding aid to the Newland-Zeuner collection is in preparation by the staff of the Library of Congress. No central record has been kept of the printed material dispersed to the general collection from Newland's library; it can only be identified by the acquisition number.
40. Pedro Antonio Daunas was a Spanish organist from Barcelona who trained at Montserrat and was organist at St. Joseph's church in Philadelphia at mid-century. J. Vincent Higginson, *History of American Catholic Hymnals* (n. p.: Hymn Society of America, 1982), 124.
41. The "Missa de Angelis" in Elliott is actually an arrangement of the mass by Bishop David; Gregorian phrases alternate with newly composed three-part homophonic phrases. Although it was not published until 1855,

Bishop David describes the mass in a letter to Bishop Fenwick dated February 10, 1833.

42. Walter's collection was in print as late as the 1870 Board of Music Trade of the United States, *Complete Catalogue of Sheet Music and Musical Works, 1870* (New York: DaCapo, 1973 [1870]).

43. The regularity with which the Gregorian Requiem appears in print may well be connected to an innate conservatism that accompanies important rituals, particularly those concerned with death.

44. The Fenwick collection is discussed in chapter three.

45. *Boston Pilot*, 13 (November 23, 1850): 5.

46. Bishop Cheverus, visiting the Passamaquoddy tribe in 1797, was surprised to find them singing Dumont's "Missa Regia," which they had learned long before from French missionaries. See J. Huen-Dubourg, *The Life of Cardinal Cheverus* (Boston: James Munroe and Company, 1839), 63.

47. *Boston Pilot*, 5 (January 31, 1842): 40; *New York Freeman's Journal*, 2 (December 25, 1841): 207.

48. *DeMonti's favorite Mass in B-flat, with an additional Alto part and English words* (Boston: Oliver Ditson, 1856); *Mass in C for 2 voices, with a separate accompaniment for the organ* (Cincinnati: A. C. Peters, 1861).

49. Entry for October 15, 1844. *Journal of the Diocese of Boston* in the Archives of the Archdiocese of Boston.

50. *Boston Pilot*, 3 (November 28, 1840): 361; 4 (January 2, 1841): 7.

51. *Boston Pilot*, 7 (February 24, 1844): 63. The composer of this mass is listed as J. B. Woodbury. It is likely that this refers to Issac Baker Woodbury, who was teaching music in Boston at the time. No other Woodbury appears in the Boston city directory; Catholic publications still occasionally used the archaic "i" for "j" spelling, which could have created the confusion. Unfortunately most of Woodbury's manuscripts were destroyed. See Robert Marshall Copeland, "The Life and Work of Issac Baker Woodbury, 1819–1858" (Ph.D. diss., University of Cincinnati, 1974), v–vi.

52. *Dwight's Journal of Music*, 21 (July 5, 1862): 109.

53. Robert Eitner, *Biographisch-Bibliographisches Quellen-Lexicon der Musiker und Musikgelehrten* (New York: Musurgia, 1898–1904), 7: 48.

54. A published essay by DeMonti, *Strictures on Mr. Logier's System of Musical Education* (Glasgow: James Hedderwick, 1817), is a strong condemnation on the Logier system; according to John W. Moore, *Complete Encyclopaedia of Music* (Boston: John P. Jewitt, 1854), one of Logier's partners was Samuel Webbe, whose dominance in the early American Catholic repertory was broken largely by the growing popularity of DeMonti's masses.

55. *Dwight's Journal of Music*, 9 (1856): 38.

56. *Boston Pilot*, 20 (October 24, 1857): 6.

57. Analysis of the Dwight-Fry debates is contained in Christopher Hatch, "Music for America: A Critical Controversy of the 1850s," *American Quarterly*,

14 (1962): 578–86, and Betty E. Chmaj, "Fry versus Dwight: American Music's Debate over Nationality," *American Music* 3 (1985): 63–84. Both articles mention Dwight's Harvard education, but neither mentions Fry's Catholic education at Mount St. Mary's College, Emmitsburg, Maryland, where an Irish immigrant, Joseph Gegan, was teacher of music. Fry, although not a Catholic, was a classmate of John Hughes and John McCloskey, who would serve successively as archbishops of New York. When McCloskey was named archbishop of New York in 1864, Fry immediately began to compose a mass setting for McCloskey's installation; Fry stopped work on his mass when McCloskey declined the offer. William Treat Upton, *William Henry Fry: American Journalist and Composer-Critic* (New York: Thomas Y. Crowell, 1954), 171.

58. William Cumming Peters, *Mass for Three Voices* (Baltimore: Geo. Willig, Jr., 1841).

59. Peters' "Mass in G" is composed in a conservative style, and as the title page notes, is based on themes from earlier British Catholic composers, such as Novello and Paxton.

60. *Boston Pilot*, 17 (August 12, 1854): 4. An ad for Donahoe's Catholic Bookstore lists "Dielman's Mass for three voices. The Mass comprises 24 large pages of plate music. It is well printed and is dedicated to Rev. John McCloskey by Dr. Henry Dielman." This is the same John McCloskey for whom Fry wished to compose a mass ten years later.

61. *New York Freeman's Journal*, 9 (October 21, 1848): 8.

62. Anonymous [Charles Constantine Pise], *Father Rowland, A North American Tale* (Baltimore: Lucas Brothers, 1841), 185–87.

63. "Literary Notices and Criticisms," *Brownson's Quarterly Review*, n.s. 1 (1847): 411.

64. *United States Catholic Magazine,* 6 (June 1847): 343.

65. "Literary Notices and Criticisms," *Brownson's Quarterly Review,* n.s. 1 (1847): 411.

66. Ibid. No evidence of any further issues has been found.

67. *Quarterly Musical Magazine and Review*, 1 (1818): 215.

68. Saint-Benoist, *Nouvel hymnaire parisien à l'usage des quatre-vingt-quatre de la République française* (Paris, 1793), p.viii. Translated and quoted in Simone Wellon, "Notes of the Performance of Plain Chant in France from 1750 to 1850," *Sacred Music,* 107 (Winter 1980): 4.

69. *The Jesuit*, 5 (May 10, 1834): 147.

70. A. E. Choron and J. Adrien de La Fage, *Nouveau manuel complet de musique vocale et instrumentale, ou encyclopédie musicale* (Paris, 1838), 2: III: 196. Translated and quoted in Abbé Jean Prim, "*Chant sur le Livre* in French Churches in the 18th Century," *Journal of the American Musicological Society,* 14 (1961): 37.

71. John Mondesir, "Memoirs," typescript of an unpublished manuscript in the library of Georgetown University, Washington, D.C., p. 92. My translation.

72. *New York Freeman's Journal,* 17 (July 19, 1856): 5.

73. The 1833 version of the "Veni Creator" is attributed to the Ursuline Convent. As discussed in chapter 3, the attribution probably suggests that the convent either transcribed the arrangement from square notation or merely provided a copy of the arrangement for inclusion in the collection. The Ursulines most likely received the version from some other source.

74. *The Jesuit,* 5 (May 10, 1834): 146.

75. *Boston Musical Gazette,* (June 21, 1847): 22.

76. *Dwight's Journal of Music,* 1 (April 24, 1852): 20.

77. Ibid., 1 (May 1, 1852): 30.

78. Ibid., 1 (April 24, 1852): 21.

79. *Kyriale; or Ordinary of the Mass: A Complete Liturgical Manual* (Baltimore: John Murphy, 1857) and *Roman Vesperal: Containing the Complete Vespers for the Whole Year* (Baltimore: John Murphy, 1857). Bishop David had hoped for a similar project much earlier. Writing to Bishop Benedict Fenwick in 1834, David said, "Let us implore the assistance of the Holy Ghost and the BVM [Blessed Virgin Mary] to form a plan. What about square gregorian notes? Graduals? Vesperals? Processionals? Method of plain chant?" "David to Fenwick, April 22, 1834" in the Archives of the Archdiocese of Boston.

80. *Roman Vesperal: Containing the Complete Vespers for the Whole Year* (Baltimore: John Murphy, 1857), v–vi.

81. Ibid., ix.

82. One exception to this is Miss Rosa Garcia, organist of St. Mary's in Boston.

83. *New York Freeman's Journal*, 9 (March 24, 1849): 5.

84. Lawrence, *Strong on Music*, 44.

85. *Boston Pilot,* 1 (March 10, 1838): 51.

86. Michael Broyles, "Lowell Mason on European Church Music and Transatlantic Cultural Identification: A Reconsideration," *Journal of the American Musicological Society,* 38 (1985): 316–48.

87. Michael Broyles, "Music and Class Structure in Antebellum Boston," *Journal of the American Musicological Society*, 44 (1991): 451–93.

88. Lawrence Levine, *Highbrow, Lowbrow: The Emergence of Cultural Hierarchy in America* (Cambridge: Harvard University Press, 1988).

89. *Boston Pilot,* 10 (May 8, 1847): 7.

90. *New York Freeman's Journal*, 16 (May 24, 1856): 4.

5. Popular Music of Ritual: The Tradition of Vernacular Song

1. James H. Stone, "The Merchant and the Muse: Commercial Influences on American Popular Music before the Civil War," *The Business History Review*, 30 (1956): 2.

2. The ultimate liturgical authority in Roman Catholicism traditionally rests with the papacy, although at times the bishops of a region have acted

together to establish ritual uniformity. Archbishop Carroll, the first United States bishop, exerted a certain amount of independence in liturgical areas. During the mid-nineteenth century, most American bishops followed the Roman position on liturgical praxis.

3. For the development of the American mission, see Jay P. Dolan, *Catholic Revivalism: The American Experience, 1830–1900* (Notre Dame: University of Notre Dame Press, 1978).

4. J. Vincent Higginson, *Handbook for American Catholic Hymnals* (n.p.; The Hymn Society of America, 1976), 46–47.

5. W. C. Peters, *Peters' Mass in G* (Cincinnati: A. C. Peters & Bro., 1860).

6. Rev. Alfred Young, *Catholic Hymns and Canticles; together with a Complete Sodality Manual* (New York: The Catholic Publication House, 1863). This work is generally cited as the first in which this text and tune were united, but the same combination was printed in Anthony Werner's *Cantate*, part II, which bears an 1862 copyright date.

7. Higginson, *Handbook for American Catholic Hymnals,* pp. 85, 254.

8. Nicholas E. Tawa, *Sweet Songs for Gentle Americans: The Parlor Song in America, 1790–1860* (Bowling Green: Bowling Green University Popular Press, 1980), 144–45.

9. James Hoerner, *Manual of Catholic Melodies, A Compilation of Hymns, Anthems, Psalms, etc. . . . with appropriate airs and devotional exercises* (Baltimore: John Murphy, 1843), iv.

10. *The Sacred Wreath; or, A Collection of Hymns and Prayers for the Use of the Youthful Members of the Sodality of the Blessed Virgin Mary, In the United States of America* (Philadelphia: Eugene Cummiskey, 1844), 5.

11. *The Catholic Harp, containing the morning and evening service of the Catholic Church, embracing a choice collection of Masses, Litanies, Psalms, Sacred Hymns, Anthems, Versicles and Motetts selected from the compositions of the first masters* (Boston: D. Reilly, 1845), iii.

12. William Cumming Peters, *Peters' Catholic Harmonist, a collection of sacred music appropriate for morning and evening service* (Baltimore: John Murphy, 1851), iii.

13. Joseph Mainzer, *Singing for the Millions* (London: Depot for the Mainzerian Publications, 1841).

14. Bernard Rainbow, *The Land Without Music: Music Education in England 1800–1860 and its Continental Antecedents* (London: Novello and Company, 1967), 104–7.

15. F. C., "Foreign Correspondence," *The Athenaeum*, no. 527 (1837): 881.

16. Lawrence, *Strong on Music*, 166–67.

17. *New York Freeman's Journal*, 3 (September 31, 1842): 109.

18. Ibid. (October 8, 1842): 119.

19. Ibid. (September 31, 1842): 109. Father Mathew and his temperance movement is discussed further in chapter 6.

20. *New World*, October 29, 1842: 288–89. Quoted in Lawrence, *Strong on Music*, 167.

21. *The Young Catholic's Vocal Class Book, Designed for the Use of Churches, Schools and Associations* (Cincinnati: W. C. Peters & Sons, 1853); *The Catholic Singing Book, containing the elements of music, progressive lessons and exercises for singing schools, a Mass by F. F. Schmid, the Vespers and other Pieces for the Use of Choirs. By A. Werner, Organist of the Cathedral in Boston* (Boston: Patrick Donahoe, 1854).

22. *Boston Pilot*, 18 (February 10, 1855): 6.

23. Ibid. (February 24, 1855): 4.

24. *New York Freeman's Journal*, 18 (March 27, 1858): 4.

25. Ibid. (March 13, 1858): 1.

26. Ibid. 1.

27. *Boston Pilot*, 13 (March 23, 1850): 3.

28. *Cantiques de Saint-Sulpice, ou opuscules lyriques sur différens de piété, a l'usage des catéchismes et des missions* (Paris, 1823).

29. *The Jesuit*, 4 (1833): 83.

30. Stevenson and Moore actually borrowed a Russian folk tune for "Hark, the Vesper hymn is stealing."

31. *New York Freeman's Journal*, 7 (October 17, 1846): 126.

32. Ibid.

33. Ibid. (November 21, 1846): 165.

34. Ibid.

35. *Ave Maris Stella, Hymn in honour of the B. V. Mary, Mother of God; from the liturgy of the Church. Translated and adapted to a celebrated French Air by Revd. M. F. W. Respectfully dedicated to the Sisters of Charity, of St. Joseph's Valley near Emmitsburg. The chorus and accompaniment by P. Kelly* (Baltimore: John Cole, 1826).

36. It is found in Garbett (1840), Hoerner (1843), *Sacred Wreath* (1844), Kirk (1845), *Sacred Melodies* (1850), *Sacred Hymns* (1853), and Rohr (1854). It was also included in hymnals published as late as 1935, e.g., *St. Basil's Hymnal*, 4th edition (Detroit: The Basilian Press, 1935).

37. *Boston Pilot*, 9 (December 26, 1846): 1.

38. *The Sacred Wreath* (1844), 7. The list also includes "Queen of the empyreal heaven," "Holy Patron, thee saluting," and "O! What could my Jesus do more." Unfortunately I have been unable to discover any pre-1844 printing of these hymns that includes a melody.

39. *The Sacred Lyre: New Hymns Harmonized for Three or more Voices. The Words translated from the Roman Breviary by Charles Constantine Pise, D.D. to whom the Music is Respectfully Inscribed by Chas. M. King (Part 1st. To be continued)* (New York: C. G. Christman, 1844).

40. *Veni Creator Spiritus: a Hymn for four voices, as usually sung before Sermon, Catechism, Spiritual Instruction, etc. Music composed and respectfully

inscribed to his esteemed friend, David R. Harrison, by Charles M. King (New York: Published by C. G. Christman, 404 Pearl Street, 1842).

41. *Boston Musical Gazette,* 4 (1850): 150. The news account agrees with the archives of Georgetown University. Dielman received this degree six years before the University of New York presented the same degree to Lowell Mason, who is often cited as the first such recipient.

42. *Lyra Catholica: containing all the hymns of the Roman Breviary and Missal... with a selection of hymns, anthems and sacred poetry* (New York: Dunigan and Bro., 1851).

43. *New York Freeman's Journal,* 10 (May 4, 1850): 5.

44. *Boston Pilot,* 14 (March 15, 1851): 5.

45. *New York Freeman's Journal,* 17 (July 5, 1856): 4.

46. Quoted in "Music in Early American Catholic Schools," *Catholic Educational Review,* 60 (1962): 581.

47. *New York Freeman's Journal,* 13 (October 2, 1852): 8.

48. *Boston Pilot,* 13 (July 6, 1850): 4.

49. An example of the extensive use of Protestant hymnody within public school ceremonies can be found in the *Musical Review and Gazette,* 9 (1858): 244–45.

50. Lord et al., *History of the Archdiocese of Boston,* 2 (New York: Sheed and Ward, 1944): 598.

51. *The Sacred Wreath* (1844), 24–25.

52. The first edition, no copy of which could be located, was advertised as "just published and for sale" in the *New York Freeman's Journal* of October 1851: *Songs for Catholic Schools, Being a Selection of those used in St. Stephen's School, New York.* It is unclear if the edition contained music, nor is there any mention of Speranza in the advertisements.

53. *Songs for Catholic Schools* (1860), no. 51.

54. *Catholic Hymns and Canticles* (1863), 165.

55. *Songs for Catholic Schools* (1860), no. 45.

56. *The Catholic Herald,* 11 (1843): 285.

57. *Boston Pilot,* 2 (1839): 191.

58. Ibid., 7 (1844): 103.

59. The information on the first edition of Kirk's collection is based on advertisements, the dictionary catalogue of New York's Union Theological Seminary library, and later editions of Kirk's work. The Union Theological Seminary copy of the first edition cannot be located.

60. *Boston Pilot,* 8 (1845): 215. This edition has often been incorrectly cited as the first edition.

61. Ibid., 14 (3/29/1851): 4.

62. Higginson, *Handbook for American Catholic Hymnals,* 303, lists two editions, one in 1851 and one in 1854. M. Camilla Verrett, "Preliminary Survey of Roman Catholic Hymnals Published in the United States of

America (M.A. thesis: Catholic University of America, 1964), does not list the work at all.

63. Information concerning Rohr's collection has been taken from advertisements and reviews of the collection, as no copy has been located.

64. Grace D. Yerbury, *Song in America from Early Times to about 1850*. (Metuchen, N.J.; The Scarecrow Press, 1971): 196–239.

65. Benjamin Carr was organist of St. Augustine Church in Philadelphia from its opening in 1801 until his death in 1831. In 1805 he compiled an important collection of Catholic church music entitled *Masses, Vespers, Litanies, Hymns, Psalms, Anthems and Motetts*. Numerous compositions by Carr for the Catholic church services circulated in manuscript form through much of nineteenth-century United States.

66. Yerbury, *Song in America,* 196–99.

67. *The Jesuit*, 5 (1834): 98–99.

68. Among Werner's collections are *The Memorare* (Boston: Oliver Ditson, 1857) and *The Cantate* (Boston: Oliver Ditson, 1862).

69. *The Catholic Choralist* (New York: E. Dunigan, 1851): ii.

70. *The Sacred Wreath* (Philadelphia: H. McGrath, 1850): 2.

71. *The Catholic Herald*, 11 (1843): 205.

72. Ibid., 253.

73. Ibid., 10 (1842): 398.

74. For example, a letter in the *Boston Pilot*, 20 (October 24, 1857): 6, noted that "the old strains are very dear. Moreover, we can have them in church. But when the choir makes such bold challenges to musical companies [i.e., public concerts], it must meet them on their own ground [i.e., Haydn, Mozart and Beethoven]."

75. James H. Stone, "Mid-Nineteenth-Century American Beliefs in the Social Values of Music," *Musical Quarterly*, 43 (1957): 38–49.

76. *New York Freeman's Journal*, 3 (1842): 173.

6. Music of Popular Ritual: Song and Parish Organizations

1. The standard biography of Mathew is Patrick Rogers, *Father Theobald Mathew: Apostle of Temperance* (New York: Longmans, Green, 1945). A more recent contextual study of Mathew is H. F. Kearney, "Father Mathew: Apostle of Modernisation," in *Studies in Irish History, Presented to R. Dudley Edwards* (Dublin: University College, 1979), 164–75.

2. C. C. Pise, "Horae vagabundae," *Catholic Expositor*, 2 (1842): 121–22.

3. Edith Jeffrey, "Reform, Renewal, and Vindication: Irish Immigrants and the Catholic Total Abstinence Movement in Antebellum Philadelphia," *The Pennsylvania Magazine of History and Biography*, 112 (1988): 420.

4. *New York Freeman's Journal*, 2 (January 15, 1842): 220.

5. *The Catholic Herald*, 11 (January 12, 1843): 16.

6. Ibid. (April 27, 1843): 136.
7. *Boston Pilot*, 6 (June 3, 1843): 173.
8. *The Catholic Herald*, 13 (April 24, 1845): 136 and 13 (May 8, 1845): 149.
9. Joseph Duffy, "19th-Century Images of Hartford's Irish Catholic Community (1827–1861)," *Éire-Ireland*, 21 (Summer 1986): 5–6.
10. *Boston Pilot*, 9 (January 3, 1846): 7. The letter also exemplifies the use of music as a diversion from drink, rather than as a propaganda device for temperance.
11. Ibid., 14 (September 27, 1851): 7.
12. *New York Freeman's Journal*, 11 (August 17, 1850): 8. Allen Dodworth was a well-known band leader in the New York area. In the *Messenger Bird* of August 1, 1849, Dodworth suggested the ideal instrumentation of a band: "Two E-flat Trebles, Two B-flat Altos, Two E-flat Tenores, One B-flat Baritone, One A-flat or B-flat Bass, Two E-flat Contra-Bass. . . . the Saxhorn . . . is made in all the different keys mentioned above."
13. *New York Freeman's Journal*, 1 (April 3, 1841): 313.
14. *Boston Pilot*, 12 (February 3, 1849): 7.
15. Ibid., 6 (October 28, 1843): 339.
16. Thomas Mooney, *A History of Ireland from its First Settlement to the Present Time* (Boston: Patrick Donahoe: 1845), 174.
17. Ibid., 177.
18. *New York Freeman's Journal*, 4 (April 6, 1844): 325. Unfortunately none of the songs in this series have been located.
19. Ibid.
20. Ibid., 323.
21. Ibid., 323–24.
22. Mooney, *A History of Ireland from its First Settlement,* 69–71.
23. *Songs of the Nation and Other Select Political Songs* (Boston: Patrick Donahoe, 1844).
24. *Boston Pilot*, 7 (March 9, 1844): 79.
25. *New York Freeman's Journal*, 4 (April 6, 1844): 325.
26. *Boston Pilot*, 7 (March 9, 1844): 79.
27. *Songs of the Nation and Other Select Political Songs* (Boston: Patrick Donahoe, 1844), 1.
28. John Hugh Campbell, *History of the Friendly Sons of St. Patrick and of the Hibernian Society for the Relief of Emigrants from Ireland, March 17, 1771–March 17, 1892* (Philadelphia: Published by the Hibernian Society, 1892), 200.
29. *The Catholic Herald*, 15 (March 18, 1847): 83.
30. *Boston Pilot*, 10 (March 6, 1847): 7.
31. Ibid.
32. Ibid., 11 (March 25, 1848): 6. American response to the famine is treated in Timothy Jerome Sarbaugh, "A Moral Spectacle: American Relief and the Famine, 1845–1849," *Éire-Ireland*, 15 (Winter 1980): 6–14.

33. *The Dying Emigrant's Prayer. Written by Henry Plunkett Grattan Esq., and respectfully dedicated to the Irish Relief Committee. Music composed by George Loder* (New York: Firth and Hall, 1847).

34. Charles Hamm, *Music in the New World* (New York: W. W. Norton, 1983), 176.

35. *New York Freeman's Journal*, 7 (December 19, 1846): 200.

36. Ibid., 8 (February 19, 1848): 270.

37. *Boston Pilot*, 10 (January 2, 1847): 1.

38. *New York Freeman's Journal*, 4 (January 27, 1844): 243.

39. *Boston Pilot*, 7 (February 3, 1844): 37.

40. In his book based on the lectures, Mooney refutes the attribution of "The Exile of Erin" to Thomas Campbell. "There was a controversy, for some time, going on about the authorship of this beautiful song. For a long while it was attributed to the Scottish poet, Thomas Campbell; and even Moore believed it; but the sworn evidence, very lengthy and circumstantial, of Miss Reynolds, the sister of the late George Nugent Reynolds, of Westmeath, proves it to have been the production of her brother, for she was in the habit of writing his poetical compositions, and took down from his lips the "Exile of Erin," which he addressed to his exiled friend, in America, Joe McCormick, the companion of Macneven and Emmet in prison." Mooney, *A History of Ireland From its First Settlement*, 1060.

41. *Boston Pilot*, 6 (October 21, 1843): 335.

42. Ibid. (November 4, 1843): 351.

43. Mooney, *A History of Ireland From its First Settlement*, 711.

44. *Boston Pilot*, 8 (February 15, 1845): 55.

45. Ibid. (November 15, 1845): 363.

46. *Catholic Herald*, 14 (April 9, 1846): 117.

47. *Boston Pilot*, 2 (February 16, 1839): 39.

48. Quoted in ibid., 2 (March 2, 1839): 16.

49. P. F. White's concerts are also discussed in chapter three.

50. *New York Freeman's Journal*, 5 (August 24, 1844): 61.

51. Ibid.

52. *Boston Pilot*, 7 (August 10, 1844): 255.

53. John Barton, "The Irish Mother's Lament: Song introducing the Irish Cry for the Dead as sung by Mrs. Seguin" (New York: Firth & Hall [1844–45]).

54. Breandán O Madagáin, "Irish Vocal Music of Lament and Syllabic Verse," in *The Celtic Consciousness* (New York: George Braziller, 1981), 311.

55. Mr. and Mrs. S. C. Hall, *Ireland: Its Scenery, Character, &c.* (London: Hall, Virtue and Co., [c. 1844]) 1: 222–23.

56. Edward Hayes, *The Ballads of Ireland* (Boston: Patrick Donahoe, 1856), 324.

57. O Madagáin, "Irish Vocal Music of Lament and Syllabic Verse," 312–13.

58. Harriet Martineau, *Letters from Ireland* (London: John Chapman, 1852), 139–40. Further details concerning the so-called "American wake" can be found in Arnold Schrier, *Ireland and the American Emigration, 1850–1900* (Minneapolis: University of Minnesota Press, 1958), 83–91.

59. John J. Kane, "The Irish Wake: a Sociological Appraisal," *Sociological Symposium*, 1 (Fall 1968): 12.

60. Allan Nevins and Milton Halsey Thomas, eds., *The Diary of George Templeton Strong: The Turbulent Fifties, 1850–1859*. (New York: Macmillan, 1952), 348.

61. *The Musical World and Journal of the Fine Arts*, 3 (March 15, 1852): 196.

62. See, for example, the notes to *Songs of Aran: Gaelic Singing from the West of Ireland* (Folkway Records FE 4002). The recording also contains two examples of keening recorded in the 1950s. Unfortunately, they appear to be the earliest examples of keening recorded.

63. Liner notes to *Songs of Aran: Gaelic Singing from the West of Ireland* (Folkway Records FE 4002), 5–6.

64. Although keening was not a common practice, as late as 1944 a journalist could recall having heard keening at a wake in her childhood in America. Jill O'Nan, "Waking the Dead," *Commonweal*, 40 (August 25, 1944): 442–43.

65. *New York Freeman's Journal*, 2 (June 18, 1842): 405.

66. *Boston Pilot*, 10 (January 2, 1847): 2.

67. Ibid., 18 (January 20, 1855): 7.

68. Ibid. (December 22, 1855): 4.

69. Quoted in John Crimmins, *St. Patrick's Day: Its Celebration in New York and other American Places, 1737–1845* (New York: Published by the author, 1902), 38.

70. Quoted in ibid., 295.

71. The name Carroll refers to Charles Carroll, the only Catholic—and longest living—signer of the Declaration of Independence.

72. *New York Freeman's Journal*, 1 (March 27, 1841): 3 (supplement).

73. Quoted in Crimmins, *St. Patrick's Day: Its Celebration*, 296.

74. John T. Ridge, *The St. Patrick's Day Parade in New York* (New York: St. Patrick's Day Parade Committee, 1988), 20. The organizations, such as the Hibernian Burial and Benevolent Society, the Roman Catholic Total Abstinence and Benevolent Society, the Young Friends of Ireland, and the Quarrymen's Union Protective Society, originally met to deal with potential violence among immigrant construction crews. The difficulties were quickly resolved, but the committee turned its attention to planning the parade.

75. *New York Freeman's Journal*, 1 (March 20, 1841): 300.

76. John D. Crimmins, *Irish-American Historical Miscellany* (New York: Published by the author, 1905), 239.

77. Ridge, *The St. Patrick's Day Parade in New York*, 20.

78. *New York Freeman's Journal*, 14 (March 11, 1854): 8.

79. John Hill Hewitt, "Autobiography." Typescript at the Music Research division of the New York Public Library, p. 27.

80. *Dwight's Journal of Music* (April 19, 1873): 8.

81. It was not unknown in Ireland for a *ban caointhe* to be hired by the mourning family. While the practice may have existed in America, no evidence of it has been found.

7. "We Hung Our Harps on the Willows"

1. *New York Freeman's Journal*, 4 (January 27, 1844): 243.

2. Roger J. McHugh, "The Famine in Irish Oral Tradition," in *The Great Famine: Studies in Irish History, 1845–1852* (New York: New York University Press, 1957), 434–35.

3. Adelaida Reyes Schramm, "Music and the Refugee Experience," *World of Music* 32 (1990, no. 3): 16.

4. See, for example, William Henry Grattan Smith, *A History of Irish Music* (New York and Washington: Praeger Publishers, 1970 [1913]), and Francis O'Neill, *Irish Minstrels and Musicians* (Cork and Dublin: The Mercier Press, 1987 [1913]).

5. *Boston Pilot*, 9 (February 21, 1846): 7.

6. Ibid.

7. Charles Hamm, *Yesterdays: Popular Song in America* (New York and London: W. W. Norton, Company, 1979), 42.

8. Peter Van der Merwe, *Origins of Popular Style: The Antecedents of Twentieth-Century Popular Music* (Oxford: Clarendon Press, 1989), 137–38.

9. Ibid., 48.

10. Schramm, "Music and the Refugee Experience," 14.

11. John Blacking, "Identifying Processes of Musical Change," *World of Music*, 28 (1986): 3.

12. Madigan's connection to St. Mary's Church and his use of the *Catholic Church Service Book* is based on a handwritten notation in the copy of the service book used at St. Mary's and preserved at the Boston Public Library; the notation identifies Madigan as conductor of the choir in 1850.

13. Francis X. Reuss, "Sketch of the Life of Professor William Augustine Newland, Last of the Old-Time Philadelphia Catholic Organists. A. D. 1813–1891," *Records of the American Catholic Historical Society*, 13 (1902): 285–324.

14. Charles Seeger, "The Cultivation of Various European Traditions of Music in the New World," in *Studies in Musicology, 1935–1975* (Berkeley: University of California Press, 1977), 205.

15. Irving Lowens, "Writings about Music in the Periodicals of American Transcendentalism (1835–50)," *Journal of the American Musicological Society*, 10 (1957): 71.

16. J. S. Dwight, "Address, Delivered Before the Harvard Musical Association, August 25, 1841," *Hach's Musical Magazine*, 3 (1841): 265. Quoted in Lowens, "Writings about Music," 76.

17. John S. Dwight, "Music," *Aesthetic Papers*, 1 (1849): 25–26. Quoted in Betty E. Chmaj, "Fry versus Dwight: American Music's Debate over Nationality," *American Music*, 3 (1985): 69.

18. The details of the Dwight-Fry debate are discussed in Betty E. Chmaj, "Fry versus Dwight: American Music's Debate over Nationality," *American Music*, 3 (1985): 63–84.

19. *Literary and Catholic Sentinel*, 1 (October 31, 1835): 3.

20. *Boston Pilot*, 10 (January 2, 1847): 2.

21. Ibid. (May 8, 1847): 7.

22. Ibid. 9 (December 12, 1846): 6.

23. Ibid. 10 (July 31, 1847): 7.

24. The list of such singers is extensive, including deBegnis, Urso, Stefani, Rossi-Corsi, and Borghesa. There were, of course, non-Italian singers as well, perhaps most notably Catherine Hayes, the "Swan of Erin," portrayed in the Irish-American press as the "Irish Jenny Lind."

25. *Dwight's Journal of Music*, 11 (July 11, 1857): 118.

26. Lawrence E. Levine, *Highbrow/Lowbrow: The Emergence of Cultural Hierarchy in America* (Cambridge, Harvard University Press: 1988), 132.

27. *Dwight's Journal of Music*, 14 (October 9, 1858): 222.

28. Ibid. 8 (October 6, 1855): 5.

29. Cited in ibid. (February 23, 1856): 164–65.

30. *New York Musical Review*, cited in *Dwight's Journal of Music*, 5 (August 12, 1854): 147.

31. *Dwight's Journal of Music*, 13 (July 31, 1858): 141.

32. Ibid. 6 (December 9, 1854): 75.

33. Robert Toll, *Blacking Up: The Minstrel Show in Nineteenth-Century America* (New York: Oxford University Press, 1974), 175–80.

34. Levine, *Highbrow/Lowbrow*, 134.

35. Lawrence E. McCullough, "European-American Music, §II, 4: Irish" in *The New Grove Dictionary of American Music* (London: Macmillan, 1986), 2:72.

36. Lawrence E. McCullough, "An Historical Sketch of Traditional Irish Music in the U. S.," *Folklore Forum*, 7 (1974): 180.

37. Nicholas Tawa, *A Sound of Strangers: Musical Culture, Acculturation, and the Post–Civil War Ethnic American* (Metuchen: Scarecrow Press, 1982).

38. John Grady, "Roman Catholic Church, Music of," in *New Grove Dictionary of American Music* (London: Macmillan, 1986), 4: 80.

Bibliography

Manuscript Sources

Fenwick, Bishop Benedict. Correspondence, 1830–1845. Archives of the Archdiocese of Boston, Brighton, Massachusetts.

Hewitt, John Hill. Autobiography (typescript). Music Research Division, New York Public Library, New York.

Journal of the Diocese of Boston, 1830–1860. Archives of the Archdiocese of Boston, Brighton, Massachusetts.

Mondesir, John. Memoirs (typescript). Copy in Special Collections, Georgetown University, Washington, D.C.

Newland, William Augustine. Collection of Musical Manuscripts. Newland-Zeuner Collection, Library of Congress, Washington, D.C.

———. Personal Papers. Newland-Zeuner Collection, Library of Congress, Washington, D.C.

Nineteenth-Century Newspapers and Periodicals

Boston Musical Gazette (Boston and Bellows Falls, Vt., 1846–50).
Boston Pilot (Boston, 1836–57).
Brownson's Quarterly Review (Boston, 1844–59).
Catholic Expositor (New York, 1841–44).
Christian Examiner and Religious Miscellany (Boston, 1830–60).
Dwight's Journal of Music (Boston, 1851–60).
Emerald Isle (Boston, 1837).
Euterpiead (New York, 1830–31).
Harbinger (New York, 1846–49).
The Jesuit (Boston, 1829–34).
Journal of the Fine Arts (New York, 1851).
Literary and Catholic Sentinel (Boston, 1834–36).
Literary and Theological Review (New York, 1834–39).
The Musical Magazine (Boston, 1839–42).

Musical Reporter (Boston, 1841).
Musical World (New York, 1852–60).
New York Freeman's Journal (New York, 1840–60).
New York Musical Pioneer (New York, 1857–60).
New York Musical Review and Choral Advocate (New York, 1854–55).
Proceedings of the American Musical Convention (Boston, 1838–45).
Quarterly Musical Magazine and Review (London, 1818–28).
Religious Cabinet (Baltimore, 1842–43).
Saroni's Musical Times (New York, 1849–52).
United States Catholic Magazine (Baltimore, 1843–49).
Western Messenger (Cincinnati, 1835–41).
World of Music (Bellows Falls, Vt., 1843–48).

Books and Articles

Adams, William Forbes. *Ireland and Irish Emigration to the New World from 1815 to the Famine.* New York: Russell and Russell, 1932.
Agonito, Joseph. *The Building of an American Catholic Church: The Episcopacy of John Carroll.* New York & London: Garland, 1988.
Arnold, Robert A. "The Kraus Organ and Church of the Most Blessed Sacrament." *Historical Review of Bucks County,* 33 (1968): 98–101.
Babow, Irving. "Types of Immigrant Singing Societies." *Sociology and Social Research,* 34 (1955): 242–47.
Berger, Max. "The Irish Emigrant and American Nativism as Seen by British Visitors, 1836–1860." *The Dublin Review,* 219 (1946): 174–86.
Billington, Ray Allen. *The Protestant Crusade, 1800–1860: A Study of the Origins of American Nativism.* Chicago: Quadrangle Books, 1964.
Bird, Isabella Lucy. *The Englishwoman in America.* Madison: University of Wisconsin Press, 1966 [1856].
Blacking, John. "Identifying Processes of Musical Change." *The World of Music,* 28 (1986): 3–15.
Brooks, William. "Wiesenthal, T[homas] V[an Dyke]." In the *New Grove Dictionary of American Music,* 4: 524. London: Macmillan, 1986.
Brown, Thomas N. "The Origins and Character of Irish-American Nationalism." *Review of Politics,* 18 (1956): 327–58.
Broyles, Michael. "Lowell Mason on European Church Music and Transatlantic Cultural Identification: A Reconsideration." *Journal of the American Musicological Society,* 38 (1985): 316–48.
———. "Music and Class Structure in Antebellum Boston." *Journal of the American Musicological Society,* 44 (1991): 451–93.
Campbell, Bernard U. "Desultory Sketches of the Catholic Church in Maryland." *The Religious Cabinet,* 1 (1842): 433–44, 478–81, 524–27, 622–36.

Campbell, Jane. "Notes on a Few Old Catholic Hymn Books." *Records of the American Catholic Historical Society*, 31 (1920): 129–43.

Campbell, John Hugh. *History of the Friendly Sons of St. Patrick and the Hibernian Society for the Relief of Emigrants from Ireland, March 17, 1771–March 17, 1892.* Philadelphia: Published by the Hibernian Society: 1892.

Cantiques de Saint-Sulpice, ou opuscules lyriques sur différens de piété, a l'usage des catéchismes et des missions. Paris: Boiste Fils, 1823.

Cantiques, ou Opuscules Lyriques, sur différens sujets de piété. Paris: Chez Nicolas Crapart, 1768.

Carey, Patrick W. "American Catholic Romanticism, 1830–1888." *Catholic Historical Review*, 74 (1988): 590–606.

Chmaj, Betty E. "Fry versus Dwight: American Music's Debate over Nationality." *American Music*, 3 (1985): 63–84.

Concilia Provinciae Baltimori, habita ab anno 1829 usque ad annum 1849: Decreta. Baltimore: apud Joannem Murphy et socium, 1851.

Connolly, Sean. *Religion and Society in Nineteenth-Century Ireland.* Dundalk: Dundalgan Press, 1985.

Copeland, Robert Marshall. "The Life and Work of Issac Baker Woodbury, 1819–1858." Ph.D. diss., University of Cincinnati, 1974.

The Core Repertory of Early American Psalmody. Edited by Richard Crawford. Madison: A-R Editions, 1984.

Crawford, Richard. "Musical Learning in Nineteenth-Century America." *American Music*, 1 (Spring 1983): 1–11.

Crimmins, John. *St. Patrick's Day: Its Celebration in New York and Other American Places, 1737–1845.* New York: Published by the Author, 1902.

Cross, Michael. "Catholic Choirs and Choir Music in Philadelphia." *Records of the American Catholic Historical Society*, 2 (1886–88): 115–26.

Cross, Virginia Ann. "The Development of Sunday School Hymnody in the United States of America, 1816–1869." D.M.A. diss., New Orleans Baptist Theological Seminary, 1985.

Curley, Michael. *Venerable John Neumann.* Washington, D.C.: Catholic University of America Press, 1952.

Dean, Talmage Whitman. "The Organ in Eighteenth Century English Colonial America." Ph.D. diss., University of Southern California, 1960.

DeMonti, Henri. *Strictures on Mr. Logier's System of Musical Education.* Glasgow: James Hedderwick, 1817.

Devitt, E. T. "Letters from the Archdiocesan Archives at Baltimore, Time of Bishop Carroll." *Records of the American Catholic Historical Society of Philadelphia*, 22 (1911): 136–37.

Dichter, Harry, and Elliott Shapiro. *Early American Sheet Music: Its Lure and Its Lore, 1768–1889.* New York: R. R. Bowker, 1941.

Diner, Hasia R. *Erin's Daughters in America: Irish Immigrant Women in the Nineteenth Century.* Baltimore: Johns Hopkins University Press, 1983.

Dolan, Jay P. *Catholic Revivalism: The American Experience, 1830–1900.* Notre Dame: University of Notre Dame Press, 1978.

———. *The Immigrant Church: New York's Irish and German Catholics, 1815–1865.* Baltimore: Johns Hopkins University Press, 1975. Rpt. Notre Dame: University of Notre Dame Press, 1983.

Duffy, Joseph. "19th-Century Images of Hartford's Irish-Catholic Community (1827–1861)." *Éire-Ireland,* 21 (Summer 1986): 1–12.

Eitner, Rob. *Biographisch-Bibliographisches Quellen-Lexicon der Musiker und Musikgelehrten.* New York: Musurgia, 1898 [preface date].

Elson, Louis C. *The History of American Music.* New York: Macmillan, 1904.

Ernst, Robert. *Immigrant Life in New York City, 1825–1863.* New York: King's Crown Press, 1949.

al Faruqi, Lois Ibsen. "What Makes 'Religious Music' Religious?" In *Sacred Sound: Music in Religious Thought and Practice,* edited by Joyce Irwin, 21–34. Chico, Calif.: Scholars Press, 1984.

Fenwick, Benedict Joseph. *Memoirs to Serve for the Future Ecclesiastical History of the Diocese of Boston.* Edited by Joseph M. McCarthy. Yonkers: U. S. Catholic Historical Society, 1978.

Ferland, David J. "Plenary, Provincial, and Synodal Legislation Concerning Liturgical Music in the United States as Causative and Resultant of the Enactments of the Third Plenary Council of Baltimore." Master's thesis, Catholic University of America, 1955.

Finney, Gretchen. "'Organical Musick' and Ecstasy." *Journal of the History of Ideas,* 8 (1947): 273–92.

Finotti, Joseph. *Bibliographia Catholica Americana: A List of Works Written by Catholic Authors and Published in the United States.* New York: The Catholic Publications House, 1872.

Flick, Lawrence F. "Minutes of St. Mary's Church, Philadelphia, 1782–1811." *Records of the American Catholic Historical Society,* 4 (1893): 245–430.

Fox, Columba. *The Life of Rt. Rev. John Baptist David (1761–1841).* New York: U. S. Catholic Historical Society, 1925.

Frankiel, Sandra Sizer. *Gospel Hymns and Social Religion: The Rhetoric of Nineteenth-Century Revivalism.* Philadelphia: Temple University Press, 1978.

Gallagher, Eugene B., S.J. "Two Hundred and Fifty Years Ago: The Beginnings of St. Joseph's Church." *Records of the American Catholic Historical Society of Philadelphia,* 93 (1982): 4.

Gould, Nathaniel D. *Church Music in America.* Boston: A. N. Johnson, 1853.

Grady, John. "Roman Catholic Church, Music of the." In the *New Grove Dictionary of American Music,* 4: 80–82. London: Macmillan, 1986.

Grassi, John. "The Catholic Religion in the United States in 1818." *Records of the American Catholic Historical Society,* 8 (1891): 98–111.

Griffith, Thomas W. *Annals of Baltimore.* Baltimore: William Woody, 1833.
Groneman, Carol. "Working-Class Immigrant Women in Mid-Nineteenth-Century New York: The Irish Woman's Experience." *Journal of Urban History,* 4 (May 1978): 255–73.
Grund, Francis J. *The Americans in Their Moral, Social, and Political Relations.* New York and London: Johnson Reprint Corporation, 1968 [1837].
Guilday, Peter. *The Life and Times of John Carroll.* Westminster, Md.: The Newman Press, 1954.
Haban, M. Teresine. "The Hymnody of the Roman Catholic Church: Historical Survey with an Analysis of Musical Styles." Ph.D. diss., University of Rochester, 1957.
Hall, Clayton Colman. *Narratives of Early Maryland.* New York: Charles Scribner's Sons, 1910.
Hall, James William. "The Tune-Book in American Culture: 1800–1820." Ph.D. diss., University of Pennsylvania, 1967.
Hall, Mr. and Mrs. S.C. *Ireland: Its Scenery, Character, &c.* London: Hall, Virtue, and Co. [c. 1844].
Hamm, Charles. *Music in the New World.* New York: W.W. Norton, 1983.
———. *Yesterdays: Popular Song in America.* New York: W.W. Norton, 1979.
Handlin, Oscar. *Boston's Immigrants, 1790–1865: A Study in Acculturation.* Cambridge: Harvard University Press, 1941.
Hatch, Christopher. "Music for America: A Critical Controversy of the 1850s." *American Quarterly,* 14 (1962): 578–86.
Hayburn, Robert. *Papal Legislation on Sacred Music, 95 A.D. to 1977 A.D.* Collegeville, Minn.: Liturgical Press, 1979.
Hayes, Edward. *The Ballads of Ireland.* Boston: Patrick Donahoe, 1856.
Hennesey, James. *American Catholics: A History of the Roman Catholic Community in the United States.* New York: Oxford University Press, 1981.
Henry, Hugh T. "A Philadelphia Choir Book of 1787." *Records of the American Catholic Historical Society of Philadelphia,* 26 (1915): 208–23.
———. "Philadelphia Choir Books of 1791 and 1814." *Records of the American Catholic Historical Society,* 26 (1915): 311–27.
Higginson, J. Vincent. "Baltimore: Catholicity in the Early Years." *Sacred Music,* 112 (Fall 1985): 19–23.
———. "Bishop John B. David—An Unknown American Composer." *Sacred Music,* 104 (1977): 8–11.
———. "Foreign Influences in Early American Catholic Hymnody." *Hymn,* 17 (1966): 16–20, 11.
———. *Handbook for American Hymnals.* N.p.: Hymn Society of America, 1976.
———. *History of American Catholic Hymnals: Survey and Background.* N.p.: Hymn Society of America, 1982.

———. "Music and Musicians at St. Mary's Church, Philadelphia." *Sacred Music*, 109 (1982): 13–18.

Huen-Dubourg, J. *The Life of Cardinal Cheverus, Archbishop of Bourdeaux*. Translated by E. Stewart. Boston: James Munroe, 1839.

Hultin, Neil C. "Mrs. Harrington, Mrs. Leary, Mr. Croker, and the 'Irish Howl.'" *Éire-Ireland*, 20 (Winter 1968): 43–64.

Jeffrey, Edith. "Reform, Renewal, and Vindication: Irish Immigrants and the Catholic Total Abstinence Movement in Antebellum Philadelphia." *Pennsylvania Magazine of History and Biography*, 112 (1988): 407–31.

The John Carroll Papers. Edited by Thomas O'Brien Hanley. Notre Dame: University of Notre Dame Press, 1976.

Johnson, H. Earle. "Early New England Periodicals Devoted to Music." *Musical Quarterly*, 26 (1940): 153–61.

———. *First Performances in America to 1900*. Detroit: Published for the College Music Society by Information Coordinators, 1979.

Kalm, Peter. *Travels into North America*. Translated by John Reinhold Forster. Warrington: William Eyres, 1770.

Kane, John J. "The Irish Wake: A Sociological Appraisal." *Sociological Symposium*, 1 (Fall 1968): 10–15.

Kearney, H. F. "Father Mathew: Apostle of Modernisation." In *Studies in Irish History, Presented to R. Dudley Edwards*, 164–75. Dublin: University College, 1979.

Keenan, Desmond J. *The Catholic Church in Nineteenth-Century Ireland: A Sociological Survey*. Totowa, N. J.: Barnes and Noble, 1983.

Kenny, Kevin G. "Religion and Immigration: The Irish Communities in N.Y.C., 1815–1840." *The Recorder*, 3 (Winter 1989): 1–49.

———. "Religion and the Rise of Mass Immigration: The Irish Community in New York City, 1815–1840." *New York Irish History*, 5 (1990–91): 29–38.

Kirlin, Joseph Louis J. *Catholicity in Philadelphia from the Earliest Missionaries Down to the Present Time*. Philadelphia: J. J. McVey, 1909.

Knobel, Dale T. *Paddy and the Republic: Ethnicity and Nationality in Antebellum America*. Middletown: Wesleyan University Press, 1986.

Larkin, Emmet. "The Devotional Revolution in Ireland, 1850–1875." *American Historical Review*, 77 (1972): 627–31, 644.

Lawrence, Vera Brodsky. *Strong on Music: The New York Music Scene in the Days of George Templeton Strong, 1836–1875*. Volume 1, *Resonances, 1836–1850*. New York and Oxford: Oxford University Press, 1988.

Lees, Lynn H., and John Modell. "The Irish Countryman Urbanized: A Comparative Perspective on the Famine Migration." *Journal of Urban History*, 3 (August 1977): 391–408.

"Letters of the Rt. Rev. John Carroll." *American Catholic Historical Society Researches*, 14 (1897): 21.

Levine, Lawrence. *Highbrow/Lowbrow: The Emergence of Cultural Hierarchy in America*. Cambridge: Harvard University Press, 1988.
Lieber, Francis. *The Stranger in America: comprising sketches of the manners, society, and national peculiarities of the United States*. London: R. Bentley, 1835.
Lord, Robert H., John E. Sexton, and Edward T. Harrington. *History of the Archdiocese of Boston in the Various Stages of Its Development, 1604–1943*. New York: Sheed and Ward, 1944.
"Lotteries for Churches." *Records of the American Catholic Historical Society of Philadelphia* 15 (1898): 161.
Lovewell, S. Harrison. "Cathedral of Holy Cross in Boston and Its Historic Organ." *Diapason,* 21 (1929): 40.
Lowens, Irving. "Writings about Music in the Periodicals of American Transcendentalism (1835–50)." *Journal of the American Musicological Society,* 10 (1957): 71–85.
Madeira, Louis Cephas. *Annals of Music in Philadelphia and History of the Musical Fund Society from its Organization in 1820 to the year 1858*. Philadelphia: J. B. Lippincott, 1896.
Mainzer, Joseph. *Singing for the Millions: a Practical Course of Musical Instruction, Adapted, From its Pleasing Simplicity and Rapid Effect, to Render Musical Reading and Singing Familiar to all Ages, Capacities, and Conditions*. London: Depot for the Mainzerian Publications, 1841.
Marryat, Frederick. *A Diary in America With Remarks on its Institutions*. London: Longman, Orne, Brown, Green and Longmans, 1839.
Martineau, Harriet. *Letters from Ireland*. London: John Chapman, 1852.
McAvoy, Thomas T. "The Formation of the Catholic Minority in the United States, 1820–1860." *Review of Politics,* 10 (1948): 13–34.
McCullough, Lawrence E. "European-American Music §II, 4: Irish." In *The New Grove Dictionary of American Music*, 2: 72–73. London: Macmillan, 1986.
———. "An Historical Sketch of Traditional Irish Music in the U. S." *Folklore Forum* 7 (1974): 177–91.
McGee, Thomas D'Arcy. *A History of the Irish Settlers in North America*. Boston: Patrick Donahoe, 1852.
McHugh, Roger J. "The Famine in Irish Oral Tradition." In *The Great Famine: Studies in Irish History, 1845–1852*, 391–436. New York: New York University Press, 1957.
McLoughlin, Philip K. "'H-A-R-R-I-G-A-N.' Glimpses of the Irish on Stage in Late Nineteenth-Century America." *Éire-Ireland,* 23 (Spring 1988): 3–7.
Meehan, Thomas F. "Early Catholic Weeklies." *Historical Records and Studies,* 28 (1937): 237–55.
Mentag, John V. "Catholic Spiritual Revivals: Parish Missions in the Midwest." Ph.D. diss., Loyola University of Chicago, 1957.

Merwe, Peter Van der. *Origins of Popular Style: The Antecedents of Twentieth-Century Popular Music.* Oxford: Clarendon Press, 1989.

Middleton, Rev. Thomas C. "Some Facts Supplementary to the Article 'Catholic Choir Music in Philadelphia.'" *Records of the American Catholic Historical Society,* 3 (1888–91): 248–52.

Miller, David W. "Irish Catholicism and the Great Famine." *Journal of Social History,* 9 (1975): 81–98.

Miller, Kirby A. *Emigrants and Exiles: Ireland and the Irish Exodus to North America.* New York: Oxford University Press, 1985.

Mooney, Hughson. "The Past as Prelude: American Popular Music, 1840–1895." *Connecticut Review,* 9 (1976): 151–67.

Mooney, Thomas. *A History of Ireland from its First Settlement to the Present Time.* Boston: Patrick Donahoe: 1845.

Moore, John W. *Complete Encyclopaedia of Music.* Boston: John P. Jewitt, 1854.

Moseley, Caroline. "The Hutchinson Family: The Function of Their Song in Ante-Bellum America." *Journal of American Culture,* 1 (1978): 713–23.

Nathan, Hans. "The Tyrolese Family Rainer and the Vogue of Singing Mountain-Troupes in Europe and America." *Musical Quarterly,* 32 (1946): 63–79.

Nemmers, Erwin Esser. *Twenty Centuries of Catholic Church Music.* Westport, Conn.: Greenwood Press, 1978 [1949].

Nevins, Allan, and Milton Halsey Thomas, eds. *The Diary of George Templeton Strong: The Turbulent Fifties, 1850–1859.* New York: Macmillan, 1952.

O Madagáin, Breandán. "Irish Vocal Music of Lament and Syllabic Verse." In *The Celtic Consciousness,* 311–32. New York: George Braziller, 1981.

O Súlleabháin, Sean. *Irish Wake Amusements.* Cork: Mercier Press, 1967.

O'Connell, Lucille. "Kealing Hurley's Scrip Book: An Irish Immigrant in America, 1847–48." *Éire-Ireland* 15 (1980): 105–12.

O'Nan, Jill. "Waking the Dead." *Commonweal* 40 (August 25, 1944): 442–43.

O'Neill, Francis. *Irish Minstrels and Musicians.* Cork: Mercier Press, 1987 [1913].

Ochse, Orpha. *The History of the Organ in the United States.* Bloomington: Indiana University Press, 1975.

Owen, Barbara. *The Organ in New England: an Account of its Use and Manufacture to the End of the Nineteenth Century.* Raleigh: Sunbury Press, 1979.

Paige, Paul Eric. "Musical Organizations in Boston: 1830–1850." Ph.D. diss., Boston University, 1967.

Perkins, Charles C., and John S. Dwight. *History of the Handel and Haydn Society.* New York: Da Capo Press, 1977 [1883].

Pise, Charles Constantine. *Father Rowland, A North American Tale.* Baltimore: Lucas Brothers, 1841.

Prim, Abbé Jean. "*Chant sur le Livre* in French Churches in the 18th Century." *Journal of the American Musicological Society,* 14 (1961): 37–49.

Rainbow, Bernard. *The Land Without Music: Music Education in England, 1800–1860, and its Continental Antecedents.* London: Novello, 1967.

Reed, Rebecca. *Six Months Residence in a Convent.* London: W. Nicholson [1836].

Reuss, Francis X. "Sketch of the Life of Professor William Augustine Newland, Last of the Old-Time Philadelphia Catholic Organists A.D. 1813–1891." *Records of the American Catholic Historical Society,* 13 (1902): 285–324.

Richards, James H. "English Catholic Church Music, from Arne to Novello." *The Diapason,* 59 (1968): 18–20.

Ridge, John T. *The St. Patrick's Day Parade in New York.* New York: St. Patrick's Day Parade Committee, 1988.

Rogers, Delmer Dalzell. "Nineteenth Century Music in New York City as Reflected in the Career of George Frederick Bristow." Ph.D. diss., University of Michigan, 1967.

Rogers, Patrick. *Father Theobald Mathew: Apostle of Temperance.* New York: Longmans, Green, 1945.

Rosalie, Sister Mary. "Music in Early American Catholic Schools." *Catholic Educational Review,* 60 (1962): 577–87.

Ruether, Rosemary Radford, and Rosemary Skinner Keller, eds. *Women and Religion in America.* San Francisco: Harper and Row, 1981.

Ryan, Thomas. *Recollections of an Old Musician.* New York: E. P. Dutton, 1899.

Saladini, Robert. "American Catholic Church Music: Baltimore Cathedral." Master's thesis, Catholic University of America, 1984.

Sarbaugh, Timothy Jerome. "A Moral Spectacle: American Relief and the Irish Famine, 1845–1849." *Éire-Ireland* 15 (Winter 1980): 6–14.

Scharf, John Thomas, and Thompson Westcott. *History of Philadelphia, 1609–1884.* Philadelphia: L. H. Evans, 1884.

Schramm, Adelaida Reyes. "Music and the Refugee Experience." *The World of Music,* 32 (1990): 3–21.

Schrier, Arnold. *Ireland and the American Emigration, 1850–1900.* Minneapolis: University of Minnesota Press, 1958.

Seeger, Charles. "The Cultivation of Various European Traditions of Music in the New World." In *Studies in Musicology, 1935–1975.* Berkeley: University of California Press, 1977.

Shaughnessy, Gerald. *Has the Immigrant Kept the Faith? A Study of Immigration and Catholic Growth in the United States, 1790–1920.* New York: Macmillan, 1925.

Shea, John Gilmary. *History of the Catholic Church in the United States.* New York: J. G. Shea, 1886–92.

Smith, Ronnie L. "Benjamin Carr." In *New Grove Dictionary of American Music,* 1: 360–61. London: Macmillan, 1986.

———. "The Church Music of Benjamin Carr (1768–1831)." D.M.A. diss., Southwestern Baptist Theological Seminary, 1969.

Smith, William Henry Grattan. *A History of Irish Music*. New York and Washington: Praeger Publishers, 1970 [1913].
Songs of the Nation and Other Select Political Songs. Boston: Patrick Donahoe, 1844.
Spalding, Martin John. *Sketches of the Early Catholic Missions of Kentucky from their Commencement in 1787 to the Jubilee of 1826–7*. Louisville: B. J. Webb & Bro. [1844].
Stevenson, E. T. *Protestant Church Music in America*. New York: W.W. Norton, 1966.
Stone, James H. "The Merchant and the Muse: Commercial Influences on Popular Music before the Civil War." *Business History Review*, 30 (1956): 1–17.
———. "Mid-Nineteenth-Century Beliefs in the Social Values of Music." *Musical Quarterly*, 43 (1957): 38–49.
Taves, Ann. "Context and Meaning: Roman Catholic Devotion to the Blessed Sacrament in Mid-Nineteenth-Century America." *Church History*, 54 (1985): 482–95.
Tawa, Nicholas E. *A Sound of Strangers: Musical Culture, Acculturation, and the Post–Civil War Ethnic American*. Metuchen: Scarecrow Press, 1982.
———. *Sweet Songs for Gentle Americans: The Parlor Song in America, 1790–1860*. Bowling Green: Bowling Green University Popular Press, 1980.
Temperley, Nicholas. "The Great Musical Divide: Channel or Ocean?" *American Music*, 8 (1990): 1–11.
———. "The Old Way of Singing: Its Origins and Development." *Journal of the American Musicological Society*, 34 (1981): 511–44.
Toll, Robert. *Blacking Up: The Minstrel Show in Nineteenth-Century America*. New York: Oxford University Press, 1974.
United States Board of Music Trade. *Complete Catalogue of Sheet Music and Musical Works 1870*. New York: Da Capo, 1973 [1870].
U.S. Bureau of the Census. *Historical Statistics of the United States: Colonial Times to 1970*. Washington, D.C.: U.S. Government Printing Office, 1975.
Upton, William Treat. *William Henry Fry: American Journalist and Composer-Critic*. New York: Thomas Y. Crowell, 1954.
Verrett, M. Camilla. "Preliminary Survey of Roman Catholic Hymnals Published in the United States of America." Master's thesis, Catholic University of America, 1964.
Walsh, Francis R. "Who Spoke for Boston's Irish? The Boston *Pilot* in the Nineteenth Century." *Journal of Ethnic Studies*, 10 (Fall 1982): 21–36.
Webber, Frederick R. "Some Early Organs in New York City Described Vividly." *Diapason*, 48 (August 1957): 16.
Weller, Philip T. "Early Church Music in the United States." *Liturgical Arts*, 7 (1938): 6–8, 29–31.
Wellon, Simone. "Notes on the Performance of Plain Chant in France from 1750 to 1850." *Sacred Music*, 107 (Winter 1980): 3–8.

Wetzel, Richard D. "The Search for William Cumming Peters." *American Music,* 1 (1983): 27–41.
Wienandt, Elwyn A. *The Bicentennial Collection of American Music,* volume 1. Carol Stream, Ill.: Hope Publishing, 1974.
Winser, Justin. *The Memorial History of Boston.* Boston: J. Osgood, 1880.
Wolf, Edward C. "The Schmahl and Krauss Organs in Old St. Michael's Philadelphia." *The Tracker,* 17 (1973).
Wolfe, Richard J. *Early American Music Engraving and Printing: A History of Music Printing in America from 1787 to 1825 with Commentary on Earlier and Later Practices.* Urbana: University of Illinois Press, 1980.
Yerbury, Grace D. *Song in America from Early Times to about 1850.* Metuchen, N. J., Scarecrow Press, 1971.

Index

Act of Union of Great Britain and Ireland, 121, 139, 144–46
African (African-American) music, 175, 199n27
Aitken, John, 46, 70, 84, 176
Allegri, Gregorio, 25–26, 46

Balfe, Michael William, 180
Bands, x, 9, 168–69, 216n12
    Hibernian, 141
    Temperance, 140–41, 169
Beethoven, Ludwig van, 26, 40, 65, 68, 178
Bellini, Vincenzo, 179
Bergé, William, 80–83
Boston Gregorian Society, 15, 16, 36–40, 71, 159, 200n8
Boston Musical Institute, 16, 45
Breviary Hymns, 10, 45, 117–18, 125
Bristow, George F., 132
    School of, 132–34, 179
Bristow, William, 132
Brown, Mrs. D. L. (Cecilia Webbe), 15, 31, 92, 177, 199n30
Brownson, Orestes, 80, 83, 158, 199n23
Bunting, Edward, 174

Caoine. *See* Keen
Carr, Benjamin, 37, 38, 40–41, 46, 74, 76, 85, 131, 133, 176
Carroll, Abp. John, 1, 60
Cathedral of the Holy Cross (Boston), 16, 30, 31, 38, 55, 66, 73, 109

Catholic Church Service Book (1833), 31–34, 40–45, 87–88, 177, 219n12
    Contents, 42–43
Catholic Harp, The (1844), 70, 72, 101, 112, 130–31
Catholic Hymns and Canticles (1863), 127–28
Catholic Melodies (1844), 130
Catholic Singing Book (1854), 108–9
Catholic Total Abstinence Society, 139–43
Chapel Choir Book (1850), 131–32
Cheverus, Bp. John Lefebvre de, 1, 46, 176
Children's Choirs, 31, 41, 92, 109–11
Choirs, 23, 55, 62
Christman, C. G., 80, 97
Church of the Immaculate Conception (Boston), 8, 53, 165–66
Comer, Thomas, 16, 34–35, 54–55, 132
Concerts (Catholic)
    benefit, 14–15, 34–35, 60, 63, 66, 92, 135, 140, 170, 180
    in Catholic churches, 14–16, 34–37, 62–63
    in concert halls, 33–34, 109–11
Cummings, Rev. Jeremiah, 68, 92, 127–29
Cross, Benjamin, 76, 114, 117, 177

Daunas, Pedro, 68, 208n40
David, Bp. John Bapst, 49, 114, 131, 208n41, 211n79
DeMonti, Henri, 33, 36–37, 40–41, 70–73, 93–94, 130–31, 200n12, 209n54
Dempster, William, 3, 142, 182

233

Dielman, Henry, 68, 74, 118, 120–23, 133, 214n41
Ditson, Oliver, x, 16, 40, 55, 67, 80
Donahoe, Patrick, 31, 39, 54, 131, 132, 148, 157, 159, 200n3
Donizetti, Gaetano, 73, 76, 179
Dos Santos, A. F., 68, 93
Dumont, Henri (*see also* "Missa Regia"), 44, 132
Dwight, John S., 21, 40, 67, 73, 89, 94, 178, 180, 209n57
Dwight's Journal, 63, 66–67, 71, 178, 181

Famine, Great Irish, 149–51, 170, 173, 176
Fenwick, Bp. Benedict, 31–34, 38, 40–41, 49, 71, 85, 87, 211n79
Fenwick, Bp. Edward, O.P., 49–50
Five Points (New York City), 4, 8, 181
Fry, William Henry, 73, 177–78, 209n57

Garbett, Richard (see also *Morning and Evening Service*), 15, 16, 40, 45, 57, 85–87, 130, 131, 133, 177
Gilmore, Patrick S., 169
Gregorian Music (*see also* plainchant), 32, 41, 44, 183
 arrangements of, 74, 85–87, 93
 difficulties with, 49
 execution of, 32, 44–45, 84–85

"Hail Glorious Apostle" (hymn), 54–55, 111, 171
Handel and Haydn Society, 14, 16, 33, 34, 36, 60, 66, 200n2
Harrison, David R., 74, 118, 121, 124
Harrison, Elizabeth (Sr. Mary John), 41, 44
Haydn, Franz J., 21, 22, 35, 37, 40, 65, 71, 73, 87, 93–94, 169, 178–79, 183
Hemans, Mrs. Felicia, 33, 49, 125, 202n39
Hewitt, John Hill, 132–33, 169
Holy Trinity (German) Church, Boston, 65
House of the Angel Guardian, Boston, 92, 109–10
Hughes, Abp. John, 6, 13, 134, 209n57
Hummel, Johann, 65, 68
Hutchinson Family, 14, 202n39
Hymns to Saints, 49, 118–20

Irish Language, 6, 164–65
Irishman, as exiles, 3, 53–54, 57, 145–46, 157, 168, 172, 175–76
Irish music (*see also* Traditional music), 53–57, 112–13, 170
 concerts of, 55–56, 108–11, 156–57, 158–59, 159–60
 histories of, 53, 155, 157, 158
 and immigrants, 3, 164, 172
 instrumental, 8, 53, 165–66
Irish Wake, 7, 162–64
Italian music, 73, 76, 94–95, 121, 133, 179–82

Jesuits, 27

Keen, 159–65, 169–71, 175
King, Charles M., 92, 118–20, 132, 144–45, 170
Kirk, Philip, 71, 130–31, 176

Lambilotte, Rev. Louis, S.J., 68, 83–84, 111
Liturgical Music, 8–10, 36, 59–95, 183
 prohibition of vernacular, 45, 135
 regulation of, 45, 52, 89–90, 135, 206n51, 207n2, 211n2
 use of vernacular, 11, 96–137, 205n41
Lloyd, George W., 131–32, 133
Loder, George, 64, 74, 76, 92–93, 130, 132, 150–54, 170
Lover, Samuel, 132, 151
Lyra Catholica (1851), 125–26, 136

Mainzer, Joseph, 107–8
Mallet, Francis, 31, 41, 44, 52
Malone, Madame Mecovino, 107–8
Manual of Catholic Melodies (1843), 101, 129–30
Mass Clubs, 67–68
Mass settings, 69
Mathew, Fr. Theobald, 108, 139
Mercadante, Saverio, 68, 73, 76, 179
Missa Regia (*see also* Dumont), 44, 70, 132
Mooney, Michael J., 110–11, 134
Mooney, Thomas, 144, 146–47, 156–58, 165, 170
Moore, Thomas, ix, 54, 56–57, 111, 143–44, 151, 156, 158, 170, 174–75, 183

234 *Index*

Morning and Evening Service of the Catholic Church (1840), 14, 16, 45–52, 85–87
  contents of, 46–48
Mozart, Wolfgang Amadeus, 21, 22, 26, 40, 49–51, 65, 76, 80, 87, 93–94, 178–79, 183
  Requiem (K. 626), 21, 60–62, 66, 73, 92, 202n28, 208n27
  "Twelfth Mass" (K. anh. 232), 61, 66, 67
Mount Benedict. *See* Ursuline Convent

National music (of Ireland), 53–57, 111
Nativism (Nativists), 2, 5, 6, 13, 26
Neumann, Bp. John, 6, 85
Newland, William Augustine, 65, 68, 76, 177
Novello, Vincent, 41, 44, 67, 76, 94

O'Connell, Daniel, 144–45, 148–49
Opera companies (touring), 179–80
Organists, 31, 32, 68, 92, 109, 118, 199n30
Organs, 19–20, 60
Ostinelli, Louis, 16, 32, 34
Ostinelli, Mrs. Sophia (Hewitt), 31, 92
Oxford Movement, 89, 118, 121, 125

Palestrina, Giovanni Pierluigi da, 23, 94
Peters' Catholic Harp (1863), 98
Peters, William Cumming, x, 57, 74–80, 93, 97–98, 101–6, 108, 132
Pise, Rev. Charles Constantine, 76, 117, 119–20, 134, 139
Plainchant (*see also* Gregorian Music), 10, 22–23, 32, 36, 41, 84–91, 94
Protestants (attending Catholic services), 7–8, 24–26, 27, 64–65, 178–79
Provincials Council of Baltimore, 58
  First (1829), 29
  Third (1837), 45, 52
  Fourth (1840), 199n1
  Fifth (1843), 140

Rainer Family, 14, 15, 200n5
Repeal Associations, 9, 121, 138–39, 143–49, 170
Requiem Mass, Gregorian (*see also* Mozart), 70, 74, 209n43
Riots, 5, 6

Rohr, Philip, 96–97, 132, 176
Roman Catholic Manual (1802), 176
Romanticism, 13, 24, 26, 29
Rosati, Bp. Joseph, 34, 49
Rossini, Gioacchino, 63, 65, 73, 76, 179–80

Sacred Melodies (1850), 111, 131
Sacred Wreath (1844), 101, 111, 114, 127
Sadlier, D. J., 40, 131
St. Andrew's Church (New York City), 65
St. Augustine's Church (Philadelphia), 65, 141
St. Francis Xavier Church (New York City), 68, 80
St. Joseph's Church (Philadelphia), 19
St. Mary's Church (Boston), 15, 30, 31, 34, 177
St. Mary's Singing Society, 14–16, 31, 39, 71
St. Patrick's Cathedral, "Old" (New York City), 61, 93
St. Patrick's Day, 10, 54, 110, 141–42, 145–46, 149–50, 166–69, 170–71
St. Peter's Church, New York City, 7, 8, 60–65, 91–92
St. Stephen's Church (New York City), 68, 92, 127
Schools, Parochial, 6, 9, 126–29
Schools, Public, 8, 9, 13, 126–27, 136
Schools, Sunday, 9, 10, 126, 134, 183
Selle, Louis, 74, 93
Singing Schools, x, 30–31, 32, 34, 68, 92, 107–9, 140
Sodality, 9, 97, 126, 134, 183
Songs for Catholic Schools (1860), 127
Stevenson, Sir John, 49, 56, 112, 171, 174
Steyermark Family, 14
Strong, George Templeton, 4, 61–64, 93, 163, 179

Taylor, Raynor, 76
Temperance Societies, x, 9, 11, 138–43, 170
Timm, Henry, 62, 74
Traditional music
  Irish, 53–57, 112–13, 135, 142, 151, 154–59, 165–66, 167–68, 169–71, 174, 183–84
  French, 111, 113–16, 135
Transcendentalism, 13, 21–22, 26, 178

Index   235

Unitarianism (Unitarians), 13, 21–22, 24, 26, 27, 41, 178
Ursuline Convent (Charleston, Mass.), 26, 30, 41, 44, 54, 211n73

Vernacular. *See* Liturgical music
Vesper Book (1836), 46, 52
Vespers, 14, 38, 76–84

Wallace, William Vincent, 180
Walter, Jacob, 36, 46, 70, 130, 176

Webbe, Samuel, 36, 40–41, 70, 76, 84, 94, 177, 199n30, 209n54
Werner, Anthony, 73, 108–9, 133, 177
White, P. F., 15, 55–57, 158–59, 170
Wiesenthal, T. V., 49, 76, 101, 133

Young Catholic's Vocal Class Book (1853), 108
Young, Charles T., 15, 31, 32, 33, 40
Young Ireland Movement, 144, 148–49

About the Author

Robert R. Grimes, S.J., is Assistant Professor of Music at Fordham University. He received his Ph.D. in musicology from the University of Pittsburgh and the present work was completed under an AMS 50 fellowship awarded by the American Musicological Society.